SOLID WASTE AS A RESOURCE

Other titles of interest

BOOKS

ASHLEY *et al.:* Energy and the Environment—A Risk-Benefit Approach

COMMISSION OF THE EUROPEAN COMMUNITIES:
  The Quality of the Environment and the Iron and Steel Industry

HENSTOCK: Recycling and Disposal of Solid Waste

KOZIOROWSKI & KUCHARSKI: Industrial Waste Disposal

JOURNALS*

CHEMOSPHERE (Chemistry, Physics, Biology and Toxicology as Focused on
              Environmental Problems)

CONSERVATION & RECYCLING

*free specimen copies available on request.

SOLID WASTE AS A RESOURCE

*Proceedings of the Conference on the Recycling and
Disposal of Solid Wastes, Dubrovnik, 1975*

Editors

MICHAEL E. HENSTOCK, B.Sc., Ph.D., C.Eng., M.I.M., M.I.M.M.
*Department of Metallurgy and Materials Science,
University of Nottingham*

and

MICHAEL W. BIDDULPH, B.Sc., Ph.D., M.A.I.Ch.E.
*Department of Chemical Engineering,
University of Nottingham*

PERGAMON PRESS

OXFORD · NEW YORK · TORONTO · SYDNEY

PARIS · FRANKFURT

U.K.	Pergamon Press Ltd., Headington Hill Hall, Oxford OX3 0BW, England
U.S.A.	Pergamon Press Inc., Maxwell House, Fairview Park, Elmsford, New York 10523, U.S.A.
CANADA	Pergamon of Canada Ltd., 75 The East Mall, Toronto, Ontario, Canada
AUSTRALIA	Pergamon Press (Aust.) Pty. Ltd., 19a Boundary Street, Rushcutters Bay, N.S.W. 2011, Australia
FRANCE	Pergamon Press SARL, 24 rue des Ecoles, 75240 Paris, Cedex 05, France
FEDERAL REPUBLIC OF GERMANY	Pergamon Press GmbH, 6242 Kronberg-Taunus, Pferdstrasse 1, Federal Republic of Germany

First edition 1978

Library of Congress Cataloging in Publication Data

Conference on the Recycling and Disposal of Solid Wastes, Dubrovnik, Yugoslavia, 1975.
Solid waste as a resource.

"Special issue of the journal Conservation & recycling, volume 1, no. 1."
Includes index.
1. Recycling (Waste, etc)--Congresses. I. Henstock, M. E. II. Biddulph, M.W. III. Conservation & recycling. IV. Title.
TD794.5.C66 1975   604'.6   77-24726
ISBN 0-08-021571-8

Published as a special issue of the journal CONSERVATION & RECYCLING Volume 1 No. 1 and supplied to subscribers as part of the normal subscription.

Printed in Great Britain by A. Wheaton & Co. Ltd, Exeter

CONTENTS

INTRODUCTION

IT is not uncommon for a book to create on publication a furore of major or minor proportions. The book itself may be shown, by remorseless hindsight, to have been less significant than at first believed. Of greater import is the effect that it has on the actions and imagination of man, whether it is itself an end or whether it points to a greater one.

Few books published this century can have made so dramatic an impact as did 'The Limits to Growth'. Its appearance prompted more widespread a concern with the environment than did the cumulative efforts of half a hundred predecessors, from Malthus onwards. The reasons for the extraordinary influence of this work are perhaps irrelevant, but the undeniable fact is that it has served to focus attention in an unprecedented way on some problems of a growth-oriented society.

One of the constraints considered by Meadows and his colleagues was an impending shortage of raw materials. The reclamation and recycling of much that is currently discarded may, in the long term, be born of sheer necessity. In the interim it can, under favourable conditions, provide materials at lower energy cost and with less environmental damage than do primary sources whose life is thereby extended. For nations lacking indigenous resources a saving of foreign exchange and a reduced vulnerability to foreign cartels form a seductive combination.

Valuable materials have always been their own incentive for reclamation, as exemplified in the long tradition of recycling of metals. It is self-evident that recovery will be practised where it is profitable so to do. When materials are abandoned it is because economics dictate the use of virgin feedstock. Price rises and recent uncertainties of supply now threaten the very basis of Western manufacturing industry depending as it does on inexpensive and, above all, abundant materials.

In April, 1975 a symposium was sponsored by the University of Nottingham and by the Inter-University Centre for Post-graduate Studies, Dubrovnik, Yugoslavia, under financial guarantees generously made by the United Nations Environmental Programme (UNEP) and by Allied Breweries. Held in Dubrovnik and entitled 'The Recycling and Disposal of Solid Wastes', the event was designed to review the entire field of resource reclamation from discarded materials.

This book contains the proceedings of the symposium, providing an overall coverage of the field and an introduction for those interested in working in this important area.

MICHAEL E. HENSTOCK
MICHAEL W. BIDDULPH

Conservation & Recycling, Vol.1, pp.3–17. Pergamon Press, 1976. Printed in Great Britain.

THE SCOPE FOR MATERIALS RECYCLING

MICHAEL E. HENSTOCK

University of Nottingham, England

Abstract—The work of Meadows *et al.* in *The Limits to Growth,* although open to severe criticism on a number of points, has focused attention on possible future shortages of materials, but the short life-time then predicted for many materials may be shown to result from oversimplification of published estimates of ore reserves. In fact, the absolute tonnages of most metals in the earth's crust are such that, with few exceptions, supplies are practically limitless, and depend largely on market forces.

Pressures are likely to come from the demand for basic amenities by the large population of the developing nations rather than from the incremental needs of the relatively sparsely populated developed lands. Shortages will probably arise from the increasing cost of energy and the higher specific energy input needed to extract from low-grade sources as richer deposits are progressively depleted. The dependence of all advanced industrial nations on a supply of relatively cheap energy, and their vulnerability to political and economic pressures through that dependence, have recently been demonstrated. Most materials may be recycled from their primary use with the expenditure of only a fraction of the energy initially required to extract from their ores; thus, they may be considered as an energy bank. This, together with concomitant benefits to the balance of payments and the improvement in environmental quality resulting from the recycling, rather than the abandonment, of materials makes the case for recycling almost irresistible in many cases

For valuable materials, such as most non-ferrous metals, the channels for recycling are already well-developed, but opportunities exist for separation and re-use of commodities whose value is less apparent. Domestic refuse may be separated into fractions rich in iron and steel, aluminium, other non-ferrous metals, glass, and combustibles. Other techniques produce saleable fractions from incinerator residues.

Perhaps the largest scope is in the field of so-called 'open loop recycling' where the waste from one process is used as raw material for another; here the possibilities for development of re-use cycles increase in number with the size of the catchment area.

INTRODUCTION

"The most difficult task that faces the governments of industrial countries in dealing with the now urgent problems of conservation and pollution is how to persuade or compel people to change many of their social habits and accept new economic concepts".

The above was written in 1973 by a former Minister of State at the Board of Trade[1]; the article that it headed reflected an awareness that, although our current preoccupation with materials stems mostly from a widespread concern with pollution, conservation of resources has emerged as a technical, social and political issue in its own right.

A great many works[2], long and short, have been concerned with pollution and lie outside the scope of this lecture. Certain specialised aspects of the subject are considered elsewhere in this symposium[3]. For the moment it is sufficient to point out that:

POLLUTION equals WASTE

If waste can be recycled, pollution will disappear since the latter is only material in the wrong place at a particular time.

DEFINITION OF WASTE

The White Paper entitled "Disposal of Solid Toxic Wastes" published by the Department of the Environment (Scottish Development Department), 1970, gives the following definition:

"The economists's definition of a waste is presumably that which it is cheaper to throw away than to make further use of. This does not mean that waste is valueless; some of it certainly is not. The situation would be quite different if raw materials became much more expensive and costs of disposal were vastly increased. But no-one wants increased prices simply in order to ease the waste disposal problem (or, indeed, for any other reason). Nevertheless we are inclined to the view that the "economist's" definition of waste is inadequate. Partly because this definition concerns one user only; it might be economic for him to throw something away but uneconomic for the nation (or for mankind) particularly in the long run".

This definition leads inevitably to the need to estimate relative costs of disposal and of reclamation and to a comprehensive study of the total costs of disposal, including social and environmental costs. This point will be re-examined in greater detail later in the paper.

AVAILABILITY OF RESOURCES

The report by Meadows *et al.,* published by the Club of Rome under the title *"The Limits to Growth"*[4], is by now so widely known that comments are almost superfluous. Problems of economic growth are considered under a number of headings, but for the purpose of this discussion it will suffice to examine the sections dealing with resources.

The work is open to criticism on a number of points, but has unquestionably served a useful purpose, whatever its faults, if it has focused attention on the problem, and this it undoubtedly has done. Some of its conclusions are questionable but manifestly true is that the growth of population this century has been substantially exponential. Concern over population growth has recently been expressed but, because of inbuilt delays in the controlling feedback loops, we cannot hope that the population will level off before A.D. 2000. Even at present mortality rates, we may expect a world population of 7000 million by that year.

Industrial production has, since 1930 at any rate, risen at 7% per annum or 5% per annum *per capita.* This does not imply that everyone's living standard will double in 14 years, since inequalities exist in distribution. Most growth occurs in industrialised countries which have, in general, low birthrates. It is in these countries, moreover, where high standards of living have already been achieved and we may expect only minor increases in *per capita* demand. In the under-developed countries, on the other hand, population is increasing rapidly; here we may expect the greatest pressure on resources, when large numbers of people demand for the first time the goods that western civilisation has long regarded as bare essentials.

It is true that developed countries consume disproportionately large amounts of materials; this is almost a definition of being developed. There is, however, evidence that the intensity of use of a material, i.e. consumption/unit of Gross National Product (GNP) may begin to fall when an economy reaches a certain stage of maturity.

The western nations, particularly the U.S.A., have been criticized as posing the largest threat to materials supply. Whilst this may once have been true it is demonstrably false if one considers future possibilities. Sales of automobiles are, in developed lands, largely for replacement; although 200 million Americans possess 80 million cars, annual sales are only *ca.* 10 million. The potential pressure on resources when the 600 millions of India, or the even greater population of China, legitimately aspire to cars or even bicycles will far exceed the incremental consumption of developed lands.

The primary resource is, of course, land, but this is outside our scope. Resources can otherwise be divided into renewable, e.g. wood, and nonrenewable, e.g. metal. Non-renewable resources (NRR) are being consumed at an exponential rate, driven by the positive feedback loops of population and capital growth.

Meadows cites, as an example, the metal chromium. This has been selected because it is a material which is not, at present, under particular pressure. It has a long static reserve index, i.e. at present rates of consumption currently known reserves would last for 420 years. Consumption is, in fact, increasing by 2.6% per annum compound, at which rate a simple calculation shows that exhaustion will occur in 95 years. The situation is, though, a good deal more complex than revealed by this simple sum since, as the material becomes scarcer, its price would rise. The effect of this would be two-fold;

(a) Efforts might be made to replace chromium by cheaper materials in certain applications.

(b) The increased price commanded by finished metal would make it economically viable to work lower grade deposits.

In this way, it is feasible that the known reserves might, by new discoveries and improved technology, as well as the incentive to exploit lower grade deposits, be increased by a factor of, say, five. Unfortunately it may be shown that this five-fold increase in reserves would not extend the life-time of the metal by a factor of five. Continued exponential growth would result in exhaustion after 154 years.

If we apply to this situation the results of an efficient recycling policy pursued from the year 1970, it may be shown that with exponential usage demand would still overcome supply in 235 years. These relationships are shown in Fig. 1.

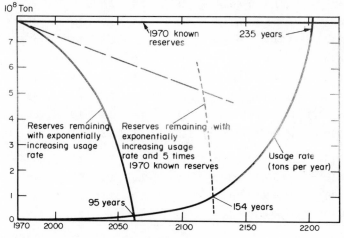

Fig. 1 Chromium reserves.

Clearly, it is unrealistic to use the static reserve index since demand is increasing exponentially. It may, with advantage, be replaced by an exponential reserve index, and Table 1 shows this for a number of common metals. From it may be drawn several interesting conclusions:

(a) A figure of nine years is given for the expected lifetime of gold. Since these figures were compiled, however, the price of gold has more or less quadrupled and, at a current price of about $150 per ounce the lifetime of the metal will be considerably extended. Gold is found in many locations throughout the world, the attractiveness of each deposit depending largely upon its richness.

(b) The projected lifetime of mercury reserves is evidently 11 years. New demands, e.g. mercury batteries, may reduce that figure.

Points for discussion also emerge for many other materials. The figures, it should be noted, are compiled not from the estimates of some environmental pressure group but from official United States Bureau of Mines statistics.

However, it has been said that figures such as these — and it should be realised that the conclusions of Meadows *et al.* are based on such — are dangerously over-simplified. They present estimates of reserves of minerals that could be used *under economic and technological conditions obtaining at a given time.* This implies that deposits of lower quality than those being exploited at that time

MICHAEL E. HENSTOCK

Table 1. Non-renewable natural resources[4]

Resource	Known global reserves		Static Index (yr)	Projected rate of growth			Exponential index (yr)	Exponential index calculated using 5-times known reserves (yr)
	tonnes litres	other units		High	Ave.	Low		
Aluminium	1.06×10^9	$(1.17 \times 10^9 \text{tons})$	100	7.7	6.4	5.1	31	55
Chromium	7.03×10^8	$(7.75 \times 10^8 \text{tons})$	420	3.3	2.6	2.0	95	154
Coal	4.5×10^{12}	$(5 \times 10^{12} \text{tons})$	2300	5.3	4.1	3.0	111	150
Cobalt	2.2×10^6	$(4.8 \times 10^9 \text{tons})$	110	2.0	1.5	1.0	60	148
Copper	279×10^6	$(308 \times 10^6 \text{tons})$	36	5.8	4.6	3.4	21	48
Gold	10.96×10^3	$(353 \times 10^6 \text{troy oz.})$	11	4.8	4.1	3.4	9	29
Iron	0.9×10^{11}	$(1 \times 10^{11} \text{tons})$	240	2.3	1.8	1.3	93	173
Lead	83×10^6	$(91 \times 10^6 \text{tons})$	26	2.4	2.0	1.7	21	64
Manganese	7×10^8	$(8 \times 10^8 \text{tons})$	97	3.5	2.9	2.4	45	94
Mercury	115×10^3	$(3.34 \times 10^6 \text{flasks})$	13	3.1	2.6	2.2	11†	41
Molybdenum	4.9×10^6	$(10.8 \times 10^9 \text{lb})$	79	5.0	4.5	4.0	34	65
Natural gas	$32.28 \times 10^{15} \text{l}$	$(1.14 \times 10^{15} \text{cu.ft.})$	38	5.5	4.7	3.9	22	49
Nickel	67×10^6	$(147 \times 10^9 \text{lb})$	150	4.0	3.4	2.8	53	96
Petroleum	$723 \times 10^8 \text{Tl}$	$(455 \times 10^9 \text{bbls})$	31	4.9	3.9	2.9	20	50
Platinum Group	13.3×10^3	$(429 \times 10^6 \text{troy oz.})$	130	4.5	3.8	3.1	47	85
Silver	171×10^3	$(5.5 \times 10^9 \text{troy oz.})$	16	4.0	2.7	1.5	13	42
Tin	4.4×10^7	$(4.3 \times 10^7 \text{lg tons})$	17	2.3	1.1	0	15	61
Tungsten	1.3×10^6	$(2.9 \times 10^9 \text{lb})$	40	2.9	2.5	2.1	28	72
Zinc	112×10^6	$(123 \times 10^6 \text{tons})$	23	3.3	2.9	2.5	18	50

† Ref. 4 calculates this value as 13.

Table 2

Element	% in average rock	Tonnes in outer 3.5 km of continental crust	% in solid deposit of minimum workable grade	Identified resources (tonnes)	1970 demand (tonnes)	Resource life at 1970 use rate (yr)
Iron (Fe)	4.65	7×10^{16}	25	3.5×10^{11}	4×10^8	875
Aluminium (Al)	8.05	12×10^{16}	23	3×10^9	1.2×10^7	250
Titanium (Ti)	0.45	6.7×10^{15}	10	1.2×10^9	1.4×10^6	857
Nickel (Ni)	0.0058	8.7×10^{13}	1.5	8.4×10^7	6×10^5	140
Copper (Cu)	0.0047	7×10^{13}	0.4	3.1×10^8	6×10^6	52
Zinc (Zn)	0.0083	1.3×10^{14}	4.0	1.5×10^9	5×10^6	300
Lead (Pb)	0.0016	2.4×10^{13}	4.0	1.3×10^8	3.3×10^6	39
Fluorine (F)	0.066	1×10^{15}	20	4.2×10^7	1.9×10^6	22
Carbon (C)	0.122	1.8×10^{15}	35	3×10^{12}	4×10^9	750

would not be included because, economically, they would be uncompetitive. There may well be vast amounts of other ores unworkable under present conditions, but requiring only modest price increases or minor technological advances to make them viable. For example, one estimate of the global reserves of bauxite, the principal current source of aluminium, is 15000×10^6 tonnes. This is equivalent to about 4000×10^6 tonnes of metal. It does not include another 5000×10^6 tonnes of bauxite presently regarded as marginal, the vast potential of the lateritic surfaces in various parts of Africa and Latin America, and large deposits in Guinea, where ore containing less than 50% Al_2O_3 is not even regarded as bauxite[5]. Further, there are massive deposits of other Al-containing minerals, e.g. anorthosite, alunite, dawsonite and clays.

In Table 2, resources for the outer crust are given[6], with 1970 demand.

Many other estimates exist, based on various criteria. An extreme view is reached[7] by considering total tonnages, irrespective of workability.

Extraction of metals from low grade ores is expensive. It has been[8] suggested that most copper will, in the 1980's, be extracted from ores of 0.5% metal, from which recovery is feasible only with large supplies of inexpensive energy.

The oil crisis of 1973, and subsequent events, may throw doubt upon that possibility.

It is, from the foregoing, clear that exponential population growth is the decisive factor in the continued availability of raw materials. It is evident that recycling will, sooner or later, become necessary for most metals. It is unlikely to occur with glass, because of the virtually limitless supplies of raw materials, although it is significant that energy accounts for 12% of the cost of glass containers. A limit to primary glass production may ultimately be imposed by the same energy shortages that could curtail the primary extraction of metals. If energy becomes the dominant factor, recycling will be attractive only if one employs routes that are less energy-intensive than those of primary extraction.

It must be noted that, since recycling cannot be 100% efficient and since demand is likely to continue to rise, recycling cannot by itself solve material shortages. Changes in usage patterns may ease the problem, and some predicted changes are given in Figs. 2 and 3.

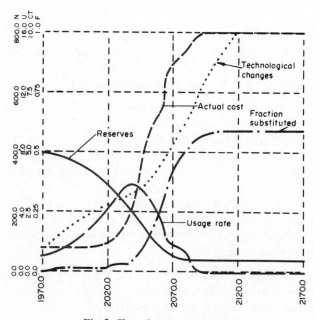

Fig. 2. Chromium usage patterns.

In Fig. 2, usage (U) grows rapidly, reserves (N) are quickly depleted. Cost (C) remains low because of assumed improvements in technology (T), facilitating the use of lower grade ores. As demand increases, T is unable to keep pace with the rising costs of exploration and extraction, so C rises slowly, then more rapidly, enforcing substitution and a more efficient use of metal. After 125 years, only *ca.* 5% of the original chromium is available and at a prohibitively high cost. Mining of new metal approaches zero and 60% of original usage has been substituted (F).

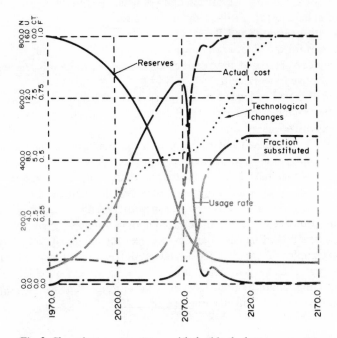

Fig. 3. Chromium usage patterns with double the known reserves.

The same exercise carried out for an assumed doubling of chromium reserves (Fig. 3) shows only an extended growth phase with correspondingly high peak usage resulting in extension of life by a mere 20 years, i.e. to 145 years.

The political implications are immense and wide-ranging. Some of the more obvious ones are:

(a) Increasing competition for limited supplies of raw materials must increase prices and result in lower overall living standards for the consuming nations.

(b) Continuous industrial growth has enabled the aspirations of the lower paid to be satisfied by continuous increases in their *absolute* standard of living. With zero or even negative economic growth, improvements in the living standards of one section of the community can be satisfied only by corresponding reductions elsewhere.

(c) A much more closely regimented society may result from the need to conserve materials. Since the prevailing political climate would seem to make rationing by price unacceptable, in the U.K. at any event, it follows that much stricter control may be exercised over the permissible materials of which a particular commodity may be made.

The advantages of recycling our waste have been outlined. It is now appropriate to examine, briefly, the cost of abandoning the wastes, i.e. of making no attempt to recover any part of them as a separate, usable fraction. In the case of UK domestic refuse, disposal costs have been estimated at £7/tonne; some 18 million tonnes is generated annually in this country.

The real cost to society of dumping industrial or domestic wastes may be very much greater than the costs usually assigned/charged. Seepage and contamination of land and water may place an additional charge on the local authority ultimately responsible. This could be avoided if waste were recycled.

General considerations of recycling

Recycling has a long history; the Bible contains references[9] to recovery of metals. Two main reasons exist for this early awareness of recycling:

(a) Metals, by their rarity to early man, who had not yet mastered large-scale extraction, have always been relatively valuable compared with other materials.

(b) Engineering practice has in the past used solid metal which, especially as process scrap, may easily be collected and reclaimed by simple melting. Modern practice has reversed this trend, possibly because the increasing value of metals has precluded the use of massive pieces of it in consumer goods.

Recycling may broadly be classified as "closed loop" and "open circuit". In the former category the shortest route is simple collection, segregation and remelting, the recycled metal being used for applications broadly similar to its original use. This procedure offers greatest flexibility but is not always possible because of the contamination of the scrap.

A somewhat longer closed loop involves the addition of a refining stage in cases where the metal is contaminated, either inadvertently during service or intentionally by alloying with metallic or non-metallic additions.

The open circuit method abandons the attempt to recycle to virgin specification material but relies for its economic feasibility on degradation to lower costs products, not themselves worth recycling. The material is, therefore, ultimately lost to the entire system and this point is taken up again elsewhere in this symposium.

The recycling of specific materials, e.g. metals, glass, paper and polymers, is already a part of our technology. More difficult in concept is the recovery of valuables from mixed materials, and the most immediate problem is posed by domestic refuse.

This provides, in principle, a raw material with considerable recycling potential. The contents of one dustbin may differ from those of the next. The proportion of glass bottles, newsprint, tin cans and plastic bags may, predictably, change with locality, ethnic group, and personal preference for fresh or packaged foods. However, a high degree of aggregation and homogenisation becomes possible when the individual transport vehicles deposit their loads at the central dump or incinerator.

The composition of domestic refuse varies with, *inter alia,* the criteria mentioned above. It is also changing with time and with changes in social and economic priorities.

The H.M. Government Working Party on Refuse Disposal provides the following average analysis for U.K. domestic refuse in 1968, and a forecast for 1980[10].

Table 3

	1968 (%)	1980 estimate (%)	2000 estimate (%)
Dust and cinder	22	12	6
Vegetable and putrescible	18	17	15
Paper	37	43	47
Metal	9	9	8
Textiles	2	3	3
Glass	9	9	12
Plastics	1	5	9
Unclassified	2	2	—

Flinthoff[11] has projected to the year 2000; in terms of relative increase/household/week, glass and plastics are notable. In absolute terms, paper is projected to increase, 1971–2000, by 3.1 kg and plastics by 1.4 kg/household/week. The relationships are shown in Fig. 4.

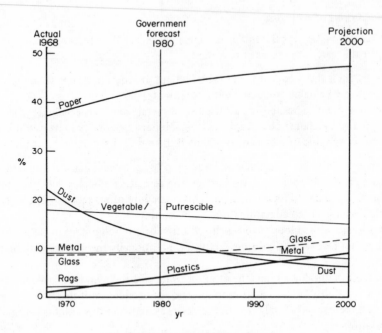

Fig. 4. Constituents of U.K. refuse.

Industrial wastes are, as stated earlier, very variable in composition; it has been estimated that quantities by weight are twice those of domestic wastes, presently running at 18×10^6 tonnes/annum for the U.K. Such estimates are thrown into perspective by the implication that for every person in Britain about a tonne of solid waste is created each year. Domestic waste in the U.S.A. may run to 300×10^6 tonnes annually.

Per capita production of solid domestic wastes has been static in Britain for about a decade; paper, glass, cans and plastics have all increased but have been offset by fall-off in ash from open fires. This offset will not continue indefinitely; a 1%/annum overall growth may ensue which, matched by industrial waste output and aggravated by population increase to, say, 65 millions, could result in 86×10^6 tonnes of solid waste by A.D. 2000. Forecasting involves provision of disposal space and several writers have erred on the side of caution in estimating a possible 100×10^6 tonnes/annum by the end of the century.

Assuming a 2 : 1 ratio of industrial and domestic refuse, some 33×10^6 tonnes of the latter may then be expected (Fig. 5). For disposal by tipping, each tonne occupies *ca.* 1.15 m^3; projected requirements by A.D. 2000 will thus be 8.7×10^6 m^3/annum, i.e. 1 km^2 covered to a depth of 8.7 m in the absence of any treatment.

Current methods of refuse disposal vary from simple uncontrolled tipping in areas with no land shortage to highly sophisticated incinerators capable of 97% volume reduction[12]. Unless recycling is possible, disposal is merely a question of relocation. Disposal never means total disappearance but only transfer from an inconvenient to a convenient site.

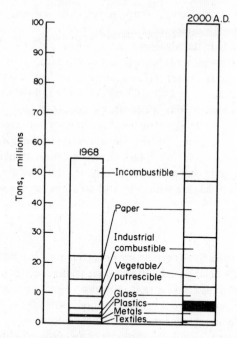

Fig. 5. Estimated total weight of solid wastes from domestic, trade and industrial sources in the U.K.

About 85% of all U.K. refuse is dumped with no prior treatment other than the almost random removal from it of large or desirable items, e.g. massive metal[11]. We may now consider the route taken by the remainder. Treatment applied to it may take several forms.

(a) Physical
(b) Biochemical
(c) Thermal.

Physical treatment may commence with removal of ferrous metals by magnetic methods. There is a wide variety of magnetic machines, developed over many years, that will remove ferrous metals too small to have justified prior manual removal. The machines are simple and relatively inexpensive but separation can be far from complete.

At this stage the remainder can be burned and further treatment applied to the incinerator residue. Methods have also been developed to process the raw, unburned refuse, and it is pertinent to examine at this point the relative advantages of treating raw waste or of first incinerating it.

Incineration provides excellent volume reduction, produces useful heat, requires no feed preparation other than the removal of items too large to enter the furnace, and is relatively pollution free, clean and immediate. The residue is innocuous and suitable for dumping. However, it has the disadvantage of so altering the form of many of the constituents of the feed that they cannot be re-used. Paper, wood, cardboard and textiles will be converted to ash and to oxides of carbon. Glass may be melted to an intractable, contaminated lump. Although some plastics do not burn readily, most are totally combustible in municipal incinerators; those, such as PVC, that release halides can initiate chemical reactions that impair metal recovery. Metals may be melted, oxidised or converted to halide compounds and lost in the gaseous effluents. Further, although combustion releases usable heat, this is normally much less than the energy input originally used to produce the material, and reconstitution requires still more energy.

Raw refuse is more bulky and heterogeneous than is incinerator ash. However, constituents remain in their original chemical state for direct recycling. A more constructive method of approach is to remove the potentially valuable materials from the raw refuse and to incinerate, pyrolyse or hydrolyse the remainder. The intensive research into segregation of raw refuse is evidence enough that incineration is, by many, considered merely as a short-term measure. In any event, only 15–20% of U.K. domestic refuse is incinerated[13], leaving some 14×10^6 tonnes/annum, the potential value of which far exceeds that of the materials contained in incinerator residues.

Pyrolysis, or the relatively low temperature heating of refuse in the absence of air, is extensively dealt with elsewhere in the symposium, but the characteristics of the residue may be mentioned. Since decomposition is essentially anaerobic, there is no oxidation of metal components. The solid product is in the form of a friable char which, unlike incinerator residues, does not require crushing to release values; there seems to be no reason why it should not be processed by the techniques applied to incinerator clinker.

Treatment of raw refuse

Any continuous process relies for its efficiency on a stream of raw material of constant quality. The size of particle efficiently dealt with by physical separation techniques, especially air classification, is such that size reduction of refuse is necessary. A device whereby a homogeneous waste material can be made from heterogeneous raw refuse is generally called a shredder or pulverizer; the municipal solid waste shredder normally combines impact with shear forces.

Municipal solid waste presents significant shredder design problems; in most industries one can design for a particular feed characteristic. The material can be hard, brittle, tough, ductile, soft, wet or fibrous. Solid refuse can, and often does, have all these characteristics in its various constituents[14].

Separation methods

Shredded raw refuse, like incinerator and pyrolysis residues, may be regarded as a multi-valuable ore, amenable to treatment by mineral engineering methods to separate it into product concentrates which, with a final cleansing, can be converted into potentially useful materials. A possible flow sheet is shown in Fig. 6.

The first stage in this method of processing raw refuse[15] is coarse shredding in a low-power machine to liberate materials contained in plastic and paper bags and boxes without damage to the equipment from solid metal objects. The coarseness of shredding should reduce paper, cardboard and plastic to a size suitable for subsequent air classification. Further, tin cans should be discharged without balling or folding, and glass shattered with a minimum production of fines. Folded cans would entrap food and other contaminants and would inhibit subsequent detinning operations. Lightly damaged cans, on the other hand, can be reshredded into short strips which are easily washed to remove food and labels. Coarse glass can be separated by colour.

A hood, positioned over the shredder discharge conveyor, controls dusting and sucks up the lightest pieces of shredded refuse from the top of the moving bed.

Shredded refuse then normally passes through a magnetic separator; the suspended belt type may suffice since, primarily, light-gauge ferrous material is involved. The heaviest iron objects remain in the waste flow. Light-gauge iron product is suitable, at this point, for final preparation prior to detinning; this is normally achieved by further milling to disrupt protective lacquer films, followed by dissolution of the tin in a caustic solution and subsequent recovery by electrodeposition.

The main refuse stream passes to a primary air classifier or elutriator that separates material in a horizontal or vertical stream of air. In the former type shredded refuse is discharged from a variable-speed belt feeder into a sloping chute entering the top at one end of the classifier. It falls into a horizontal air stream entering the chamber from the same side as the refuse. Airflow rates can

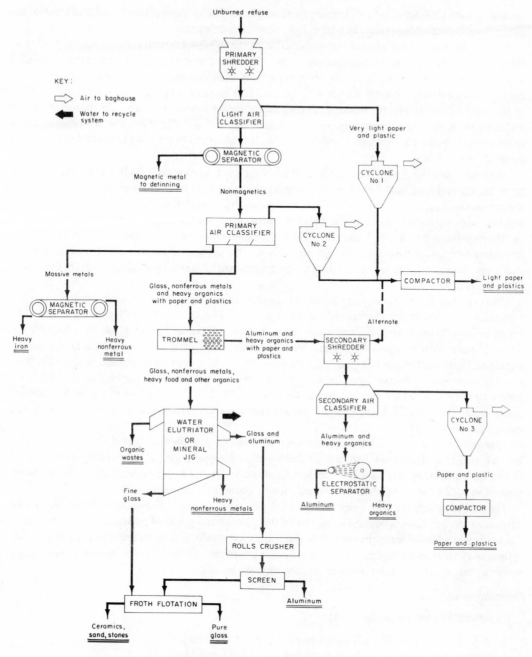

Fig. 6. United States Bureau of Mines raw refuse separation flowsheet.

be varied from 29–141 m³/min (1000–5000 ft³/min). At rates > 141 m³/min, turbulence reduces efficiency.

Very heavy objects fall vertically through the airstream to a conveyor that takes them to storage. Lighter material is blown laterally past a divider where a carefully controlled stream of air, created by a suction fan at the end of the processing system and rising from an opening in the base, carries off the lightest shredded material. It passes to a cyclone, where solids are collected, the air then traversing a dust collector before escaping to atmosphere. The cyclone product includes most of the paper from the incoming refuse, as well as light plastics and fabrics.

Material blown past the divider but not lifted with the lightest fraction falls through the rising air-stream to a conveyor; this fraction includes most of the glass, aluminium, food waste, heavy plastics, wood, rubber, and heavy paper articles such as partially shredded magazines. These are carried by conveyor to a rotating trommel screen with 5.7 cm (2.25 in.) holes. Glass, food wastes and small amounts of the other materials pass the screen and, via conveyor, pass to storage. Water elutriation of this product yields a glass concentrate and an organic waste containing soil and fine glass. The glass concentrate is dried and screened on a 4–mesh screen (*ca.* 0.6 cm, ¼ in. holes). Oversize is processed in electronic colour sorters.†

The colour-sorting system has been described in the context of glass, which may be identified by its transparency and separated from opaque particles. A simple adaptation of the optical system enables the device also to grade scrap glass (cullet) into various coloured fractions, e.g. flint, amber and green, and two-stage separation could deliver these and products from the glass concentrate. The use of electromagnetic sensor heads, however, permits the same basic system to separate non-ferrous from ferrous metals; future developments will probably involve the use of ultra-violet, X-ray transmission and X-ray fluorescence as rejection criteria. The system works best on particles of 0.6 cm diameter or greater[16].

Oversize from the trommel joins the light materials collected by the cyclone and passes to a secondary shredder, which further reduces the size to 2.5–7.6 cm (1–3 in.). Secondary air classification follows; heavy material (aluminium, wood, leather, rubber and heavy plastics) is discharged to a further water elutriator yielding organic wastes and metallic aluminium. Light material is trapped in a cyclone. Principally paper and plastics, it may be split by high tension electrodynamics[17], this recently developed technique operates at up to 200 kV. Paper is drawn to the electrode while plastics adhere to the drum and are brushed free at the bottom. On 2.5–7.6 cm (1–3 in.) shredded material concentrates averaging 99.4 and 99.9% paper are claimed, with plastics recovery of up to 99.4% and paper recovery of 100%.

Recovered plastics can be burned to provide heat but, despite the fact that their present value as fuel is higher than that as raw material, of much greater long-term appeal is separation by type and re-use. Encouraging results have been achieved, using a variety of aqueous media, in a float-and-sink separation of the five most plentiful components of waste thermoplastics.

The particular scheme here described is a pilot plant[15] of the U.S. Bureau of Mines; a detailed analysis of the products is beyond the scope of this paper but a point of particular significance is that the trommel undersize was predominantly glass and food residues, demonstrating the ability of the system to capture and concentrate at a single point essentially all the glass and putrescibles of the incoming refuse. The organics are then readily removed by elutriation.

Operating costs

Two situations were examined[15];

1. A 550 tonne/day plant working a single 8 hr shift, 6 d/week.
2. The same plant two 8 hr shifts, 6 d/week, i.e. 1100 tonne/day.

The refuse was processed into fractions as shown in Table 4.

Conservative estimates are given for probable values of the products. Those assigned to paper and plastics are values as fuel, and those for glass and metal are figures assumed for products reclaimed from incinerator residues. No value has been ascribed to fine glass residues although they might well be usable in low value products, e.g. building materials.

† At the time of editing (January 1976) it is understood that colour sorting has been abandoned because of unfavourable economics.

Table 4

Product	Value ($/tonne)	kg recovered, per tonne of refuse	Value per tonne of refuse ($)
Iron	44.10	72	3.17
Aluminium	264.61	8	2.11
Heavy nonferrous metals	661.52	2	1.32
Glass, colour sorted	22.05	35	0.77
Fine glass, mixed colours	11.03	59	0.65
Combustibles (fuel)	4.41	758	3.34
Waste, ceramics, dirt, etc.	−	66	−
Gross value with colour sorting of coarse glass	−	−	11.34
Gross value with no colour sorting of glass	−	−	10.84
Operating cost (550 tonne/d) including amortization, 20 yr, with colour sorting of glass	−	−	6.50
with no colour sorting of glass	−	−	4.30
Operating cost (1,100 tonne/d) including amortization, 20 yr, with colour sorting of glass	−	−	4.30
with no colour sorting of glass	−	−	2.98
Net value (550 tonne/d) with colour sorting of glass	−	−	4.84
with no colour sorting of glass	−	−	6.54
Net value (1100 tonne/d) with colour sorting of glass	−	−	7.04
with no colour sorting of glass	−	−	7.86

Final computation of operating costs must include costs of alternative methods of disposal, e.g. landfill. Some tentative economics are summarized in Table 5.

Table 5

Refuse processed	550 tonne/d ($)	110 tonne/d ($)
Net revenue from sale of products	6.54	7.86
Savings in hauling to landfill	1.10	1.10
Savings in landfill operation	2.20	2.20
Total/tonne	9.84	11.16

Indirect savings are impossible to quantify. It should be noted that judicious choice of amortization period can produce, within limits, profit figures at any desired level.

The number of operational RRS continues to increase[18]; best known is probably that at Franklin, OH, using the Black Clawson process to a design maximum of 165 tonne/d of refuse. Pulpable and friable materials in the waste stream are first converted to a slurry by a high-speed rotor. Large, heavy objects are removed via a bottom opening, ferrous metals are removed magnetically and glass, sand and small pieces of non-ferrous metals extracted in a liquid cyclone. Slurry is screened and channelled into primary and secondary fibre selectors to remove most of the long and short chemical fibres, which are dewatered and baled. Sludge is burned in a fluid bed reactor. A facility for glass colour sorting is to be added.

Treatment of incinerator residues

The incineration process virtually destroys all but the metal content of refuse so far as possible recycling is concerned. The scope for separation of useful fractions is thus severely limited. Incineration is normally designed only for drastic bulk reduction with or without utilisation of the heat so generated.

Magnetic treatment can reclaim ferrous material such as tin cans; the residual clinker is essentially unsaleable, although it contains non-ferrous metals amounting, for a town of 100,000 inhabitants, to an estimated 0.5 tonne/d in copper and aluminium alone.

Work carried out by Warren Spring Laboratory showed that the non-ferrous metal fraction contains 45% aluminium, 25% copper, 4.5% lead, 8.4% zinc and 1.4% nickel.

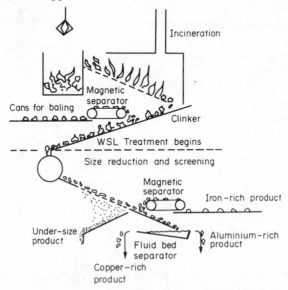

Fig.7. Warren Spring Laboratory system for metallic recovery from incinerator clinker.

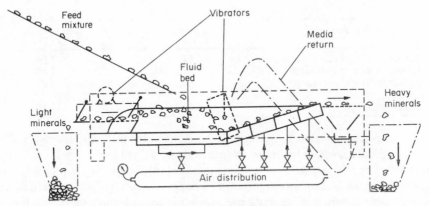

Fig. 8. Warren Spring Laboratory dry fluid bed separator.

This fraction can be treated on classification principles (Fig. 7) using a fluidised bed (Fig. 8) to produce two products containing, respectively, 95% aluminium and 60% copper. Valuations by metal merchants were, respectively, £61 and £203/tonne and an operating surplus of £0.74/tonne is feasible in a plant processing 25 tonne/h of clinker. The United States Bureau of Mines has also devised a flowsheet for treating incinerator residues and this was to be implemented†, first, at Lowell, MA[19].

† At the time of editing for publication (January 1976) it is understood that the Lowell incinerator has closed. owing to an inability to comply with EPA emission requirements. Thus, the residue plant will not go into operation in that locality.

THE M.I.T. LARGE ITEM SORTER

Traditionally, reclamation plants have separated solid wastes in the as-received condition. Hand picking has long been relied upon to extract from the flow of refuse certain classes of large saleable items, e.g. newspaper, cardboard, metals and glass, and much interest has been shown in MIT's attempt to automate this process, work that was carried out under an EPA grant. Large items of refuse are carried in bottom-opening carts and are scanned by a number of sensors in series, each evaluating a specific physical property. Sensor output is fed to a computer which decides to which of perhaps 25 different categories the item should be switched as the carts pass over a series of hoppers. The criteria for acceptance into a given category are, of course, set subjectively by the plant operator; large heterogeneous items are thus rejected by the sensing system and pass to a hammer mill for further size reduction and subsequent classification [20].

A significant feature of this process is that the materials being separated or the purity of these materials can be changed from day to day according to changes in market condition. The current limitations of the process are imposed by the need to develop both more sophisticated sensing devices and acceptance/rejection criteria for a broader variety of materials and objects, and one doubts whether it represents a realistic segregation process for domestic refuse.

REFERENCES

1. G. Darling, Bridging the persuasion gap, *Reclamation Industries International,* May/June (1973).
2. See, e.g. G. R. Taylor, *The Doomsday Book,* Thames & Hudson, (1970), or Panther Books (1972).
3. P. J. Boden, Toxic and Radioactive Wastes, paper delivered in the present Symposium (April 1975).
4. D. H. Meadows *et al., The Limits to Growth,* Earth Island Ltd., London (1972).
5. B. Balkay, Raw materials supply of the aluminium industry up to the year 2000, *8th World Mining Congress,* Lima, (November 1974).
6. Sir Kingsley Dunham, Non-renewable mineral resources, *Resources Policy* **1,** 1 (September 1974).
7. F. Callot, The problem of the world supply of ores in the year 2000 is basically a question of relative prices, *8th World Mining Congress,* Lima, (November 1974).
8. Sir Ronald Prain, The future availability of copper supplies, *Metals and Materials,* November (1970).
9. See, e.g. *Isaiah,* Chapter 2, verse 4.
10. *Waste Disposal,* HMSO, (1971).
11. F. L. D. Flinthoff, *The Disposal of Solid Wastes,* The British Plastics Federation, (1973).
12. Incineration: Fact Sheet, The National Center for Resource Recovery Inc. (March 1973).
13. J. E. P. Miles, Recovery of non-ferrous metals from domestic refuse, *Surveyor,* December (1972).
14. Shredders: Fact Sheet, The National Center for Resource Recovery, Inc. (April 1973).
15. P. M. Sullivan and Harry V. Makar, Bureau of Mines process for recovery of resources from raw refuse, *Proc. 4th Mineral Waste Utilization Symp.* Chicago, (May 1974).
16. Gunson's Sortex, private communication, (1974).
17. M. R. Grubbs and K. H. Ivey, Recovering plastics from urban refuse by electrodynamic techniques, U.S. Bureau of Mines, TPR 63, (December 1973).
18. Resource Recovery Systems: Fact Sheet, The National Center for Resource Recovery, (March 1973).
19. K. B. Higbie, Status of municipal refuse processing in the United States, World Conference *Towards a Plan of Action for Mankind. Needs and Resources – Methods of Forecasting,* Paris, (September 1974).
20. David Gordon Wilson and Stephen D. Senturia, Design and performance of the M.I.T. process for separating mixed municipal refuse, *Proc. 4th Mineral Waste Utilization Symp.,* Chicago, (May 1974).

Acknowledgements–Figures 1–3 and Table 1 are taken from *The Limits to Growth: A Report for THE CLUB OF ROME'S Project on the Predicament of Mankind,* by Donella H. Meadows, Dennis L. Meadows, Jorgen Randers and William W. Behrens III. A Potomac Associates book originally published by Universe Books, NY, 1972. Graphics by Potomac Associates. Figures 4 and 5, and Table 3 are after F. L. D. Flinthoff. Original publication issued by the British Plastics Federation. Figure 6 is reproduced by courtesy of the United States Bureau of Mines. Figure 7 and Figure 8 are Crown copyright. Reproduction by permission of the Director, Warren Spring Laboratory, Statistics originally quoted in Imperial have been converted by the present author to SI units. The Imperial values are given, where appropriate, in parenthesis.

Conservation & Recycling, Vol.1, pp.19–30. Pergamon Press, 1976. Printed in Great Britain.

COMPOSITION OF WASTES AND SOME POSSIBILITIES
FOR RECOVERY

B. G. KREITER
SVA, Amersfoort, Holland

INTRODUCTION

In 1969 the Institute for Waste Disposal (Stichting Verwijdering Afvalstoffen) was founded in the Netherlands. This Institute is a governmental organisation under the jurisdiction of the Ministry of Public Health and Environmental Hygiene.

The objective of the Institute is, primarily, to give advice and assistance to government departments, provinces and municipalities concerning waste disposal problems, and other bodies requesting help.

The advisory task comprises:

(a) The supplying of data for the drafting of legal regulations;

(b) The drafting of alternative projects for disposal of different categories of waste, having regard to environmental, planning and economic aspects;

(c) The giving of assistance (in evaluating, designing, contracting, testing and managing of transportation and treatment plants) to municipal and private services, that are in charge of an executive task in the field of waste disposal;

(d) The supply of general information, by publications, lectures, symposia and the promotion of education;

(e) The promotion of the training of executives;

(f) The coordination and evaluation of research in the field of collection, transportation and treatment of solid waste;

(g) The study of possibilities for better use of raw materials through recovery.

At present, the quantity of municipal solid waste in Holland amounts to about 300 kg per inhabitant per year, which totals approximately 3.5 million tonnes.

In terms of percentages the waste is disposed of as follows:

(a) 17% by composting on the Van Maanen system in two large plants, situated in more or less isolated rural regions;

(b) 3% by composting on the pulverising principle. This is still done in two municipal composting plants;

(c) 30% by incineration in modern installations in eight regions in which several municipalities cooperate;

(d) 50% by dumping on municipal and regional dumping sites; about 5% of these dumping sites comply with the necessary environmental and regional planning demands.

COMPOSITION OF DOMESTIC WASTE

One of the main tasks of SVA is the collection of basic data on the composition of domestic waste. This type of waste, collected in bins or plastic bags, forms a substantial part (60–70%) of municipal waste.

Data about composition are of real interest to determine whether recovery of some components might be feasible. Further, valuable information may be obtained in relation to disposal methods, including

(a) *Incineration,* whereby organic matter is burned, often with energy recovery;

(b) *Sanitary landfill,* whereby the waste is discharged and piled in thin layers at a suitable site, compacted and covered;

(c) *Composting,* a biological process whereby the organic material is biologically decomposed. Coarse inorganic matter has to be separated and treated.

It must be understood that a continuous determination of the composition of domestic refuse on a nation-wide scale is impossible. Therefore, three typical "pilot" districts were chosen for a thrice-yearly determination of the composition. These districts were located in the following communities:

(a) A village, *Overasselt,* number of inhabitants: 3 300;

(b) A medium-sized town, *Arnhem,* number of inhabitants: 128 000;

(c) A large town, *Amsterdam,* number of inhabitants: 771 000.

In the last case two districts are involved: an old and a new district.

By so doing it was hoped to determine possible differences in composition caused by factors such as:

(a) standard and modes of living;

(b) degree of industrialisation;

(c) size of community;

(d) seasonal variations.

The most important components for determination were:

(a) paper and board;

(b) ferrous metal;

(c) plastics;

(d) glass;

(e) textiles;

(f) putrescible material.

In the absence of a mechanical device available for this separation, hand-sorting was employed. Figure 1 depicts the procedure used. As an average over the above-mentioned districts the principal results were as follows:

	1971	1972	1973	1974
Paper and board	25.5	26.1	25.6	22.6
Ferrous metal	3.1	3.3	3.2	3.1
Plastics	4.7	5.2	5.1	5.3
Glass	10.0	11.7	11.9	13.0
Textiles	1.9	2.3	2.2	1.8
Vegetable	49.7	45.0	45.5	48.1
Unclassified	5.1	6.4	6.5	6.1

Figures 2–7 show the above-mentioned components as a function of district.

We may now establish the following:

(a) New districts, characterised by high living standards, show considerable quantities of paper and glass (sherry and gin bottles) in domestic waste.

(b) Small communities produce refuse containing more putrescible material.

In addition to this hand-sorting analysis the following examinations were recently commenced:

(a) A granular classification of the putrescibles, obtained by a sieving analysis:

        fraction 1   −3mm

        fraction 2   3–8mm

        fraction 3   8–20mm

        fraction 4   +20mm.

(b) Separation of the paper and plastic component in packing and non-packing material.

(c) Determination of moisture content, dirt content and fibre-quality of the paper component.

(d) Separation of the plastic component into:

 (i) polyvinylchloride

 (ii) polystyrene

(iii) polyethylene and polypropylene.

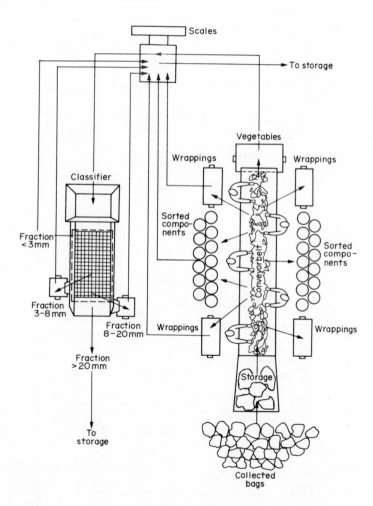

Fig. 1. Outline of the analysis procedure.

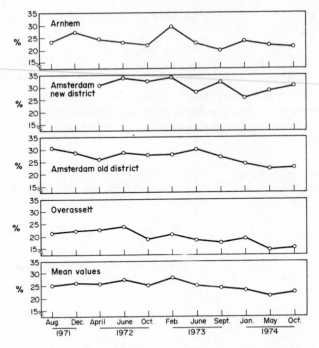

Fig. 2. Percentage (wt) of paper and board in domestic waste.

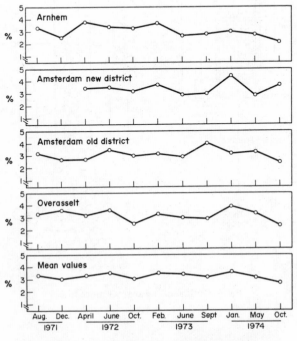

Fig. 3. Percentage (wt) of ferrous metal in domestic waste.

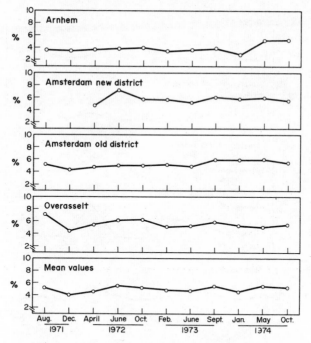

Fig. 4. Percentage (wt) of plastics in domestic waste.

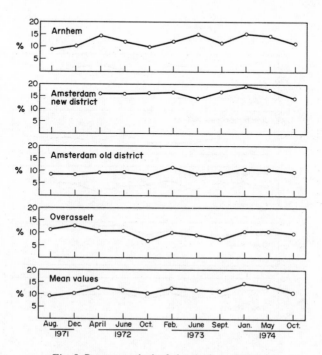

Fig. 5. Percentage (wt) of glass in domestic waste.

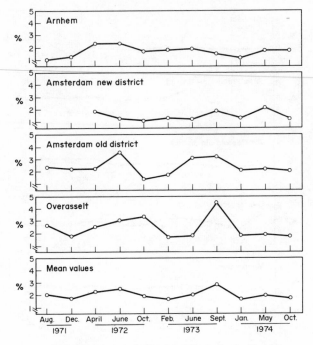

Fig. 6. Percentage (wt) of textiles in domestic refuse.

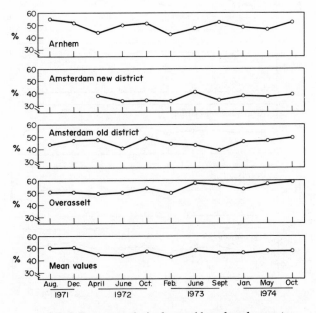

Fig. 7. Percentage (wt) of vegetable and garden waste.

POSSIBILITIES FOR RECOVERY

The recovery of wastes has become a focal point of interest for two reasons:

(a) The recovered wastes take the place of an equivalent quantity of virgin raw material.
(b) Less waste remains to be disposed of by other means.

Both these aspects are important when considering the various methods or systems of reuse.

In view of the general interest shown in this subject, it seemed desirable to draw up a summary of the research coordinated or encouraged by SVA into the reuse of wastes. This research, and the usual advisory work on the disposal of waste, are a major part of the work of the SVA. It cooperates closely for the purpose with a number of institutes that have facilities for carrying out such research.

This paper does not deal with recovery by the method of separate collection. It is based on recovery before or after the usual treatment methods.

Any process for the recovery of certain components of waste will, of course, have to be incorporated into a waste treatment *system*. Separating plants can generally treat only domestic waste. Industrial and bulky wastes present insuperable difficulties owing to their varying composition and dimensions. Figure 8 indicates the categories of waste to which specific separation techniques might be applied. Further, some percentages relating specifically to the situation in the Netherlands are quoted.

(a) Incineration + sanitary landfill

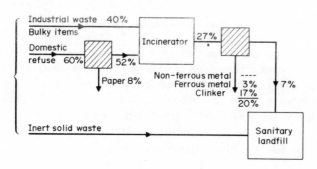

(b) Only sanitary landfill

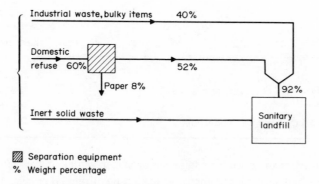

Separation equipment
% Weight percentage

Fig. 8. Possibilites for integration of separation methods in a solid waste disposal system.

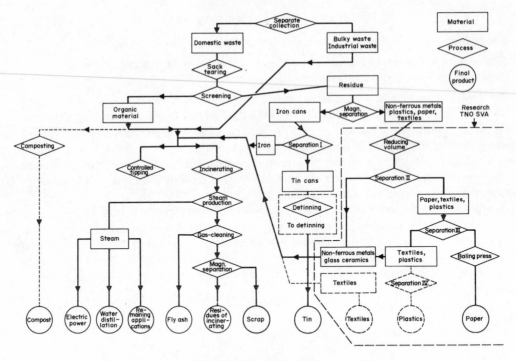

Fig. 9. Possibilities for reuse of wastes.

Figure 9 gives further details on the recovery of certain components and on possible uses of wastes. It assumes the desirability, even in the case of incineration, of the separate collection of domestic waste and bulky wastes, and it divides recovery activities into the following three phases:

(a) *Mechanical pre-separation of certain components*. Separation of the following components is

(b) Treatment of the remaining material, together with industrial and bulky wastes, either by controlled tipping or by incineration (eventually with heat recovery).

(c) Separation of certain materials from incinerator residues.

These phases are considered below:

(a) *Mechanical pre-separation of certain components*. Separation of the following components is considered feasible:

	Percentage of domestic waste by weight
Paper	20–25
Tin cans (for recovery of tin and ferrous metal)	3– 4
Plastics	5– 6
Organic material (for compost production)	45–50

The separation of plastics and organic material has been disregarded in view of the present great uncertainty (in the Netherlands at least) about the marketing of these products. The amount of excess organic material in the Netherlands is already so great (manure, organic sludge, etc.) that the production of an additional quantity of organics from domestic waste hardly seems appropriate.

The recovery of tin from tinplate is at present being studied by a working group composed of representatives of the steel industry, the tinplate industry and the SVA. The results of the study will be made known in due course.

It thus becomes apparent that paper is the most favourable component for possible recovery; it accounts for 20 to 25% of the weight of domestic waste, and it also produces a reasonable yield which, according to available data, may account to approximately * Dfl. 80/tonne.

In 1972 about 1 600 000 tonnes of paper and cardboard was produced in the Netherlands, about 34% of this quantity from waste paper [22]. It appears that, in the near future, either the supply of raw materials from abroad (cellulose, groundwood) will decrease or the prices of these raw materials will rise sharply [2]. An increasing demand for waste paper can consequently be expected. The obvious course, therefore, is to establish whether paper can be recovered from domestic waste, and the purposes for which it might be used. It may thus be concluded that a separation plant for domestic waste has to be designed to deal mainly with paper, and that the recovery of other components has little effect on the economic feasibility of a separation plant. It should be noted that a close correlation exists between the price for mixed waste paper and the paper content of domestic refuse (see Fig. 10). This phenomenon can probably be observed for other components, too, and should be incorporated in any feasibility study.

(b) *Treatment of the residuces after a pre-separation process.*

Sanitary landfill:

This comprises the storage of wastes at such a place and in such a manner that (at least when there are no objections on environmental or aesthetic grounds during and after the landfill procedure) the completed landfill project may be an improvement to the landscape and may be regarded as a form of utilisation of wastes.

Incineration:

The following forms of recovery are relevant to incineration:

(i) utilisation of the heat released during incineration.

(ii) treatment of incineration residues in order to recover certain materials.

Two principle variants regarding heat recovery are conceivable:

(i) supply of heat for purposes such as district heating or

(ii) generation of electricity.

If the heat is used for domestic heating systems, it will usually be possible, in summer, to use only part of it owing to the very low demand at that time. About 80% of the expenditure on heat for the production of distilled water, using multistage flash evaporators, is accounted for by fuel costs. If in any region, there is a shortage of water of a high degree of purity, either for the processing industry or for improving the quality of drinking water, it may, from the point of view of cost, be worth while using a refuse incinerator to supply the heat. The feasibility of this procedure has been demonstrated by detailed calculations for certain regions.

The generation of electricity has become less attractive in recent years owing, on the one hand, to the ever increasing essential additional expenditure involved (on investment, staffing and maintenance) and, on the other hand, to the proportionally decreasing price per MJ (kWh) of electrical energy. The two effects mentioned are shown approximately in Fig. 11, which gives (as a measure of the additional capital expenditure) index figures for the metalware products group for MJ (kWh) prices. The effect of the extra staff employed and the additional maintenance is not expressed in this graph. Furthermore,incineration systems without a specific form of heat utilisation have been found at least as dependable as systems with heat utilisation.

The growing scarcity of fossil fuels gives rise to the view that the MJ price may have to be reviewd in the near future. Whether the resulting evaluation will justify the additional expenditure where electricity is generated is still uncertain.

*$U.S. = 2.7 Dfl. at date of editing (January 1976). 1 Dfl. = 100 cents.

Combinations of the various forms of heat utilisation are the subject of constant attention, and the energetic and economic implications are being studied case by case. Some further points closely connected with heat-recovery in the incineration of waste, and methods such as pyrolysis are dealt with elsewhere in this symposium.

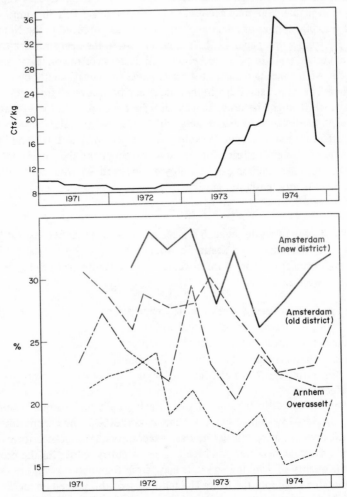

Fig. 10. Official price for mixed waste paper (upper graph) and paper content in domestic waste (lower graph).

(c) *Recovery of certain materials from incinerator residues* The composition of incineration residues is approximately as follows:
glass—approximately 20%.
iron—approximately 20% (provided that no pre-separation of tin cans has been performed), a small percentage of non-ferrous metals (aluminium, copper and zinc).
residue (including stone and pottery)—approximately 58%.

Partly as a result of the research findings of institutions in other countries, regarding recovery of materials such as glass, iron and non-ferrous metals from incinerator residues, a thorough study of the subject has been undertaken in close cooperation with the department of Mineral Technology, Delft University of Technology.

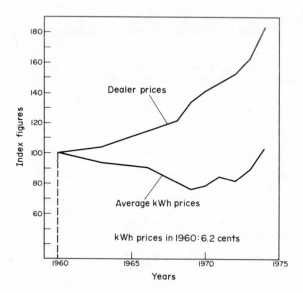

Fig. 11. Index figures of kWh prices (industry and trade) and dealer prices (metals).

CONCLUSIONS

An attempt has been made in the foregoing to bring the various modes of waste recovery into a logical connection with one another, and particularly to relate them to the treatment methods generally used, especially to sanitary landfill and to incineration. Certain priorities have also been recognised, and these are reflected in research projects.

Experiments on a commercial scale are needed in almost every case, for accurate weighing of costs against benefits. It is hoped that the knowledge thus gained will help to ensure the most efficient evaluation of the many new ideas and systems regarding utilization of wastes.

BIBLIOGRAPHY ON UTILIZATION OF WASTES

1. National Centre for Resource Inc, Washington, D.C., "Materials Recovery System" (Dec. 1972).
2. E. Vecchi, R. Baldo & E. Balducci, "Utilizzazione cartaria delle Paste da Fibre Urbane". *Cellulose e Carta* (Feb. 1973).
3. Elio Mensurati, "A contribution by the Administration of Rome Municipality to the preservation of natural resources. Disposal of solid refuse and production of natural resources. Disposal of solid refuse and production of paper pulp" (May 1973).
4. J. A. Dijkstra, "Terugwinning en hergebruik van oud papier en karton" (recovery and reuse of waste paper and cardboard). Centraal Technisch Instituut" (Central Technical Institute), T.N.O., (June 1972).
5. "Stichting Verwijdering Afvalstoffen" (Institute for Waste Disposal), "Enkele belangrijke aspecten inzake toepassing van het 'Hydrasposal-Fibreclaim process' als verwekings-methode voor afvalstoffen, alsmede een aantal in Duitsland en Zwitserland toegepaste methoden van hergebruik en recirkulatie" (Some important aspects of applying the 'Hydrasposal-Fibreclaim process' as a method of processing wastes, and of a number of methods of reuse and circulation used in Germany and Switzerland (SVA/383), (Nov. 1972).

6. W. Herbert, The Franklin Environmental Control Complex. "A process for recovery of paper, metals and glass from municipal wate". *Tappi,* **54,** No. 19 (Oct. 1971).

7. "Black Clawson Waste Systems"–The Black Clawson Company.

8. R. C. McKee, "Effect of repulping on sheet properties and fiber characteristics", *Paper Trade Journal* (May 1971).

9. B. W. Recknagel, "Recycling fibers–Economics and the environment",, *Paper Trade Journal,* (Feb. 1971).

10. "Papermakers study recycling", *Chemical Engineering* (Dec. 1970).

11. A. Porteous, "W. P. Disposal Process Turns Cellulose Material into Alcohol".

12. N. D. Drobny, H. E. Hull & R. F. Testin, "Recovery and Utilisation of municipal waste," U.S. Environmental Protection Agency (1971).

13. A. Darnay, "Recycling. Assessment and Prospects for Success", U.S. Environmental Protection Agency (1972).

14. A. Darnay & W. E. Franklin, "Salvage Markets for Materials in Solid Wastes", U.S. Environmental Protection Agency (1972).

15. P.M. Sullivan & M.H. Stanczyk, "Economics of recycling metals and minerals from urban refuse", U.S. Bureau of Mines, TPR 33 (April 1971).

16. G. Berman & J. Gony, "Les rejets solides, recyclage et réutilisation" (Solid wastes, recycling and reuse), Bureau de Recherches Geologiques et Minières (March 1973).

17. M. R. Grubbs & K. H. Ivey, "Recovering plastics from urban refuse by electrodynamic techniques", U.S. Bureau of Mines, TPR 63 (Dec. 1972).

18. Battelle-Institut e.V., Frankfurt am Main (publication of the Federal Ministry of the Interior), "Verwertung von Altpapier" (Utilisation of Waste Paper) (1973).

19. Vereniging van Nederlandse Papierfabrikanten V.N.P., (Union of Dutch Papermakers), "Struktuuronderzoek in de Nederlandse papierindustrie", (Structural research in the Dutch Paper Industry) (May 1973).

20. "Werkgroep Hergebruik Afval" (Working Group on the Reuse of Waste), "Centrum Milieuzorg Leiderdorp" (Environmental Care Centre, Leiderdorp): "Kan het ook anders met papier?" (Can paper be dealt with in some other way?) (May 1973).

21. "Stichting Verwijdering Afvalstoffen", (Institute for Waste Disposal) "Hergebruik van Afvalstoffen" (Reuse of Wastes). (SVA/568) (July 1973).

22. G. H. van Dorth, "De plaats van oud papier als grondstof". (The place of waste paper as a raw material), *De Ingenieur,* No. 7 (Feb. 14, 1974).

23. F. J. Colon, "Het TNO-scheidingssysteem voor huishoudelijk afval", (The T.N.O. separation system for domestic refuse), *De Ingenieur,* No. 7, (Feb. 14 , 1974).

24. B. G. Kreiter, "Onderzoek naar mogelijkheden tot hergebruik van afvalstoffen". (Research on possibilities for reuse of wastes), *De Ingenieur,* No. 7, (Feb. 14, 1974).

Conservation & Recycling, Vol.1, pp.31–54. Pergamon Press, 1976. Printed in Great Britain.

PRINCIPLES OF RECYCLING PROCESSES

MICHAEL W. BIDDULPH

Department of Chemical Engineering, The University of Nottingham,
Nottingham NG7 2RD, England

Abstract—The processes which are available for use in some aspects of recycling of solid materials are described. The techniques are explained with some elementary design criteria included where approiate. Size reduction equipment for use with various types of solid material is covered, including some basic principles of comminution. The methods of moving quantities of solids from one place to another during a process are included, with a comprehensive list of the types of conveyor in use. Storage of solids in bins and hoppers and the problems encountered in the removal of solids from storage and the presence of stagnant zones are noted. The drying of solids to form a process intermediate or a final product is described in some detail. Separation processes as applied to systems containing a solid phase are considered in detail. The processes which are available for solid/liquid, solid/gas and solid/solid systems are described, including diagrams and design details where appropriate.

INTRODUCTION

This paper is concerned with the Recycling and Disposal of Solid Waste Materials, and considers the general engineering principles on which the various physical processes involved are based. Some understanding of basic principles is desirable when the selection of a process scheme is being made, and the object here is to present an overall coverage for the general reader.

Two main topics are covered: (1) Size Reduction, Materials Handling, Drying and (2) Separation Processes. The former is obviously important in solids recycling and the latter is covered for processes which may be used when solid particles provide one phase.

1. SIZE REDUCTION

Most continuous processes require a feed which is homogeneous. In the processing of solid materials, this means avoiding large lumps, and so size reduction is used to make the feed more homogeneous.

Size reduction, or comminution, is achieved by a variety of different techniques, the choice being dictated by the·nature of the material.

The four main methods used are:
1. Compression
2. Impact
3. Attrition or rubbing
4. Cutting

These are typified in everyday life by
1. Nutcracker
2. Sledgehammer
3. File
4. Pair of shears.

On a larger scale, the principal types of size reduction machines are (1),

I. *Crushers*
    (A)   Jaw crushers
    (B)   Gyratory crushers
    (C)   Crushing rolls

II.   *Grinders* (intermediate and fine)
      (A)   Hammer mills, impactors
      (B)   Rolling compression mills
      (C)   Attrition mills
      (D)   Revolving mills
            1. Rod mills
            2. Ball mills; pebble mills
            3. Tube mills; compartment mills.
III. *Ultrafine grinders*
      (A)   Hammer mills with internal classification
      (B)   Fluid energy mills.
IV.   *Cutting machines*
      Knife cutters: Dicers.

Some of these individual machines will be considered later, but first some of the basic principles of comminution.

Principles of comminution

Energy and power requirements. The cost of power is a major expense in crushing and grinding, and is particularly significant at the present time.

Particles being crushed are distorted and eventually a new surface is created. This requires the appropriate new surface energy, with any extra energy appearing as heat. This leads to the concept of a 'crushing efficiency' which is defined as the ratio of the new surface energy created to the total energy absorbed by the solid. Since the surface energy is small compared with the energy stored in a particle at the time of rupture, crushing efficiencies are usually low, and have been found to be in the range 0.1–2%. Further energy is lost in friction forces in the equipment.

An early law associated with crushing was proposed by Rittinger [1] who stated that the work required in crushing is proportional to the new surface created. This is equivalent to assuming that the crushing efficiency is constant for various sizes of crusher. It has been shown to apply reasonably well unless the energy input per unit mass of solid is very great.

A more recent approach has been made by Bond [1] who found that the work required is proportional to the square root of the surface/volume ratio of the product. It is easy to see that this can only apply when the feed is in very large pieces compared with the product, and it does work quite well for commercial crushers and grinders.

It is readily understandable that it is very difficult to develop any sort of rigorous theoretical basis for the principles of comminution, and this is especially so when dealing with solid waste containing a wide range of articles and materials.

SIZE-REDUCTION EQUIPMENT

The broad classification of types of equipment has already been given. The boundaries between the classes are indistinct, and the same type of machine is sometimes found in more than one class. A few types of equipment available are now considered.

Crushers

Crushers are slow speed machines for the coarse reduction of large quantities of solids. The main types are jaw crushers, gyratory crushers, smooth roll crushers, and toothed roll crushers. The first three operate by compression. The toothed roll crushers tear the feed as well as crushing, and so these are used in the case of softer feeds (coal, bone, soft shale).

Jaw crushers. The most common type of jaw crusher is the Blake [1] crusher, shown in Fig.1. There is a V formed by the fixed jaw and the moving jaw. An eccentric drives the moving jaw back and forth, perhaps 250-400 times/min. These machines come in large sizes with feed openings perhaps

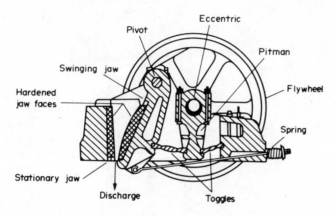

Fig. 1.

2 x 3m. The largest forces are applied near the pivot, as in a nutcracker, and this is where the largest particles are crushed.

Gyratory crusher. This may be looked upon as a jaw crusher with circular jaws, between which the material is being crushed at some point at all times. A diagram is shown in Fig. 2. A conical crushing head gyrates inside a funnel shaped casing, open at the top. The bottom end of the drive shaft is on an eccentric, so that it moves nearer to and further from points on the casing. Solids are broken up and pass out of the bottom. The speed of the crushing head would be 100-400 rpm. The power requirement per ton of material is less than for the jaw crusher. They may handle around 3000–4000 tons/h. The capacity varies with the jaw setting, the impact strength of the feed, and the speed of the gyration. The capacity is almost independent of the compressive strength of the material being crushed.

Smooth roll crushers and toothed roll crushers are self-explanatory.

Grinders

The term 'grinder' describes a variety of size reduction equipment for intermediate duty. It is often used as a follow up to a crusher. The commonest type of grinder is probably the hammer mill. These take the form of a horizontal shaft which has a rotor disc attached to it. A number of swing hammers are located on the rotor disc and the shaft rotates at high speed. The material entering the hammer mill is smashed by the swinging hammers. A discharge opening is covered by a grill which only allows material which has been reduced below a specified size to escape. These machines are versatile and can accept a wide variety of objects, but they can become jammed by heavy metal objects. Furthermore the grill can become blocked, and this can intensify any explosion which may occur.

A machine designed to overcome these problems is the 'Tollemache Pulveriser'. A diagram is shown in Fig. 3. This consists of a vertical shaft rotating in a conical casing surmounting a cylindrical casing. Hammers rotate in the conical section and these break up the large pieces. Heavy metal objects are rejected through a shute and the broken pieces of the other objects are ground by hammers re-

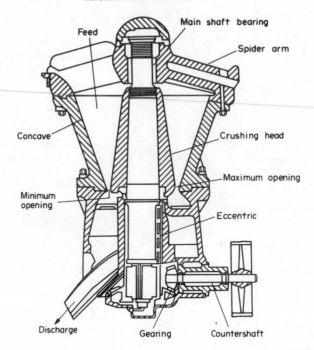

Fig. 2.

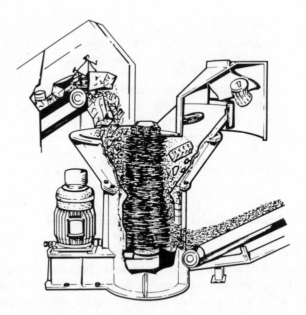

Fig. 3.

volving in the cylindrical section. All the material is ground to such an extent within the machine that grills are not necessary, and blockages are avoided. Furthermore explosions are less serious. These machines are produced to process between 10 and 75 tons/h.

Heat transfer. Much of the energy put into grinding machines ends up as heat. This heat is often removed by cooling water or brine circulated through cooling coils. Solid carbon dioxide may be admitted with the feed to remove heat. Very low temperatures can be achieved by using liquid nitrogen, with the object of changing the breaking characteristics of solids, making them more friable.

Sometimes heat is deliberately added during grinding in order to dry a moist solid during the process of size reduction. This may be achieved by passing gas at high temperature through the equipment. This is an efficient way of drying, but it may not be satisfactory if the solid feed contains appreciable amounts of moisture.

HANDLING OF SOLIDS

Solids, in general, are much more difficult to handle in processing operations than liquids or gases. Solids exist in many forms—large pieces, fine powders, sheets and so on. The mass of solids may have difficult properties; it may be abrasive, sticky and may be explosive. This section is concerned with the problems associated with moving solids from one location to another and with storing of solids.

Bulk solids are often treated as though they were fluid, since they will 'flow' to some extent. The theory of flow of solids has advanced considerably in recent years, and it is now possible to predict with certainty the behaviour of solids in storage bins and hoppers. The effects of particle size, moisture content, temperature and time of storage at rest on the flowability of a solid can be predicted with precision [10].

There are some major fundamental differences between the properties of a mass of solids and the properties of a liquid.

1. *Pressure* is not the same in all directions as it is in the case of a liquid.
2. A mass of solids can transmit an applied shear stress at rest, whereas a liquid cannot.
   (One result of this is that solids form a pile at rest whereas liquids form a level surface).
3. The *density* of a mass of solids may vary from place to place whereas this is not so in a liquid.

These differences lead to the result that solids possess quite different flow patterns from those in liquids. In addition some particulate masses may have cohesive properties. For example sticky wet clay has cohesive properties whereas grain, sand and plastic chips do not. A cohesive mass can form arches or holes which a liquid cannot.

STORAGE OF SOLIDS

Large masses of insoluble solids, like sulphur and coal in pulverised form, are usually stored in enormous heaps out in the open. The solids are removed from the pile when required by tractor shovel and delivered to a conveyor [1].

Solids which are too valuable or too soluble to store in this way are usually placed in bins, hoppers or silos. Basically these are cylindrical or rectangular vessels made from concrete or metal.

A *silo* is tall and has a relatively small diameter.

A *hopper* is a small bin with a sloping bottom, used for providing a feed to a piece of processing equipment.

A *bin* is usually a simple large diameter storage container.

We usually feed solids into these containers from the top and the material leaves from an outlet at the bottom when required. It is of interest to look briefly at the way that solids flow out of a vessel. A *liquid* flowing out of a container retains a level top surface and simply drains out completely. A mass of *solids* does not do this [10]. If it is free flowing (not cohesive) then we have a flow pattern developing as shown in Fig. 4. Flow towards the outlet takes place within a conical core expanding upward from the outlet. Note that the vessel illustrated has a flat bottom. The angle of the cone formed is dependent on the solid properties and is usually 10–30° only. The solid mass surrounding the cone is completely at rest. Solids fall into the cone from the top surface and a crater is formed. If

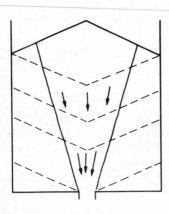

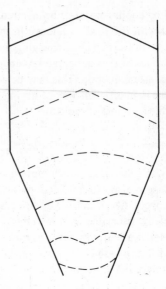

Fig. 4.   Fig. 5.

the solid is sufficiently free flowing then the crater gradually descends, shown by the dotted lines, and eventually the final crater around the outlet remains. Dry sand behaves in this way.

If the solid is not free flowing, we may get an arch formed across the outlet, preventing any flow, or the initial cone may empty out and the solid may form a stable empty pipe. Even if this does not happen, the final 'angle of repose' around the outlet will be much greater in the case of a nonfree-flowing solid.

If the solid is stored in a hopper with a converging region at the bottom then a different situation can exist. If the angle of the converging part is sufficiently great and if the surface is smooth then we get more uniform flow through the outlet. All the solid is in motion and no stagnant regions develop (Fig. 5). This is important since we may get parts of the solid being in the bin so long that caking and deterioration occur.

Conveying of solids

Bulk solids are usually moved from one location to another by means of some form of conveyor. It is possible also to move solids by suspending them in a fluid, liquid or gas.

A classification of the various types of conveyors and elevators is given below (1).

1. Conveyors that carry.
   A.   *Upper surface*
       1. Belt conveyors.
       2. Slat, apron and pan conveyors.
       3. Pivoted bucket conveyors.
       4. Vibrating conveyors.
       5. Gravity roller conveyors.

   B.   *Inside closed tube*
       1. Zipper conveyors.
   C.   *By suspension from above*
       1. Chain conveyors.
       2. Overhead monorails.

II. Conveyors that drag or push.
    A.   *Drag and flight conveyors*
    B.   *'En masse' conveyor*
    C.   *Screw and ribbon conveyors*
III.   Conveyors depending on fluidization
    A.   *'Boiling-Bed' type*
        1. Airslide
    B.   *Pneumatic conveyors*
        1. Vacuum system.
        2. Pressure system.
IV.   Elevators.
    A.   *Bucket elevators*
        1. Centifugal discharge
        2. Positive discharge
        3. Continuous-bucket type
    B.   *Pivoted bucket conveyor-elevator*
    C.   *Zipper conveyor elevator*
    D.   *Screw elevator*
    E.   *'En masse' elevator*
    F.   *Pneumatic conveyor-elevator*
Some of these are described and illustrated below.

1. Conveyors: carrying type

Belt conveyor. A typical belt conveyor system is illustrated in Fig. 6. The rubber belt or canvas belt passes round two pulleys, the left hand one being driven. The solids are deposited on the belt and

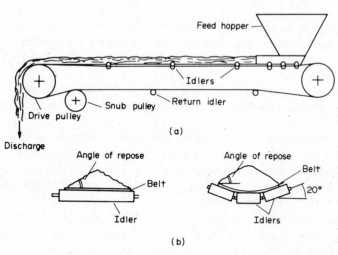

Fig. 6.

discharged at the end. The weight of the solids is carried on idler pulleys. A flat belt has a capacity limited by the angle of repose of the material, and so some belts are troughed to increase the carrying capacity.

Vibrating conveyors. Some solids must be kept enclosed or must be totally in an inert atmosphere. In order to achieve this, the vibrating conveyor was developed. The particles of the solid are propelled

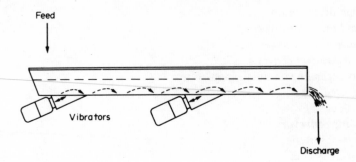

Fig. 7.

upwards and forwards by the motion of the conveyor. During the flight of a particle, the conveyor moves back. In this way the solids are moved along at velocities in the range 0-25 m/s. The vibration may be produced electrically or mechanically. A diagram is shown in Fig. 7. For long conveyors, a vibrator is required about every 3 m.

Screw conveyors. Solids are moved in a trough or tube by means of a metal helix. The revolving helix moves the solid particles along and the design of the helix depends on the properties of the solid phase.

Elevators

While many designs of conveyor will transport solids upwards at an angle, they will generally not lift vertically. The most obvious type of elevator consists simply of a series of buckets on an endless chain. The solid is scooped up at the bottom and discharged at the top.

Pneumatic conveyors. Solids are moved along by being suspended in a stream of liquid, or more commonly, air. They have a number of advantages over mechanical conveyors:
1. They are completely enclosed and dustless.
2. They occupy less space.
3. They may pick up material from several points and deliver to several points.
4. They can carry material long distances through awkward locations where mechanical conveyors could not go.
    However, they use considerably more power than mechanical conveyors. The air may be either sucked through the pipe (vacuum system) or blown through the pipe (pressure system).
    A typical multiple inlet vacuum system is illustrated in Fig. 8 (1). The solids and dust are collected in cyclones before the vacuum pump or blower. Thus this pump handles only dust-free air. Figure 9 shows a multiple discharge pressure system.
    If the gas velocity is high then relatively large amounts of solids can be moved. Commercial systems are often designed to have the solids occupy 3-12% of the volume of the pipe [1]. The main problem is that of erosion of the pipe wall at the bends. If the air velocity is too low, then operation is unstable. When this happens solids tend to build up at localized points causing the gas to be slowed and increasing the pressure. The solids are then suddenly and violently blown out of the system. The cycle then repeats itself. The larger the particle sizes, the greater the required air velocity to ensure stable operations.

Drying of solids

This is usually the final step in a product preparation. Although it is possible to remove water from a solid using presses, this section will only be concerned with the more common method of thermal

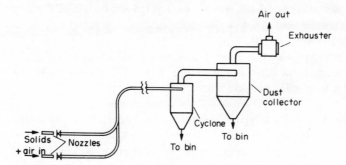

Fig. 8.

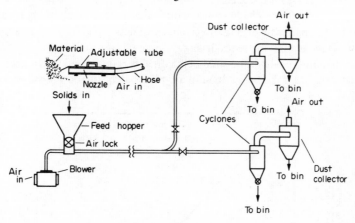

Fig. 9.

vaporization. However, as much water as possible should be removed mechanically before thermal drying since vaporization is expensive. Of course, the final product may not necessarily be 'bone-dry' but may contain some residual water [1].

The major types of driers have been classified by McCabe and Smith [1].

Material dried	Batch or cyclic operation	Continuous operation
Rigid or preformed cakes or shapes	Tray drier	Tunnel drier
Granular solids or pastes:		
Material not agitated	Tray drier	Screen-conveyor drier
Material agitated	Pan drier	Screw conveyor
		Flash drier
		Tower drier
		Festoon drier
Continuous flexible sheets		Cylinder drier
Solutions or slurries		Drum drier
		Spray drier

In the most common type of drier, water is evaporated and carried off by a stream of air. Super-heated steam may also be used as the carrier phase, or a vacuum pump may be used to reduce the pressure and cause the water to boil.

The heat required to provide the latent heat of vaporization is usually provided by heating the carrier gas before it enters the drier. In some driers the solid is in contact with hot metal surfaces, so some of the heat is provided by conduction.

Batch operation. The simplest type of drier is the Tray drier, consisting simply of a metal box containing racks on which trays are placed. These trays are typically 1m square and a drier may contain perhaps 50 trays. Air is drawn in, passes over heaters and is guided over the material on the trays by means of baffles. They can be used to dry almost anything but manual labour is required to load and unload the trays. This is made easier by mounting the racks on wheels so that they may be wheeled into and out of the drier. The length of a drying cycle may be anything from 4 to 48 h. They are often used for fairly small scale drying of valuable products. They may be used under vacuum, and in the specialized application of freeze-drying.

A *Pan-drier* is a variation in which the solid being dried is agitated and steam heated.

The moisture content of a solid being dried in a typical batch situation is shown in Fig. 10 [11].

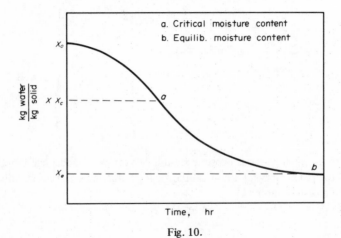

Fig. 10.

From this curve, by taking the slope of the line, a 'drying-rate' curve is obtained, see Fig. 11 [11]. After an initial 'induction-period' when the system is adjusting itself to the drying conditions, then there is a 'constant-rate' period. At this time the surface of the solid is flooded with liquid, and water is carried away as a liquid surface. Furthermore, during this constant rate period, water is arriving from the solid fast enough to maintain the surface completely wet. This constant rate period may be extended if the solid starts to shrink and squeezes water out to the surface.

At a certain time, a 'critical moisture content (X_c)' is reached. This is when dry patches begin to appear on the surface and the rate of drying begins to fall. The liquid surface goes down into the pores in the solid phase, and water vapour must now diffuse through very narrow channels in order to escape. Eventually the entire surface is dry, and after this point the drying rate falls more rapidly. The heat required for the vaporisation must pass through the solid by conduction. It is very difficult to predict the drying rates in the falling rate period, and usually experiments are essential to determine the batch drying time.

It can be seen from Fig. 11 that the rate of drying becomes zero before the moisture content has

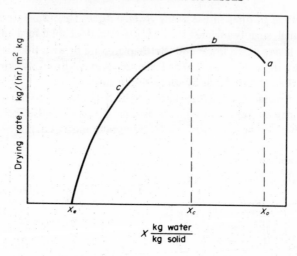

Fig. 11.

become zero. The 'equilibrium moisture' content for a given solid is determined by the temperature and relative humidity of the drying air.

Continuous drying. Continuous operation is usually desirable. For solids or pastes, the tray drier may be made continuous by simply elongating the drying chamber to form a tunnel, while the trays are moved through. Hot air is admitted at the dry end of the tunnel and leaves at the wet end. If the drier is operating at 'steady-state', then the conditions at any point in the drier do not vary with time.

A more satisfactory type is the *Continuous belt drier.* This is illustrated in Fig. 12 [11]. A layer of 2–15 cm of the material to be dried is carried slowly along on a metal screen through a long drying chamber. This chamber consists of a number of different sections, each with its own fan and air

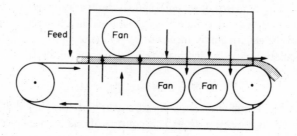

Fig. 12.

heaters. At the wet end of the drier the air usually passes upwards through the bed while at the dry end, the air flow is usually downwards. This is to avoid excessive dust formation from the dry solids. These driers can be quite large, perhaps 2 m wide and 4.50 m long. Drying times may be 5 min to 2 h. Coarse solids or fibrous materials can be placed directly on the screen, but pastes or filter cakes of fine particles must be pre-formed in some way before they can be handled by this type of drier.

These driers are quite economical to operate, requiring perhaps 2 kg of steam per kg of water evaporated. The fact that the drier contains a number of different sections makes this a flexible type, able to tolerate changes in duty.

Another common type of drier in use is the *Rotary drier,* This usually consists basically of a revolving cylindrical shell, slightly inclined to the horizontal. Wet solid feed enters at the higher end and dry solid product leaves at the lower end. Baffle plates are fitted inside the shell in such a way that as the shell rotates, the solids are lifted and showered down through the interior of the shell. The drier may be either heated externally or by using hot air through the drier. Figure 13 [11] shows an illustration. The heated surfaces in the drier improve the heat transfer to the solid and improve the drying. The diameter may be from 0.5 to 3 m. This type of drier is very effective for free flowing granular materials, and unless heat sensitive, the solid usually moves countercurrently to the air.

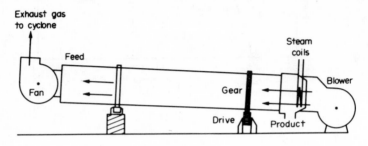

Fig. 13.

A variation is the *Screw-conveyor drier,* in which the solid is moved through the drying shell by means of a horizontal screw. They will handle solids which are too fine and too sticky for a conventional rotary drier. Since they are completely enclosed they can be used in applications where recovery of the evaporated solvent is required, and so they are sometimes called 'desolventizers'.

Another class of driers contain the *Flash drier.* In this type, the solid is pulverised and is mixed with very hot gas and is blown up a fairly long duct during which time drying takes place very rapidly. This is illustrated in Fig. 14 [1]. Sufficient dry solid is mixed with the wet feed to make the solids easy to handle, and a hammer mill provides the pulverization. With the gases very hot, perhaps 650°C, the drying only takes a matter of seconds and the temperature of the actual solid does not rise by a large amount, and so heat-sensitive materials can be dried in a correctly controlled system. The solids are removed from the gas stream by means of a cyclone separator. An intermittant timer may control the solids recirculation ratio, which may be 4–5 kg/kg of product.

Driers for slurries

Slurries present a different problem from a drying standpoint, and they require particular consideration. A common type is the *Drum drier.* This consists of one or more heated metal rolls on the outside of which the liquid is evaporated to dryness, and the solid scraped off continuously. The feed may be simply put into a reservoir containing the drums, as illustrated in Fig. 15 [1]. The two drums revolve independently and the solids adhere to the roll surface. Obviously this type is only satisfactory if the slurry spontaneously forms a sufficiently thick layer on the submerged drum. If this is not so, a splasher may be used to splash slurry onto the drum surface.

The drums may typically be 0.5–1.5 m dia. and 1–4 m long. They revolve at 4–10 rpm and the time of contact of the solid is thus 6–15 s and this is short enough to result in little decomposition with many heat sensitive materials. The drying capacity may be 50 kg/pm^2 of drum surface per hour.

A common type used for slurries industrially is the *Spray drier.* In this type the slurry is dispersed into a stream of fine droplets. Moisture is rapidly vaporized and residual particles of dry solid are then separated from the gas stream by means of a cyclone. The droplets are formed by an atomiser at the

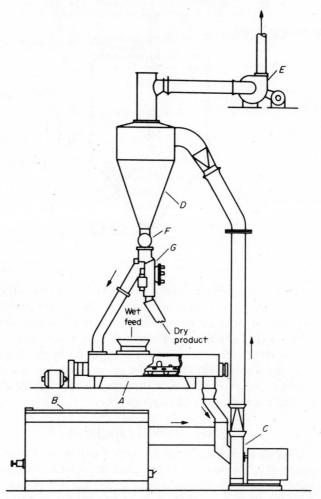

Fig. 14. Flash drier with disintegrator: *A*, Paddle–conveyor mixer. *B*, Oil-fired furnace. *C*, Hammer mill. *D*, Cyclone separator. *E*, Vent fan. *F*, Star feeder. *G*, Solids flow divider and timer.

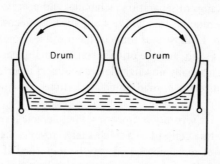

Fig. 15.

top of a cylindrical chamber. The diameter is large to prevent liquid drops striking the walls, possibly 2-10 m. An illustration is shown in Fig. 16 [1]. A hot gas stream is admitted at the top of the chamber, and cooled gases leave lower down. Much of the dried solids collect at the bottom of the main drying chamber.

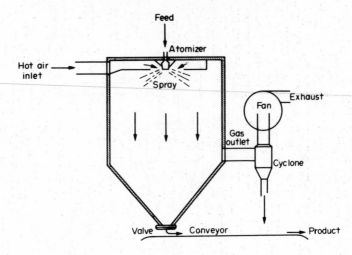

Fig. 16.

There are other designs of spray drier available. The advantage is a short drying time, perhaps 2–20 s. This again means applications for heat sensitive materials and the production of spherical particles. If the final consistency of the product is important, this may make the spray drier a good choice. The spray drier will yield a final product from a slurry in a single step.

The performance of a spray drier depends on the time the drops spend in the chamber. This depends on the size and shape of the chamber, the size and terminal velocities of the drops and the flow pattern and velocity of the air. In general the droplets will cover a range of sizes, which may result in over drying small drops and under drying large drops.

2. SEPARATION PROCESSES

'Separation' has been defined as 'the division of a system into at least two parts, significantly different in composition' [2]. The two parts end up physically separate from each other. We may subdivide out 'physical separations' which use forces to produce differential motion. Systems in which physical separation techniques are likely to be useful will in general by heterogeneous. That is, they generally have two phases present.

There is, of course, a wide range of separation techniques and processes available, and the ultimate selection of the best technique requires that all the alternatives are recognized and that a specific evaluation is carried out. Figure 17 illustrates some of the possible choices available for phase separation when one of the phases is solid, and the other is solid, liquid or gas.

It is important to note that normally no single device produces a perfect separation in one operation, this being particularly noticeable in solid/liquid separations. This means that separating devices are usually combined to provide a complete separation process.

In the evaluation of alternative separation processes, the tolerable levels of imperfection are considered. For example, the moisture content of a solids sludge governs the cost of subsequent treatment. Also the solids content of remaining liquid may be important if it approaches maximum allowable limits on effluent. Guidlines on equipment selection have been provided by Fitch [2].

FILTRATION

In filtration, solid particles are removed from a fluid medium by passing the fluid through a filtering medium. The fluid medium may be liquid or gas. It is a process which is of considerable interest in waste recycling of solids, typically in metals recovery from sludges.

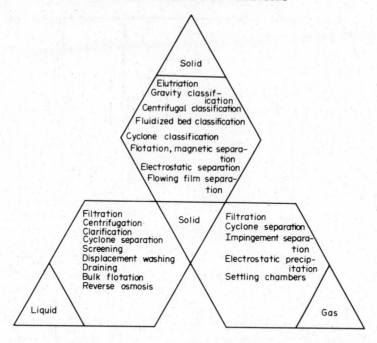

Fig. 17.

There are four main groups of filters:

(A)   Strainers
(B)   Clarifiers
(C)   Cake filters
(D)   Filter thickeners

Strainers and clarifiers are simple screening equipment, usually with the object of retaining a clear liquid stream. In solid waste recycling we shall be more interested in cake filters which produce a 'cake' of crystals or sludge. There may be facilities for washing the solids, and for removal of residual liquid from the cake.

A pressure difference must be applied to assist filtration. This may be achieved by applying an increased pressure to the upstream side, or by reducing the pressure on the downstream side—a vacuum filter. Further, they may be used in a continuous or a dis-continuous way. In the former type, the cake is removed continuously while in the latter, the filtering process must be interrupted to remove the filter cake.

A filter-thickener gives partial separation of a thin slurry, discharging some clear liquid and a thickened but still flowable suspension of solids.

An important influence on the cost of the operation is the moisture content of the resultant sludges (which will proceed for further treatment). A guide to typical moisture contents of solids produced by various methods is shown in Fig. 18.

Therefore a series of considerations must be taken into account when a choice of filtration equipment is made, and this particular section will be mainly concerned with these considerations.

Feed properties

A number of properties of the slurry feed are significant:

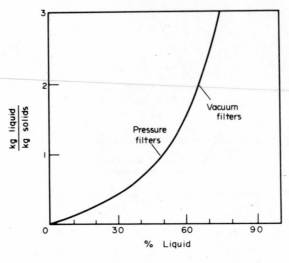

Fig. 18.

1. Suspended solids concentration. This governs the *rate* at which filtration can take place. The problem in high solids concentration slurries is in liquid removal from the cake. In the case of low solids content, some initial sedimentation is desirable.

2. Size of particles. Very coarse particles are best handled by simple screening, but if there are large quantities of fine particles (smaller than 5–10μm), this will govern filter performance.

3. Solids and liquid properties. Influences scaling problems and the pressure and rate of filtration, also the material of construction.

4. Feed rate. Governs the equipment size which must be specified.

Product quality requirement

The liquid product is called the filtrate, and limitations on this are important. If this filtrate must be very clear, then a precoat filter is used. The filtration takes place through a bed of free filtering material such as kieselguhr or asbestos. The passages through this medium are small enough to trap all the particles, and the thin layer of cake is scraped off.

If fabric is used as the filtering medium, then some fine solids may pass through. For high solid content slurries, the coarse particles settle on the fabric and assist in the removal of the fine particles.

Cake washing

When thorough washing of the cake is required, then drum type filters are often used. During washing most is achieved in the first 3–5 displacement wash volumes. Additional washing liquid tends to pass through the channels already washed. For even more thorough washing, the cake may be re-deposited on a second filter.

As mentioned previously, usually the cake moisture content must be minimised, for subsequent treatment. Other important factors to be considered are capital limitations, total process flowsheet, the possible use of slurry pre-treatment, such as thickening, etc. all this leading to a choice between batch and continuous filtration.

Laboratory scale tests are essential in the final selection of a filtration set-up for treating a given slurry. This then presents some scale-up problems. The details of this need not be considered in any depth here, except to mention that nearly all filter cakes are compressible. This is to say that the resistance to flow provided by the filter medium plus the cake is a function of pressure. This means that an increase in pressure driving force may even decrease the filtering rate due to an increase in the resistance of the bed. The theory of flow of fluids through porous beds has been studied in some depth, and many different factors are involved.

Types of filter

Figure 19 shows a Plate and Frame filter press [1]. It contains a set of plates designed to provide a series of chambers, or compartments in which solids may collect. The filter medium may be canvas. The slurry is admitted to each compartment and liquid passes through the filter medium leaving a cake behind. The compartments are formed by alternate plates and open frames.

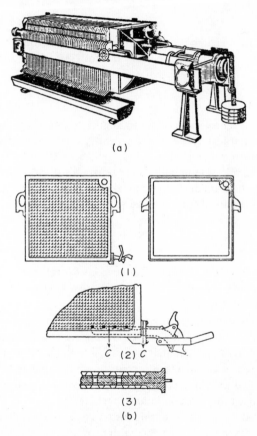

(a)

(1)

C (2) C

(3)

(b)

Fig.19.

Filtration is continued until the solids build up and the pressure suddenly rises. The cake may then be washed. The press is then opened and the cake dumped into a storage bin.

Figure 20 shows a continuous vacuum rotary filter [1]. A horizontal drum with a slotted face turns at 0.1–2 rpm in an agitated slurry trough. A filter medium such as canvas covers the face of the drum, which is partially immersed in the liquid. Inside the main drum is an inner drum. The space between the two drums is divided into a number of compartments. Vacuum and air are alternately

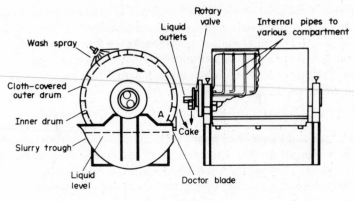

Fig. 20.

applied to each compartment. Vacuum is used to draw the liquid through the filter medium, and also to draw wash liquid through. Air is applied to blow the cloth out a little and ease the removal of the cake by the scraper knife.

Centrifugation

The force which is used to achieve a phase separation in the centrifuge is centrifugal force. The mixture of phases is revolved at high speed, and any density difference between the phases causes relative motion. The centrifuge can be used in liquid/liquid separation for immiscible liquids, but we shall be concerned with its application in liquid/solid separations.

Separations using a centrifuge are much more rapid than separation by gravity settling. The ratio of the centrifugal to the gravitational force is equal to:

$$S = \frac{Xw^2}{g},$$

where X is the radial distance of a particle from the axis of rotation
          w is the angular velocity of rotation of the centrefuge (rad/s)
          g is the acceleration due to gravity.

The value of S often has a value of several thousand. In addition to increased speed of separation, some separations which are impossible using gravity settling are possible in a centrifuge. Very fine particles may be maintained in suspension under gravity, due to the random molecular motion.

Centrifuges were first used in the nineteenth century, and all the early machines were batch processes. This involves wasted time in slowing the machine down to a stop to remove the collected solids. Recent trends have been towards continuous machines.

If a suspension of solids in liquid is fed continuously to a centrifuge, there is a maximum rate at which separation can be achieved which coincides with providing the particles with sufficient time to get to the outer periphery before the liquid leaves the machine. It can be shown that the radial velocity of a particle is given by

$$\frac{RADIAL}{VELOCITY} = \frac{dh}{dt} = \frac{d^2 (\rho_s - \rho) w^2 b}{18\mu}$$

where d is the particle diameter, ρ_s, ρ are the densities of solids and fluid respectively, w is the angular velocity, b is the radius of the centrifuge and μ is the fluid viscosity.

This leads to the following expression for the maximum volumetric rate of feed to the centrifuge:

$$Q = \frac{d^2 \, (\rho_s - \rho) \, b \, w^2 \, V}{18\mu h},$$

where V is the volume of the centrifuge and h is the radial distance from inner liquid surface to the wall.

These equations are given in order to illustrate the important variables, and the form of the dependence.

It will be noted that d the particle diameter and w the angular velocity have a pronounced effect on Q.

Commercial centrifuges

The two most likely types of centrifuge to be used in recycling applications are probably the Solid Bowl Conveyor Type and the Disc-Nozzle Type.

In the Solid-Bowl type, solids are continuously removed by a spiral conveyor. This type has the flexibility to handle a wide range of particle sizes, and can accept concentrated and dilute slurries. It is used in recycling dust from furnaces in steel works, which can amount of 2% of the steel production. Typical sizes range from 60 X 95 cm handling *ca.* 2500 kg/h up to 90 X 240 cm handling 12000 kg/h solids. The cake produced may have 18–25% water.

The disc-nozzle centrifuge has a set of conical discs. The rotation causes one phase to move up one side of the cone and the other phase to move down the other side of the cone. They are basically designed to thicken dilute streams.

Reverse osmosis

Another process which has been applied in solid/liquid separation is 'Reverse Osmosis'. This process, which uses the convenient properties of a membrane, has been applied in the recovery of cheese whey [3] and other applications.

The handling of cheese whey has been a considerable problem because of the extremely large quantities involved. The estimated production of cheese whey in the United States is 11 billion kg/y [3]. This presents enormous *disposal* problems apart from the fact that the whey contains valuable materials. The estimated constituents in this whey per year are lactose (0.45 billion kg), soluble protein (77 million kg) amino acids, vitamins and milk solids. It can be used, if condensed, as animal food, it can be made into processed cheese, lactose for pharmaceuticals, baby food, etc.

Reverse osmosis is a technique which is suitable for use in this type of application. Alternatives would be evaporation followed by drying or fermentation to yield protein. Reverse osmosis is a relatively cheap process which will remove part of the water. It has the major advantage that it involves no phase change. Thus the energy which is required to achieve a change of phase, e.g. evaporation, is saved. It depends on the property of some polymer membranes, typically celluose-acetate, to allow passage of water molecules but impede the passage of salts and small molecules. The actual mechanism of the selectivity is quite complicated and depends upon hydrogen bonding between the water molecules and the polymer molecules. Reverse osmosis became a practical proposition in the late 1950s when membranes were developed which combine good selectivity with low resistance to mass transfer through the membrane. This latter property is essential to keep the membrane area down and hence keep the equipment cost low. Membranes are now available which combine excellent selectivity with low resistance, high physical strength and long lifetimes.

The process of reverse osmosis may be illustrated with the diagram shown in Fig. 21 [3]. Figure 21 shows the initial condition with water and mixture separated by the membrane. If the situation is left to develop, then water ions pass from the pure water side into the mixture side because of the

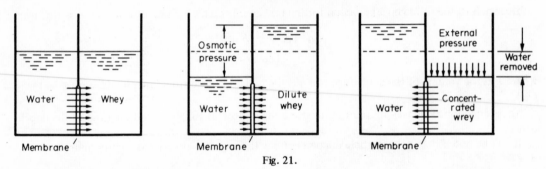

Fig. 21.

fact that the concentration of water is greater on the pure side. This results in a pressure difference being created, which is called the 'Osmotic pressure'. At equilibrium this is about 100 lb/in^2 (*ca.* 7 atm) for dilute whey. We may reverse the flow by exerting a pressure on the mixture side greater than the osmotic pressure. Thus water flows through the membrane from the mixture. Thus the whey is concentrated from 6.3 to 23% total solids in a typical case. Lactose concentration goes from 4.7 to 18.7%. The products then require further processing which may be centrifugation and drying or evaporation, and this subsequent operation will be assisted by the preliminary reverse osmosis.

Continuous reverse osmosis is illustrated diagrammatically in Fig. 22 [4].

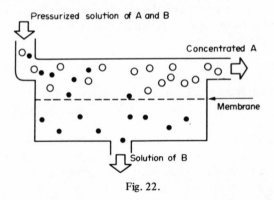

Fig. 22.

Applications of reverse osmosis include treatment of municipal sewage [6], treatment of plating wastes [7], concentration of orange juice [8] as well as the concentration of whey.

Comparison of membrane processes with other methods

Membrane processes are useful for heat-sensitive materials, for which evaporation or distillation are not usable. Furthermore, as mentioned above, energy is saved by avoiding a phase change. Costs are lower for small and medium sized plants. Evaporation usually produces higher concentration of solute.

Figure 23 shows the particles size ranges which are effectively treated by the various separation processes.

Considering now solid-solid separation techniques, one possibility is the:

ELUTRIATOR

The elutriator separates solid particles on the basis of their settling velocity in a fluid. The 'terminal velocity' of a particle in a fluid, which is the constant falling velocity attained in the fluid, is governed by density, size and shape.

It is sometimes not possible to make a complete separation by this method. Suppose that we desire to separate particles of a relatively dense material X from particles of a less dense material Y. If there is a large range of particle sizes present, the terminal velocity of the largest particles of Y

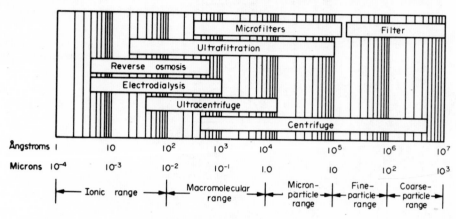

Fig. 23.

may be greater than the terminal velocity of the smallest particles of X. Therefore, if this is the case, complete separation is not possible. We can calculate the maximum range of sizes which can be separated by finding the sizes which have the same terminal velocity.

Taking an 'ideal' situation, with the fluid fully turbulent, the terminal velocity (U) of a particle of dia. d is given by:

$$ U = \sqrt{\frac{3dg\,(\rho - \rho_F)}{\rho_F}} \quad , $$

where: g = acceleration due to gravity
ρ = density of particle
ρ_F = fluid density.

The elutriator consists basically of a vertical tube. Liquid is pumped up the tube and the mixture of particles to be separated is fed into the middle of the tube. Any particle which has a terminal velocity less than the velocity of the fluid will be carried upwards and will appear at the top of the elutriator. Any particle which has a terminal velocity greater than the fluid velocity will fall to the bottom of the elutriator.

Particles of the same shape and size but of different density can be separated due to the difference in the above equation. Similarly particles of the same material and shape but different sizes can obviously be separated. Furthermore particles of the same material and size but different shape can be separated because the 'equivalent diameters' are different.

Gas-solid separations

We are often required to remove solid particles from a gas stream. A commonly used piece of equipment for this service is the cyclone separator. This simply uses centrifugal forces to assist separation, Fig. 24 [5]. The gas is introduced tangentially into the cylindrical casing at approximately 30 m/s, and clean gas leaves through a central outlet at the top. It is very effective for particle sizes greater than *ca.* 10μm.

Some considerable amount of work has been devoted to studying the way that these separators operate and the effect of the dimensions of the cyclone. By means of smoke injection into the inlet

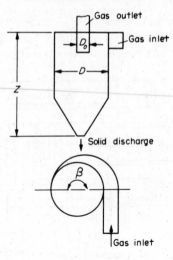

Fig. 24.

gas stream and photography it has been shown that the gas tends to spiral downwards around the wall of the cylindrical vessel, and then it moves inwards down the cone to leave up the centre of the separator.

The particles which will be retained in the separator are those whose terminal falling velocity is greater than a critical value.

This critical value is given by

$$U_o = \frac{0.2G\,D_o\,g}{\pi\rho ZDU_{to}^{\,2}} \quad ,$$

where G = mass rate of flow of fluid

         D_o = diameter of outlet of cyclone separator

         g = acceleration due to gravity

         ρ = density of fluid

         z = total height of separator

         D = vessel diameter

         U_{to} = tangential component of gas velocity at circumference.

This gives an indication of the way that the various dimensions and conditions influence the performance of a cyclone separator. Thus we can see that decreasing the size of the inlet and outlet improves the separating power of the cyclone, but this is limited by the pressure drop which is allowable for the separator. Also it can be seen that the depth and diameter of the cyclone should be as great as possible. This will be limited in the end by the cost of the equipment. Another indication from the above equation is that the performance of a cyclone separator is directly related to the throughput of gas. This means that cyclones are not particularly flexible, and so it is usually better to have cyclones in parrallel so that the load on each can be maintained approximately constant.

The efficiency of collection is defined as

$$\eta = \frac{\text{collected material}}{\text{total feed material}} \quad ,$$

and it varies with particle size as shown in Fig. 25 [9]. The dotted line is the manufacturers' curve while the solid curve represents some experimental results on coal fired boiler fumes. The tests were

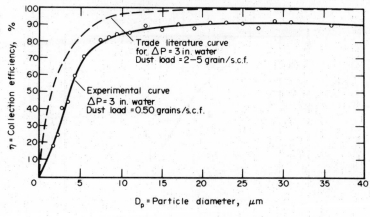

Fig. 25.

with a lower solids content than the manufacturers' specifications, and this illustrates the reduction in efficiency of cyclone separators due to 'bounceout'. When the solids load is small, some particles, particularly larger ones can bounce off the walls and find their way out. This effect is reduced with heavier solids loads.

A double cyclone separator is sometimes used when the range of particle sizes is large. This consists of two cyclone separators, one inside the other. The gas first enters the outer cyclone where the heavier particles are deposited. The partially cleaned gas then passes to the inner separator through tangential openings, where although the diameter is less, the velocity is greater. An extension of this is the multi-cyclone which has a series of tubular units.

Electrostatic precipitation

When very fine particles are to be separated from a gas, an electrostatic precipitator is often used. Its efficiency is highest when the particle size is very small. The capital costs and the running costs are fairly high, and so it is usual to remove the coarser particles first by using a cyclone separator.

In the electrostatic precipitator, the gas/solids stream is passed through a gap between two electrodes. These may be in the form of flat plates, but it is more common for one electrode to be a metal tube, and the other electrode to be a wire running along the axis of the pipe. A potential difference of from 10 000-60 000V is applied between the electrodes and ions formed in the gas attach themselves to particles and carry them to the receiving electrode. The potential difference is determined by the tendency to arcing. As the solids build up on the receiving electrode, they must be removed to avoid a significant reduction of the gap between the electrodes. The electrodes are vibrated or irrigated to remove the collected solids.

The gas velocity over the electrodes is usually maintained between 2 and 10 ft/s, and the average contact time is of the order of 2 s. The maximum velocity is determined by the maximum distance through which any particle must move in order to reach the electrode, and by the force exerted on the particle. This varies as the particle moves through the field. Collection efficiencies of 99% are usually employed.

The migration velocity of particles is related to the collection efficiency by the Deutsch equation

$$\eta = 1 - e^{(-wA/V)},$$

where w is the migration velocity

A is the collecting electrode area

V is the gas flowrate.

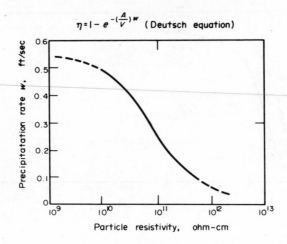

$$\eta = 1 - e^{-(\frac{A}{V})^w} \quad \text{(Deutsch equation)}$$

Fig. 26.

It can be seen from this equation that as A increases, the efficiency increases, while as V increases the efficiency decreases. This is to be expected. Furthermore this equation also reflects the dependence of efficiency on migration velocity. The dependence of migration velocity on resistivity of the particles is shown in Fig. 26 [9]. Therefore resistivity of less than 10^{11} seems to be desirable for successful precipitation.

REFERENCES

1. W. L. McCabe, and J. C. Smith, *Unit operations of Chemical Engineering,* McGraw-Hill, N.Y. (1956).
2. B. Fitch, Choosing a separation technique, *Chem. Engng. Prog.* **70** (12), 33 (1974).
3. G. F. Bennett and L. Lash, Industrial waste disposal made profitable, *Chem. Engng. Prog.* **70** (2), 75 (1954).
4. R. E. Lacey, Membrane separation processes, *Chem. Engng* Sept. 4 p. 56. (1972).
5. J. M. Coulson and J. F. Richardson, *Chemical Engineering,* Pergamon Press, Oxford (1962).
6. W. M. Conn, Raw sewage revers osmosis, presented at 69th Annual meeting of A.I.Ch.E. at Cincinnati, Oh. (May 1971).
7. L. T. Rozelle, *Ultrathin Membranes for Treating Metal Finishing Effluents by Reverse Osmosis,* Environmental Protection Agency Report 12010 DR11 11/71.
8. R. L. Merson and A. I. Morgan, *Food Technol.* **22,** 631 (1968).
9. R. L. Lucas, Gas-solids separations: State-of-the-art, *Chem Engng Prog* **70** (12), 52 (1974).
10. A. W. Jenike and J. R. Johanson, *Chem Engng Prog* **66** (6), 31 (1970).
11. C. O. Bennett and J. E. Myers, *Momentum, Heat and Mass Transfer,* McGraw-Hill, N.Y. (1962).

ACKNOWLEDGEMENTS–The author wishes to acknowledge permission to use diagrams from the following:
    McGraw-Hill Book Company
    (*Unit Operations of Chemical Engineering* McCabe and Smith).

American Institute of Chemical Engineers
(Chemical Engineering Process).

Pergamon Press Ltd.,
('Chemical Engineering' Vols. I and II Coulson and Richardson).

Morgan-Grampian Ltd.,
(Process Engineering).

Conservation & Recycling, Vol.1, pp.55–69. Pergamon Press, 1976. Printed in Great Britain.

THE RECYCLING OF METALS—I. FERROUS METALS

MICHAEL B. BEVER

Department of Materials Science and Engineering,
Massachusetts Institute of Technology, Cambridge, MA 02139, U.S.A.

Abstract—This paper treats the recycling of ferrous metals as an integral part of the iron and steel industry. The flows of home, prompt industrial and old scrap are analyzed. The industrial organization of ferrous scrap recycling is also described.

Scrap is one of the two major raw materials of the iron and steel industry. The various steelmaking processes however, consume scrap in different ratios to other raw materials in the charge. The price sensitivity of scrap and the growing importance of automotive scrap are also considered.

The advantages of using scrap in steelmaking include savings of energy, pollution abatement measures and processing which would otherwise be required in producing raw iron in the blast furnace. As a disadvantage, scrap can cause technical difficulties by introducing impurities into the steel.

The paper also deals with international aspects of ferrous scrap markets. Finally, it assesses the supply–demand relation as a function of such developments as the shift in the balance of steelmaking processes, the adoption of continuous casting, the use of prereduced ores and further improvements in the processing of ferrous scrap.

1. THE IRON AND STEEL INDUSTRY

The recycling of ferrous metals is an integral part of the operations of the iron and steel industry and can be understood only in relation to the structure of the industry [1]. We shall, therefore, begin our discussion by considering the flow diagram shown in Fig. 1.

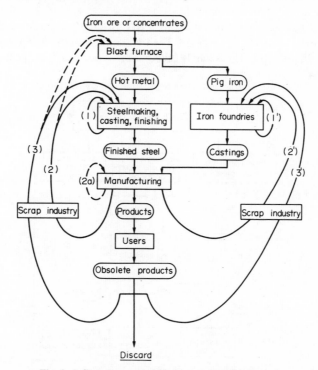

Fig. 1. A flow diagram of the iron and steel industry.

The iron in all industrial ferrous metals — plain-carbon steels, alloy steels and cast irons — is originally derived from iron ore or concentrates as seen in the flowsheet. In a modern integrated steel plant, iron minerals are reduced in a blast furnace to "hot metal". This, usually together with ferrous scrap, is refined in a steelmaking furnace. The raw steel is solidified by casting into ingot molds or by continuous casting. It is finished by shaping operations which produce such products as rails, bars, rod, wire, plate, sheet and pipe. Some of these products are used without further conversion; others are used in the manufacture of various types of goods. When these products and goods become obsolete, they are discarded or recycled.

Two features of the supply of raw materials for steelmaking deserve special mention. Modern electric furnace practice depends entirely on cold metal, usually scrap, as its raw material. Prereduced iron ore, the production and utilization of which are being developed, may in the future serve as a partial substitute for scrap in various steelmaking processes.[2]

Cast iron foundries are the second major component of the iron and steel industry (see Fig. 1). At one time they used hot metal from blast furnaces directly or as solidified pig iron ("merchant iron"). They now depend mostly on scrap. Although the volume of production of the iron foundry industry is much smaller than that of the steel industry, the foundry industry is a large consumer of ferrous scrap. Steel castings are made mostly from steel scrap.

2. FERROUS SCRAP

The production of steel and cast iron is inevitably accompanied by the generation of scrap. This is called "home scrap", "circulating scrap", "revert scrap" or "in-house scrap". It presents no major problems of collection, transportation or sorting and is always recycled.

The conversion of steel into various parts and products also generates scrap. This is called "prompt industrial scrap", "processing scrap" or "new scrap". It is recycled as part of normal industrial housekeeping as well as for economic reasons.

Obsolete goods containing iron are discarded by many different classes of users: utilities, transportation services, industrial concerns, households. The iron content of discarded goods can be recovered by recycling, at least in principle. This scrap is called "old", "obsolete" or "post-consumer" scrap.

Iron and steel scrap flow diagram

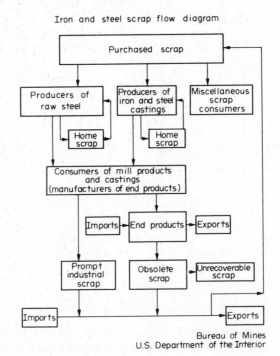

Bureau of Mines
U.S. Department of the Interior

Fig. 2. A flow diagram for iron and steel scrap. Source: Ref. [9].

In Great Britain old scrap is further classified as "merchant scrap" and "capital scrap". Merchant scrap is short-term and medium-term scrap ranging from cans to automobiles. Capital scrap arises after long-term service of such structures as bridges or ships.

The flow of home, prompt industrial and old scrap is shown in Fig. 1 by the loops marked (1), (2) and (3), respectively, for steelmaking and loops (1'), (2') and (3') for iron foundries. The ferrous scrap industry generally acts as an intermediary between the generators and consumers of scrap and thus finds its place in loops (2), (3), (2') and (3'). This industry carries out the functions of collecting, sorting and processing prompt industrial and old scrap. It also contributes to the balancing of supply and demand by exporting or importing scrap and to a limited extent by adding to or reducing inventories.

Major trade associations of the ferrous scrap industry are the Institute of Scrap Iron and Steel (ISIS) in the United States and the British Scrap Federation in the United Kingdom. The interests of the scrap consuming industry are represented by such organizations as the American Iron and Steel Institute, the British Steel Corporation, the British Independent Steel Producers Association and various foundry associations. Some of these organizations issue periodical publications containing information on ferrous scrap.[3—6] Such information is also published by various government agencies.[7—9]

A detailed flow diagram for iron and steel scrap is shown in Fig. 2.[9] The information contained in this diagram is consistent with that in Fig. 1. The category of purchased scrap comprising prompt industrial and obsolete scrap and the inclusion of exports and imports should be noted.

3. PROMPT INDUSTRIAL SCRAP (PROCESSING SCRAP)

The generation of prompt industrial scrap is closely tied to manufacturing. In 1954 a survey of United States industries reported scrap generation ratios, i.e. typical percentages of the steel used in manufacturing that ends up as scrap.[10] For example, structural and ornamental work had a scrap generation ratio of less than 5%, while the ratio for the production of screw machine parts was approx. 50%. The current emphasis on the conservation of energy and materials is focussing attention on metal working processes with low scrap generation ratios.[11]

The supply of prompt industrial scrap is closely related to the level of industrial activity. However, there is a time lag in the availability of prompt industrial scrap when business conditions change. When activity improves after a slump, the supply of prompt scrap picks up only after several months, which are required for the increased volume to move through the industrial system. The rate of prompt industrial scrap generation depends on the relative maturity of an economy and is different for different countries.

Prompt industrial scrap is usually consumed as it becomes available. In the mass production industries such as automobile plants, prompt industrial scrap cannot be allowed to accumulate. The supply of this type of scrap, therefore, is price inelastic (which we will discuss later). Consistent with this, automobile manufacturers in the United States sell their scrap at auction.

Manufacturing industries are becoming interested in the possibility of using some of their prompt industrial scrap in their own operations. A recent development by an automobile manufacturer in the United States is directed at the use of machining chips which are cleaned and processed by modified powder metallurgy: for example, the chips are pressed and sintered for the production of a pole shoe for a starter motor, but apparently the process is not limited to nonstructural applications.[12] Another use of prompt industrial scrap was developed by the same manufacturer: clippings generated in the production of automobile bodies are melted in an electric furnace and solidified by continuous casting ("strand casting") into bars from which gears can be made.[13] Similar developments are being reported from other countries and other industries. For example, comminuted scrap has been reconstituted without melting by rolling into sheets. Such developments are represented by loop (2a) in Fig. 1.

4. OLD SCRAP

Old ferrous scrap comprises many kinds of discarded articles and structures. The main categories are: general, railroad, shipbreaking, demolition, automotive. Ferrous materials in municipal solid wastes are a category that is attracting much current interest.

General ferrous scrap consists of obsolete machinery, industrial equipment, agricultural equipment and household appliances.

Railroads generate large amounts of scrap, much of which is of good quality. The abandonment of railroad lines results in the tearing up of track, which yields large quantities of scrap in the rails and other structures. Similarly, large-scale modernization of industrial production facilities can release substantial amounts of scrap.

In some locations such as Taiwan the steel industry is largely based on scrap from shipbreaking. For a number of years the price of this scrap has been highest in the Far East, intermediate in Southern Europe and lowest in Northern Europe reflecting the relative importance of this scrap in these regions. [14] The reclamation of scrap by shipbreaking is labor intensive.

Scrap arising from the dismantling of structures and demolition scrap can be important. No practicable way, however, has yet been found for recovering reinforcing bars from concrete.

Automotive hulks present problems of disposal and recycling.[15, 16] These problems were particularly severe in the United States where annually about eight to ten million automobiles are discarded (deregistered) and ca. one million abandoned. About 1970 estimates of the accumulated total of abandoned cars throughout the country ranged from twelve to twenty million. These hulks would have posed an even more serious problem if the steel shortage of 1972–74 had not provided economic incentives for recovering them. Processing improvements, in particular the development of shredders, have facilitated the recovery of automotive scrap and have improved its quality. We shall consider the contribution of automotive scrap to the supply of ferrous materials further in Section 6 and certain associated technical problems in Section 9.

Municipal solid wastes are a large potential source of ferrous scrap.[17–19] In the United States an estimated maximum potential of ca. 11 million tons per year of ferrous materials is currently being discarded.[18] The potential maximum contribution of ferrous materials from municipal solid wastes to total consumption of iron has been estimated as 6–7%, but this is not likely to be realized. The additional supply of ferrous scrap from municipal wastes is viewed by the established ferrous scrap industry as potentially destabilizing. For the steelmaker the ferrous material recovered from municpal solid wastes raises technical problems because of the effects of contaminants on the quality of the steel produced. We shall discuss these problems in Section 9.

5. GRADES OF SCRAP

In the United States the Institute of Scrap Iron and Steel has established a grading scheme for ferrous scrap consisting of a large number of grades; a few of these, however, account for the bulk of scrap traded.[3, 5] Another scheme applies to railroad scrap. The British grading scheme for ferrous scrap is built on 13 standard specifications agreed upon by the British Scrap Federation, the British Steel Corporation and the British Independent Steel Producers Association.

The grading schemes are based on the nature and origin of the scrap and on its physical and chemical characteristics. The physical characteristics are primarily concerned with maximum and minimum dimensions and the overall density of the scrap, which determines its behavior during charging and melting. The chemical specifications are primarily intended to limit the concentration of contaminants, which will be discussed further in Section 9.

Table 1 gives statistical data on U.S. ferrous scrap arranged by types and grades[3] Number 1 heavy melting, stands out by its high tonnage. Number 1 and 2 bundles are also important. Number 1 bundles, especially from auto stamping plants, are of good quality and desirable. Number 2 bundles contain much automotive scrap but shredded automotive scrap is rapidly gaining in importance. Turnings and borings are of poor quality and are often charged to a blast furnace rather than a steel furnace (see Fig. 1). Corresponding data for the steel industry only may be found in Ref. [5].

Table 1. Purchased scrap receipts, home scrap production and ferrous scrap consumption by grade
(Thousands of net tons)

Total – All Types of Manufacturers GRADE OF SCRAP Carbon steel:	1970			1974		
	Purchased Scrap Receipts[1]	Home Scrap Production	Total Scrap Consumed	Purchased Scrap Receipts[1]	Home Scrap Production	Total Scrap Consumed
Low-phosphorus plate and punchings	1,597	250	1,861	2,343	316	2,658
Cut structural and plate	1,469	77	1,530	2,288	512	2,807
No. 1 heavy melting steel	6,046	20,961	26,544	8,871	20,485	29,016
No. 2 heavy melting steel	2,172	1,038	3,228	3,346	1,149	4,254
No. 1 and electric furnace bundles	5,312	775	5,943	7,745	2,741	10,297
No. 2 and all other bundles	3,459	373	3,918	4,097	476	4,314
Electric furnace 1 foot and under(not bundles)[2]	–	–	–	489	103	611
Railroad rails[3]	–	–	–	269	34	305
Turnings and borings	2,129	591	2,779	2,652	405	2,990
Slag scrap (Fe content 70%)	1,250	2,042	3,292	1,681	2,436	4,087
Shredded or fragmentized	878	–	841	3,410	5	3,249
All other carbon steel scrap	4,182	13,715	17,449	5,075	12,520	17,541
Stainless steel scrap	432	500	950	552	773	1,286
Alloy steel (except stainless)	359	2,447	2,841	540	2,114	2,623
Ingot mold scrap[2]	–	–	–	538	2,950	3,823
Cast iron (includes borings)	4,253	9,228	13,194	–	–	–
Cast iron borings[2]	–	–	–	2,120	1,973	4,082
Motor blocks[2]	–	–	–	836	396	1,230
Other iron scrap[2]	–	–	–	1,575	4,686	6,263
Other scrap	610	578	1,189	2,907	1,174	4,046
Total scrap[3]	34,148	52,575	85,559	51,334	55,250	105,482

[1] Receipts less shipments
[2] These grades not reported individually prior to 1974
[3] Data may not add to totals because of independent rounding.

Source: Ref. [3].

The trade press reports prices for several important grades of steel scrap. A composite price index is based on the price of Number 1 heavy melting scrap in Chicago, Pittsburgh and Philadelphia; the index is an average quoted in dollars per ton.

There are also several grades of cast iron scrap. For example, the British specifications include heavy cast iron scrap, light cast iron scrap and cast iron borings.

6. THE CONSUMPTION OF SCRAP IN THE PRODUCTION OF STEEL AND CAST IRON

Figure 3 shows the major types of ferrous raw materials supplies in the United States in the period 1950–1974. [7] The importance of old scrap in the total supply of ferrous materials for the steel industry can readily be seen. This scrap moves through loops (3) and (3′) in Fig. 1. The absolute amount of scrap consumed throughout this period was fairly constant, but its relative contribution decreased because of an increase in the total volume of ferrous materials consumed, which resulted from an appreciable increase in the imports of ore and finished steel. During this period the United States exported substantial amounts of ferrous scrap.[3] Great Britain has also been an exporter of scrap[6].

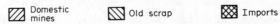

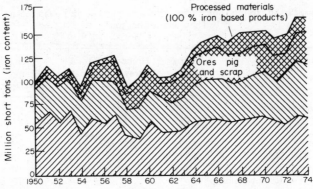

Fig. 3. United States supplies of iron, 1950–1974. Source: Ref. [7].

Figure 4 presents more detailed information on the composition of the total iron supply to the United States steel industry.[8] "Net receipts of scrap", or "purchased scrap", are the sum of prompt industrial and old scrap (e.g. loops (2) and (3) in Fig. 1). The net receipts of scrap are appreciably smaller than the home scrap consumed in steel production. If we add net receipts of scrap to home scrap, we obtain total scrap consumption. Throughout the period 1955–1972 pig iron consumption, which was almost entirely hot metal consumption, and scrap consumption were nearly equal. We should not expect to get total steel production by adding pig iron and scrap consumption. The true curve is lower because home scrap must be subtracted since it merely circulates. (In Fig. 4 each curve has its zero value at the abscissa whereas in Fig. 3 the values are plotted as bands lying one above the other.)

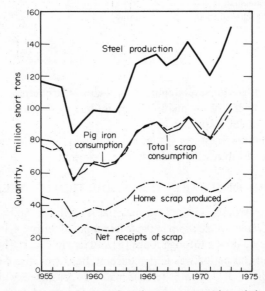

Fig. 4. Steel production; Total iron and steel scrap consumption. pig iron consumption; home scrap production; net scrap receipts–U.S.A. Source: Ref. [8].

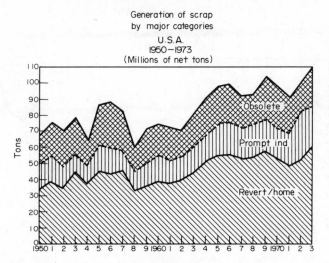

Fig. 5. Generation of scrap by major categories – U.S.A., 1950–1973. Source: Ref. [20].

Figure 5 reports prompt industrial and old scrap separately.[20] It can be seen that home scrap is by far the largest of the three types of scrap consumed.

Figure 6 shows automotive scrap as a fraction of total old scrap. This fraction had a steadily increasing trend from 1960–1972. The current level is approx. 35%. According to a study of automobile scrap[16], approx. 57% of old scrap is automotive scrap, which seems excessively large in relation to the values in Ref. 20. The importance of automotive scrap for the United States steel industry, however, is clearly established. A decrease in the weight of U.S. cars will have major implications both for the demand for steel and the supply of scrap – the latter with a time lag of approx. ten years.

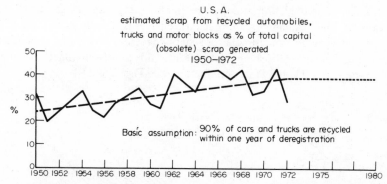

Fig. 6. Estimated scrap from recycled automobiles, trucks and motor blocks as percent of total capital (obsolete) scrap generated, U.S.A. 1950–1972. Source: Ref. [20].

We have seen in Sections 3 and 4 that essentially all home scrap and a very large fraction of prompt industrial scrap are recycled. The operational necessity to dispose of them and the obvious economic benefit are adequate incentives and price is generally not a consideration. The recycling of home and industrial scrap thus is not sensitive to price and these two classes of scrap may be considered as essentially price inelastic. The supply of old scrap has some price elasticity. In Fig. 7[20] the time series of the price index of scrap and the amount of scrap generated show a parallel course: a change in price is accompanied by a corresponding change in the amount of scrap generated. A plot of price

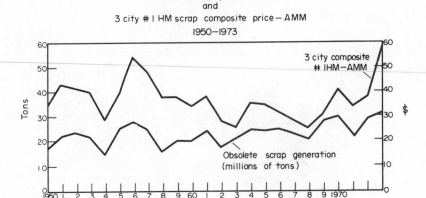

Fig. 7. Obsolete scrap generation and No. 1 heavy melting scrap composite price – American Metal Market, 1950–1973. Source: Ref. [20].

vs amount of old scrap shows a high degree of correlation.[20] Since the amount of old scrap available at any time, however, is limited, its price elasticity applies only over the short term. The size of the total pool of ultimately available ferrous scrap is not well known. Appreciably different estimates have been made. Such an estimate must take into account the amounts of ferrous materials which cannot be expected to be recovered because they are permanently committed or lost. Also in some applications losses due to corrosion are likely to be appreciable, a feature in which ferrous materials differ significantly from copper.

7. SCRAP IN STEELMAKING PROCESSES

Scrap plays different parts in different steelmaking processes. The basic open hearth process, which produces steel by the oxidation of impurities in a furnace heated by gas or oil, is most flexible in its capacity for consuming scrap. It can use charges ranging from all scrap to all hot metal, but these extremes are generally undesirable for economic reasons. In typical open hearth practice the charge consists of from 40–60% scrap. Until recently this process dominated steel production accounting for up to 90% of United States production (See Figs. 8 and 9).

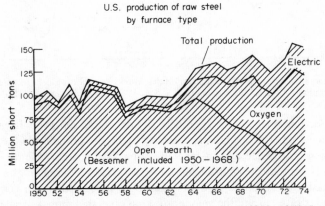

Fig. 8. United States production of raw steel by furnace types. 1950–1974. Source: Ref. [7].

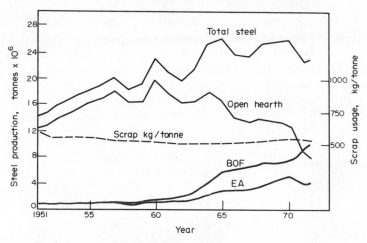

Fig. 9. Scrap usage in steelmaking – Great Britain. Source: Ref. [21].

The basic oxygen process emerged in the 1950's and was soon widely adopted. It is a pneumatic process, resembling the Bessemer process, but oxygen rather than air is used. In the following the designation B.O.F. will refer to all variants of this process such as the LD, Kaldo and Q-BOP processes. The B.O.F. process is limited in the amount of scrap that it can consume, because the heat required for melting the scrap is provided by the oxidation of the impurities in the hot metal. On the other hand, some scrap is needed to prevent overheating of the charge and the vessel. The necessity to balance these opposed thermal effects limits the flexibility in the amount of scrap used. The consumption of scrap can be increased by preheating the scrap in a separate furnace. The Swedish Kaldo process can use up to 40% scrap whereas other variants of the B.O.F. are limited to 25–30%.

Steel production by the electric furnace has grown steadily since its inception about the turn of the century. The electric furnace process, which originally was a quality process, used pig iron or

Table 2. Industry consumption of scrap and pig iron by types of furnaces.
(Thousands of net tons)

Year	Type of Furnace	Consumed		
		Scrap	Pig Iron	Total
1974	Open hearth	18,922	23,383	42,305
	Basic oxygen process	26,448	65,443	91,891
	Electric	28,920	1,060	29,980
	Cupola	705	263	968
	Direct castings	–	1,877	1,877
	Blast	4,447	–	4,447
	Other (incl. air furnace)	696	499	1,195
	Total	80,138	92,525	172,663
1970	Open hearth	21,935	31,494	53,429
	Basic oxygen process	21,124	49,136	70,260
	Electric	18,834	288	19,122
	Cupola	1,695	115	1,810
	Air	41	6	47
	Blast	5,302	–	5,302
	Other	392	8	400
	Total	69,323	81,047	150,370

Source: Ref. [5] (after U.S. Bureau of Mines).

scrap. Currently, most electric furnace installations operate exclusively with scrap. The process can consume the scrap that other processes fail to absorb and thus can act as a sink for scrap. The development of minimills depended on the use of electric furnaces and the availability of scrap. In the United States most of these plants, which do not have blast furnaces, were established in locations where steel had not been produced previously. These mills are not designed to produce high-quality steel but such products as reinforcing bars for local markets.

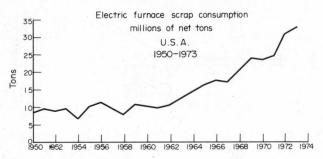

Fig. 10. Electric furnace scrap consumption (millions of net tons) – U.S.A., 1950–1973. Source: Ref. [20].

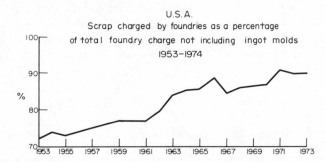

Fig. 11. Scrap charged by foundries as a percentage of total foundry charge not including ingot molds – U.S.A., 1953–1973. Source: Ref. [20].

Table 2 lists for two recent years the amounts of scrap consumed by various steelmaking processes in the United States. [5] Figure 9 shows the amounts of steel produced by the three major steelmaking processes, the total steel production and the scrap ratio for the British steel industry.[21] In spite of large changes in the amounts produced by the three processes, the scrap ratio has been approximately constant at 50% while the shares of the processes have changed (Fig. 8).

The scrap ratio is lower than 50% for the steel industries of some countries, for example, the French industry, and higher for others, which depend heavily on scrap as a raw material, such as the industries of Italy and Spain. Electric furnace steel production has been increasing steadily in the United States, Canada, Japan and the EEC and this increase is expected to continue. This implies a corresponding increase in the scrap consumption by electric furnaces, which is shown in Fig. 10 for the United States.[20]

In considering the total consumption of ferrous scrap the iron foundry industry must be included. Figure 11 shows an appreciable increase in the use of scrap by United States foundries.

8. ADVANTAGES AND DISADVANTAGES OF SCRAP IN STEELMAKING

The most obvious advantages of using scrap in the production of steel result from bypassing the blast furnace. This bypassing has economic and environmental effects. It eliminates the costs of using expensive equipment, labor and energy required by the blast furnace process. Although there is no threat of world-wide shortage of iron ore, the use of scrap rather than ore as a source of iron climinates mining operations, the generation of mining wastes and transportation expenditures. Both mining and transportation are energy intensive. Bypassing the blast furnace also eliminates the need for coke and thus results in further resource savings which are significant because metallurgical grades of coal are not plentiful. Finally, pollution due to blast furnace operation and coke production is also eliminated.

The use of scrap also yields direct savings in the steelmaking process. Since scrap has the approximate composition of steel, it needs less refining than hot metal, from which approx. 4% carbon and 1% silicon must be removed. Scrap must be melted, but this expenditure of energy is made up by other savings. The presence of contaminants in the scrap poses serious problems which will be discussed in the next section.

The use of scrap provides greater flexibility in adjusting the volume of steelmaking operations than the use of hot metal from a blast furnace, which has a relatively fixed output. On the other hand the price of scrap is subject to large fluctuations whereas the cost of hot metal in an integrated steel plant is comparatively fixed.

9. TECHNICAL PROBLEMS

The major technical problems resulting from the use of scrap are caused by contaminants which cannot be removed in steelmaking and which adversely affect the quality of the steel produced. The most important tramp elements can also cause furnace damage; in particular, lead can penetrate the furnace bottom. Lastly, some tramp elements complicate the slag chemistry; this would be true of aluminum if bimetal cans were present in the furnace charge. The most important contaminants present in scrap are copper and tin. Automotive scrap contains copper from the electrical systems. Scrap may also introduce other copper-bearing parts, for example, in the form of brass. Bearings and solder introduce tin and lead. Tin would also be added, if tin cans were recycled without prior detinning.

How harmful these impurities are depends upon the intended application of the steel. Reinforcing bars, for example, may contain impurities which would make steel entirely unsuitable for automobile body sheet. The adverse effects of copper and tin reinforce each other. Cast iron has a higher tolerance for tin.

Copper and tin are not the only elements which are not removed in steelmaking, as shown in Table 3.[22] Alloy elements in Group 3 such as nickel and molybdenum which are essential constituents of certain alloy steels are generally undesirable if present in other steels; one reason is that they cause unpredictable responses to heat treatment. These elements, therefore, are undesirable constituents in scrap.

The problem of contaminants should not be viewed only in terms of single furnace charges. While given charges may stay within allowable limits, they may nevertheless add to the average concentration of contaminants in steel, which tends to rise as scrap is recycled repeatedly. Such an increase has been shown by statistics for the average copper content of steel produced in the United States.

The contamination due to automotive scrap deserves special consideration because of the large amounts of such scrap used. The substitution of aluminum for copper in the electrical system, which has been proposed, is not likely to be adopted; also it would not solve the problem which automobiles now in service will create. Although the quality of shredder scrap has been somewhat variable in the past, improved equipment and operation of automobile shredders will produce acceptable scrap. Similar claims have been made for the cryogenic processing of automotive scrap.

Table 3. Behaviour of alloy elements and impurities in steelmaking

Group 1. Elements almost completely taken up by the slag:	silicon aluminum titanium zirconium boron vanadium
Group 2. Elements distributed between the slag and metal:	manganese phosphorus sulfur chromium
Group 3. Elements remaining almost completely in solution in the steel:	copper nickel tin molybdenum cobalt tungsten probably arsenic and antimony
Group 4. Elements eliminated from slag and metal:	zinc cadmium lead

Source: Ref. [22].

Figure 12 shows a schematic life cycle of ferrous materials starting with iron and steel products produced from ore and scrap. The average contamination increases from a relatively low level as steel is converted into consumer and other products. The average contamination is shown in the figure to be reduced as obsolete products are processed into scrap products which implies a satisfactory performance by scrap processors. This scrap is combined with new iron produced from ore, thus further reducing the average contamination. The cycle then can resume once more. The average life cycle of ferrous goods has been estimated as 15–20 years, but the concept seems to have limited usefulness for materials with such widely differing applications as the ferrous materials.

10. INTERNATIONAL ASPECTS OF FERROUS SCRAP

Figure 13 shows world trade in ferrous scrap about 1965.[23] The large movements of scrap from the United States to Japan and Europe are the main features of this chart. Scrap was also imported by countries that had no appreciable accumulations of old scrap or no adequate blast furnace capacity. Typically the movement of ferrous scrap is from the older industrial countries to countries currently in the process of industrialization.

The ferrous scrap industry relies heavily on exports during periods of depressed domestic demand. This is generally acknowledged to be a desirable means for assuring the economic viability of the industry. However, periods of booming steel production and heavy demand for scrap have usually been accompanied by scrap shortages. In such a situation, the domestic steel industry tends to seek an embargo or quotas on scrap exports in order to protect its own scrap supplies. In these circumstances the steel industry comes into conflict with the scrap industry. Similarly, the requirement of free movement of scrap within the European Economic Community appears to be unsettling for scrap supplies in Great Britain.

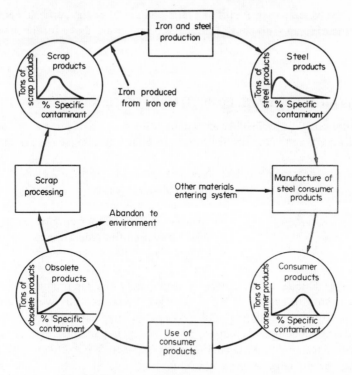

Fig. 12. Stages in life cycle of steel. Source: Ref. [16].

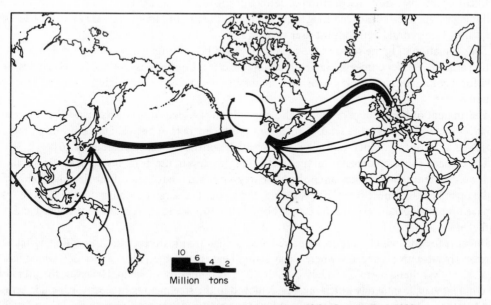

Fig. 13. World trade in iron and steel scrap about 1965. Source: Ref. [23].

   The export of finished steel for use by foreign manufacturers is equivalent to the export of prompt industrial scrap. The export of manufactured goods means that prompt industrial scrap is retained by the exporting country. The import of steel rather than manufactured goods is equivalent to the import of prompt industrial scrap.

The export of ferrous scrap is an export of a large amount of energy, probably equal to *ca.* 12×10^6 B.T.U./ton of scrap. This consideration has been advanced as a further argument against scrap exports.

11. AVAILABILITY AND COMPETITIVE POSITION OF FERROUS SCRAP

The factors influencing the availability and competitive position of scrap are technical developments and organizational and industrial developments. Some of these factors are imperfectly understood.

The major technical developments are: New scrap processing techniques
                                       Improved scrap quality
                                       Continuous casting
                                       Changes in relative importance of steelmaking processes
                                       Direct reduction (prereduced ore)
                                       Effects of operating procedures.

Scrap processing techniques affect the amount and quality of scrap produced as well as its cost. Scrap when first discarded is worth less than when it is delivered to a steelworks because processing has upgraded its quality. The techniques of processing steel scrap have been greatly improved in recent years. New types of equipment, automobile shredders in particular, greater capacity for rapid analysis and improved techniques for separating mixed scrap are some of these developments. New types of equipment reclaim large volumes of ferrous scrap but they are capital intensive. Current efforts are aimed particularly at improving the quality of ferrous scrap by removing harmful contaminants. Examples are the separation of ferrous from nonferrous materials by cryogenic processes. Detinning by chemical means has long been applied to the prompt industrial scrap of tin plate users and is now being considered for post-user tin cans.

The generation of home scrap at the casting stage has been estimated as 6% for continuous casting against 20% for conventional ingot casting practice. Continuous casting also eliminates the need for ingot molds and stools which are a source of scrap exceeding one million tons a year in the United States.

The amount of home scrap produced also depends on the kind of products made. A plant that produces sheet generates more scrap than a plant producing rails or beams. Steel conversion factors, expressed as ingot-to-product multipliers, are available for the British steel industry.[6]

The demand for scrap depends on the steelmaking process in use as discussed in Section 7 above. We have seen that the introduction of the basic oxygen process has reduced the demand compared to the open hearth furnace. On the other hand, the amount of scrap consumed by the electric furnace process depends only on the amount of electric furnace steel that can be produced and marketed.

Direct reduction, which produces a prereduced or high-iron material without melting, is becoming increasingly attractive especially where cheap natural gas is available.[2] The product, which has been called "synthetic scrap" is widely considered as a competitor of scrap. However, the prereduced ore contains gangue minerals which must be removed in the steelmaking process. High-grade scrap used together with prereduced ore would reduce the amount of gangue to be eliminated and such balancing of prereduced ore and scrap may in fact favor the consumption of scrap.

Industrial and organizational developments also affect the availability of ferrous scrap. Improved operating skills in steelmaking — both in casting liquid steel and converting raw steel into finished steel — reduce the amount of home scrap. On the other hand, more stringent specifications tend to have the opposite effect.

Materials conservation strategies will affect the amounts of scrap that become available. Increased efficiency of production methods reduces the amount of prompt industrial scrap. [11] The reuse of components without remelting reduces the supply of old scrap but may be considered to be preferable to the recycling of the component materials when it is more efficient. Strategies aimed at increasing the life of products by improving their repairability and durability will not reduce the ultimate amount of old scrap but will extend the time at which it will become available.

REFERENCES

1. H. E. McGannon, (Ed.), *The Making, Shaping and Treating of Steel,* United States Steel Corporation, 9th edn. (1971).
2. J. R. Miller, Changing patterns of demand for iron and steelmaking metallics in the 1975/1985 decade, *Proceedings of the Council of Economics,* AIME, 177–192 (1975).
3. *Facts, 1974 Statistical Yearbook,* Institute of Scrap Iron and Steel Inc., 32nd edition (1974).
4. Phoenix Quarterly, Institute of Scrap Iron and Steel, Inc., 7 vols. (1970–76).
5. "Annual Statistical Report – 1974", American Iron and Steel Institute (1975).
6. Iron and Steel Industry Annual Statistics for the United Kingdom – 1974, British Steel Corporation, Published on behalf of the Iron and Steel Statistics Bureau, Croydon (1975).
7. Mining and Minerals Policy 1975, Annual Report of the Secretary of the Interior under the Mining and Minerals Policy Act of 1970 (P. L. 91–631) 1975.
8. Minerals Yearbook 1973, **1**, Metals, minerals, and fuels, U.S. Bureau of Mines (1975).
9. H. T. Reno and D. H. Desy, Iron and steel, a Chapter in *Mineral Facts and Problems,* U.S. Bureau of Mines 1975.
10. Industrial Scrap Generation: Iron, Copper, Aluminum. A Statistical Study, U.S. Dept. of Commerce, 1957.
11. P. E. Becker and H. J. Pick, Resource implications of material waste in engineering manufacture, *Resources Policy* **1**, 142–153 (1975).
12. P. Vernia, *Macromesh – Metal Powder from Machining Chips,* General Motors Research Laboratories, Warren, MI, February (1972).
13. J. Webbere and G. Williams, *Steel Scrap Reclamation Using Horizontal Strand Casting,* General Motors Research Laboratories, Warren, MI, October (1971).
14. H. P. Drewry (Shipping Consultants) Ltd., *The Scrapping of Ships,* London (1973).
15. Automobile Disposal – A National Problem, U.S. Bureau of Mines (1967).
16. J. W. Sawyer, *Automobile Scrap Recycling: Processes, Prices and Prospects,* Johns Hopkins Press. (1974).
17. Resource recovery and source reduction, *2nd Report to Congress,* U.S. Environmental Protection Agency (1974).
18. Resource recovery and waste reduction, *3rd Report to Congress,* U.S. Environmental Protection Agency (1975).
19. Committee on Mineral Resources and the Environment (COMRATE), Commission on Natural Resources, National Research Council, Mineral resources and the environment, Supplementary report: Resource recovery from municipal solid wastes, *Nat. Acad. Sci.* (1975).
20. H. B. Jensen, Analysis of ferrous scrap supply/demand balance – USA, *Report for 31st Electric Furnace Conference,* Metallurgical Society of AIME, December, 1973, revised (1974).
21. R. S. Barnes, *Material Resources for the Iron and Steel Industry, Resources Policy,* **1**, p. 66–74 (1974).
22. G. Derge, (Ed.), *Basic Open Hearth Steelmaking,* 3rd edn., *AIME* (1964).
23. G. Manners, *The Changing World Market for Iron Ore 1950–1980,* Johns Hopkins Press (1971).

Conservation & Recycling, Vol.1, pp.71–81. Pergamon Press, 1976. Printed in Great Britain.

ENERGY RECOVERY FROM MUNICIPAL AND INDUSTRIAL WASTE

B. G. KREITER

S. V. A., Amersfoort, Holland

Abstract—A detailed analysis is given of the economics of heat recovery and utilisation in the inciner-ation of waste materials. Energy may be recovered as heat with or without electricity generation but, since electricity may be generated at little marginal cost, only the alternatives involving its production are considered. Detailed calculations are made for the economic implications of treating 140,000 tonnes of waste annually, and a net saving of 23 million m^3 of natural gas indicated.

It is not yet possible to compare incineration with pyrolysis since much information regarding the latter is still unavailable, but published figures indicate that an energy saving of 430 kWh per tonne of waste is attainable by combustion of fuels produced by pyrolysis in a utility power station. Inciner-ation for steam production, followed by electricity generation, can save *ca.* 730 kWh per tonne of waste.

1. INTRODUCTION

In principle, methods exist for the processing of waste materials where energy can be recovered either directly or indirectly.

The *direct* method of energy recovery, namely by incineration in specially designed installations, has been applied on a very large scale since the beginning of this century, and such installations are still being built.

Energy can be recovered from waste materials *indirectly* by means of:

(a)   *pyrolysis* (liquid and gaseous products by heating in an oxygen-free or oxygen-deficient at-mosphere).

(b)   *fermentation* (production of methane gas).

Since the fermentation process has little importance today, this process has not been included in this paper. On the other hand, the pyrolysis of waste materials seems particularly important at present, as evidenced by the considerable amount of research being conducted both in laboratories and at pilot plants. In the United States some fairly large installations are either under construction or already in operation.

The preferred method of energy recovery from waste materials will perhaps be evident from the technical and economic operating results of these installations.

Some of the most important aspects to be considered when comparing incineration and pyrolysis are:

(a)   *Reliability.* From the point of view of environmental hygiene, continuity in processing waste materials is essential.

(b)   *Net operating costs.* The gross operating costs and the profits from energy supply or sale of pyrolysis products must also be considered.

(c)   *The savings of primary energy,* related if possible to national energy requirements.

2. RECOVERY OF HEAT FROM INCINERATION

Incineration of wastes takes place normally in specially designed installations (furnaces). The heart of the furnace is a grate, mostly of a sloping, reciprocating type, which allows the waste to make close contact with the so-called primary air during the combustion process.

Grates in incinerator furnaces usually have controls for:

(a)   feed velocity,

(b)   grate speed,

(c)   speed of ash removal.

The more fundamental information on incinerators is readily available in the literature.

A particular case of energy recovery from wastes is the use of the light fraction (paper, plastic) from domestic refuse as supplementary fuel in suspension-fired power boilers. One tonne of this material with a calorific value of approx. 12.55 MJ/kg (5400 B.t.u/lb) equals a quantity of primary energy of approx. $400m^3$ of natural gas. A research program has been initiated by SVA to study the possibilities for this method in the Netherlands.

It is noteworthy that the quantity of waste incinerated in the Netherlands at the present time (10^6 tonnes/annum) derives primarily from the large urban areas of the country (Amsterdam, Rotterdam, The Hague and environs). These cities have incineration plants where the heat produced during the incineration process is utilized for generating electrical energy. Moreover, in the near future incineration of 1,500,000 tonnes/annum of municipal waste will be achieved, so that any present consideration of heat utilization in the Netherlands should be related to the difference in the quantities mentioned, namely 500×10^3 tonnes.

Figures 1 and 2 show cross sections of incineration plants respectively *without* and *with* heat recovery.

2.1 *Possibilities for heat utilization in the incineration of waste materials*

In regard to heat utilization the following alternatives may in principle be considered:
(a)   supply of heat;
(b)   supply of electricity;
(c)   supply of heat and electricity (the so-called 'heat-power' combination).

Case (a) will be ignored in the following, since electricity can simultaneously be generated at relatively small marginal cost, particularly for in-plant use.

2.2 *Economic aspects*

2.2.1 *Cost factors.* In respect of cost the following factors play an important role in any form of heat utilization:
(a)   extra investment (boilers, turbogenerators, buildings);
(b)   increased staff;
(c)   extra maintenance costs;
(d)   possible energy production;
(e)   yield from the energy supplied;
(f)   saving in energy;
(g)   the development of profits and the extra costs with time in terms of wages, material and fuel prices.

The following may be calculated from the factors mentioned when compared with an installation without heat utilization;
(a)   the extra annual fixed costs, consisting of capital, personnel and maintenance costs.
(b)   the net extra operational costs, as opposed to the above-mentioned extra fixed costs, with savings and yields of unconsumed energy and supplied energy respectively.

2.3 *Derivation of some formulae*

2.3.1 *The net additional operating costs.* Compared with the situation without heat utilization, the net extra operational costs ΔE may be calculated as follows:

ΔE = extra fixed charges—saving in energy not purchased—profit from sale of energy.
This may be represented as follows:

$$\Delta E = \Delta V - G(P.K._1 + Q) \text{ per annum.} \tag{1}$$

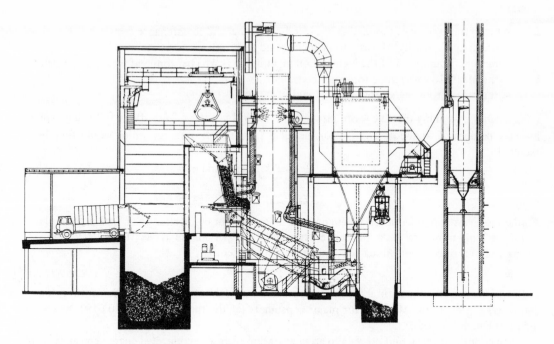

Fig. 1. Incineration plant without heat recovery. Capacity 6t/h, maximum calorific value 2000 kcal/kg, maximum gross thermal load 12.10^6 kcal/h.

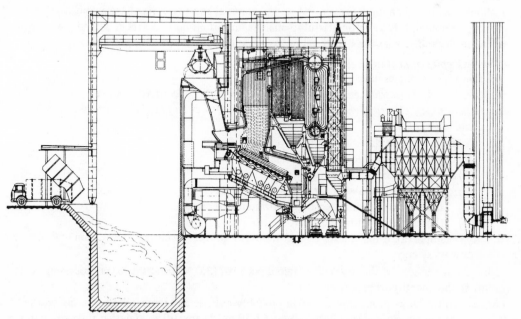

Fig. 2. Incineration plant with heat recovery. Capacity 5t/h, maximum calorific value 2500 kcal/kg, maximum gross thermal load $12,5.10^6$ kcal/h.

where:

ΔV = the extra fixed costs (consisting of capital, personnel and maintenance costs).
G = the annual quantity of waste to be incinerated (tonnes).
P = power consumption of the incineration plant in MJ (kWh) per tonne of incinerated waste.
K_1 = the MJ (0.28 kWh) price for major consumers.
Q = the profit from energy supply (heat and/or power) per tonne.

2.3.2 *Savings*. Assuming that the waste processing costs will not rise ($\Delta E = 0$) the following expression may be derived from equation (1) for the yield from supplied energy which would then be required·

$$Q = \frac{\Delta V}{G} - P.K_1 \text{ per tonne of waste}$$

or
$$Q' = Q.G = \Delta V - P.G.K_1 \text{ per annum.} \tag{2}$$

Furthermore, assuming that a certain energy consumer without connection to an incineration plant consumes $X \, m_0^3$ of natural gas as primary energy, and Y MJ per annum as electrical energy, this means, in terms of costs, an annual amount for this consumer of:

$$X.A + Y.K_1 \text{ per annum.} \tag{3}$$

In this expression A is the natural gas price per standard m^3 (about f 0.11 at the moment for new contracts) and K_1 is the MJ price for major consumers (at the moment about f 0.019), where f indicates Dutch Guilders.*

When connected ('heat and power') to an incineration plant the connected energy consumer saves annually:

$$X.A + (Y + P.G) K_1 - \Delta V. \tag{4}$$

The size of this saving, whether positive or not, depends of course to a great extent on the values to be substituted in equation (4).

It should be borne in mind however that wages, material and fuel prices have a considerable effect on this cost problem. It is therefore useful to analyze important cost factors in detail in terms of components dependent on wages, material prices, capital and fuel costs.

2.4 *Two examples of heat utilization*

The following examples have been considered:

(a): Generation of electrical energy with supply to the public electricity system.

(b): Generation of electrical energy with the supply of power and heat to a nearby water desalination plant.

A number of calculated results are given in Table 1.

Among other things the following values are given:

(1)   the extra fixed charges (gross).
(2)   the yields and savings for different fuel costs.
(3)   the net extra running costs for different fuel costs.
(4)   the savings in primary energy.

Considering example (a), it may be stated that the waste processing costs increase even with increased costs for primary energy.

Figure 3 gives an idea of the payment required per kWh (3.6 MJ) and the extra processing costs according to the quantity of processed waste.

For case (b) the waste processing costs will probably not rise and there will be a saving on the water cost, but the remaining water costs (about f 1.50 m^{-3}) are still so high that the marketability of this water might cause some problems.

*$U.S. = 2.7DF1 at date of editing (January 1976).

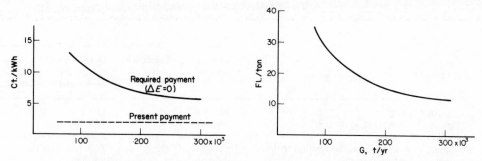

Fig. 3. kWh payments/left graph/and additional processing costs/right graph/at present kWh
payment both as a function of the average quantity of incinerated waste.

Figure 4 presents an overall breakdown of production costs of distilled water and indicates the
cost-saving attained. Mainly due to the very high water cost, the possibility of achieving a combined
installation according to example (b) is still remote.

The application of heat from incineration for other industrial purposes or even for urban
heating are often much more feasible.

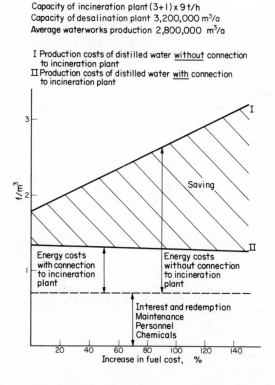

Fig. 4. Overall breakdown of production costs/Dfl/m^3/for distilled water.

	A	B
	Generation of electrical energy	Generation of electrical energy with heat supply for a waterworks
Capacity of incineration plant	(3+1) × 9 t/h	(3 + 1) × 9 t/h
Average quantity of incinerated waste G t/a	140,000	140,000
Design of turbine installation	Condensing turbines	Backpressure turbines
Extra investment } With regard to installation without	f 29,100,000.00	f 13,100,000.00
extra personnel } heat utilization	19 men	15 men
Installed capacity	2 × 5 MW	2 × 1.4 MW
Specific extra investment	f 2,910.00/kW	f 4,680.00/kW
Energy to be supplied to public system (average)	43,400,000 kWh/a	0
Extra annual fixed charges ΔV:		
Interest and redemption (8%, 25 y.)	f 2,910,000.00	f 1,310,000.00
Personnel costs f 31,200.00/man./annum.	f 594,000.00	f 468,000.00
Maintenance 3%	f 873,000.00	f 399,000.00
ΔV	f 4,377,000.00	f 2,177,000.00
Indexing coefficients for extra fixed charges:		
To be calculated according to variations in: { wages	28.5%	35.3%
{ material costs	5.0%	4.6%
Not calculable	66.5%	60.1%
Yields and savings:		
At present-day fuel cost	f 1,260,000.00	
At 50% higher fuel cost	f 1,750,000.00	f 2,177,000.00
At 100% higher fuel cost	f 2,240,000.00	
Net extra charges ΔE:		
At present-day fuel cost	f 3,117,000/a f22.20/t	
At 50% higher fuel cost	f 2,627,000/a f18.80/t	0
At 100% higher fuel cost	f 2,127,000/a f15.20/t	
Increase in fuel cost for ΔE = 0	316%	
Saving in primary energy (natural gas)	14,700,000 m_o^3/a	1,700,000 m_o^3/a
Data: water desalination plant:		
Average water production	—	2,800,000 m^3o/a
Energy production (without connection):		
Primary energy (natural gas) x^1	—	8 m_o^3/m^3 water
Electrical energy y^1	—	3 kWh/m^3 water
Total primary energy $(x^1 + 0.3 .y^1)$	—	8.9 m_o^3/m^3 water
or		24,900,000 m_o^3 gas/a
average saving with 'heat-power' connection:		
At present-day fuel cost (f 0.11/m^3_o, f 0.07/kWh)	—	f 0.45/m^3 water
At 50% higher fuel cost	—	f 0.95/m^3 water
At 100% higher fuel cost	—	f 1.45/m^3 water
Summary:		
Saving in primary energy (natural gas)	14,700,000 m_o^3/a	26,600,000 m_o^3/a

2.5 *Savings in primary energy*

In 1972 the following quantities of primary energy were consumed in Holland according to statistical figures:

coal	12.9	x 10^{10}MJ
oil	130	x 10^{10}MJ
gas	120	x 10^{10}MJ

total   262.9 x 10^{10}MJ (627 396 kcal).

In the near future *ca*. 1.5 x 10^6 tonnes of waste per annum will be incinerated.

In the case of heat utilization by the generation of electrical energy, and where about 1.116 x 10^3 MJ/tonne (310 kWh/tonne) of waste is supplied to the public generation system with an average energy consumption of 2.68 MJ/MJ, this implies an annual saving of primary energy of:

$$1.5 \times 10^6 t \times 1.116 \times 10^3 \text{ MJ/t} \times 2.68 \text{ MJ/MJ} = 4.486 \times 10^9 \text{ MJ} \text{ (1070 kcal)}$$

At present about 10^6 tonnes of waste is incinerated, the heat being used primarily for generating electricity. These installations were built some ten years ago and range from 'large' to 'very large' capacity. At that time an alternative flue gas cooling method (water injection) had not yet been sufficiently developed for large-scale application. Moreover, the ratio between the extra operational costs deriving from energy generation and the profit from the energy supplied to the public system has since developed most unfavourably.

Any electrical energy produced in *new* installations would produce a saving of primary energy, related to the total consumption mentioned, of the order of

$$\frac{500 \times 10^3 \times 1.116 \times 10^3 \times 2.68}{262.9 \times 10^{10}} \times 100 = 0.06\%.$$

If the electrical energy is generated in all incineration plants, then this percentage rises only to 0.18%.

3. RECOVERY OF FUEL FROM PYROLYSIS

Pyrolysis, i.e. heating in an oxygen-free atmosphere, is not in itself a new process. For example, it has been applied for over 100 years to pit-coal. When this process is applied to waste materials, a number of problems may arise in connection with:

(a)   pretreatment of waste materials,
(b)   plant feeding,
(c)   treatment of effluent,
(d)   heat transfer,
(e)   marketability of the pyrolysis products.

Currently it appears that the most effective designs will, of necessity, be based on particular objectives as well as on the types of wastes to be treated. For example, by pyrolysing domestic refuse, solid, liquid, and gaseous products can be produced in different weight proportions and with different fuel potentials depending on the operating conditions. In this context, the general trends associated with increasing rates of heating and with increasing temperatures of pyrolysis indicate increased gas volume and, up to a point, calorific value and lower char, distillate and oil production [24]. According to some investigators, specific wastes such as plastics and rubber (car tyres) lend themselves particularly well to pyrolysis. One of the advantages of the pyrolysis process is that the liquid and solid fuels obtained can be retained and burnt efficiently elsewhere.

Regarding the pyrolysis of municipal wastes, much research has been done both in Europe (among others Kroyer-Destrugas, Denmark, and Warren Spring Laboratory, UK) and in the US.

In the meantime, research in the US has led to the construction of plants, some of which are detailed in the following table:

Project	System	Capacity (tonnes per day)
San Diego	Garrett R and D	200
Charleston	Union Carbide Corp.	200
Baltimore	Monsanto Envirochem. Systems	1000
Orchard Park	Torrax Inc.	75

References [21] and [28] provide a detailed survey of systems and designs. It should be noted that the construction of the American plants was made possible largely by grants from the US Government (Environmental Protection Agency).

It is of considerable importance to know the details of plants which are operating on a practical scale, to establish the following:
(a)   environmental aspects
(b)   reliability
(c)   net operating costs
(d)   net energy to be supplied.

In a comparison, aimed at assessing the situation in Europe, it should be borne in mind that the composition of waste materials in the USA is often entirely different from that in European countries.

4. PROCESS COMPARISON

Although some information is not available with regard to the pyrolysis process, it seems logical to try to indicate, on the basis of some important parameters, a comparison of the processes considered in the earlier sections.

The parameters used are as follows:
(a)   environmental hygiene (emissions)
(b)   reliability
(c)   net energy production
(d)   net operational costs
(e)   volume reduction
(f)   recycling possibilities of materials from waste or residues.

Where possible and practical, information from existing processes (namely an incineration plant of European design and a well-known pyrolysis process, both plants operating at a heat value of H_u = 10 475 kJ/kg (2500 kcal/kg, 4500 B.t.u/lb) according to circumstances, in the USA) were used.

It was also assumed that, at an early stage, a decision would have been taken for a waste processing system with a volume reduction as large as possible and using the energy present in the waste materials.

Table 2 (energy balance) gives figures for possible savings on primary energy (parameter c), which make use of natural gas data normally used in the Netherlands.

Whereas the calculations presented in Table 2 are only relevant to pyrolysis, it may be concluded that in some cases the energy balance is clearly in favour of incineration. Furthermore, it should be noted that Table 2 is an example of a comparison of different processes with regard to energy consumption, energy supply and savings on primary energy.

In some circumstances it is possible that other parameters might be used.

Table 2. Energy balance (example)

Process	Heat value of waste (kJ/kg) and pyrolytic oil	Boiler efficiency (%)	Steam generation			Electricity generation		
			Energy to run process (kJ/kg)	Net heat production (kJ/kg)	Saving in primary energy (natural gas) (m_o^3/kg)	Energy to run process (kJ/kg)	Net electricity production (kJ/kg)	Saving in primary energy (natural gas) (m_o^3/kg)
Incineration								
Steam supplied to own power station	10 475 (2 500 kcal/kg)	70	108 (0.03 kWh/kg)	7 040 (1 680 kcal/kg)	0.247		1 656 (0.46 kWh/kg)	0.140
Steam supplied to utility power station						144 (0.04 kWh/kg)	2 646 (0.735 kWh/kg)	0.247
Pyrolysis	5 870 (1 400 kcal/kg)	85	511 (0.142 kWh/kg)	3 620 (864 kcal/kg)	0.127	324 (0.09 kWh/kg)	1 548 (0.43 kWh/kg)	0.153

Assumptions

Heat value of pyrolytic oil: 24.4 MJ/kg (5 830 kcal/kg, 10 500 B.t.u/lb)
Heat value of natural gas: 31.7 MJ/m_o^3 (7 560 kcal/m_o^3, 850 B.t.u/ft^3)
Production of pyrolytic oil: 24% of as-received waste
Overall thermal efficiency of utility power station: 32% (using pyrolytic oil as a fuel and including its own consumption)
Thermal efficiency of natural gas-fired boiler: 90%
Consumption of pyrolysis process: 324 MJ/tonne (90 kWh/tonne) of as-received waste.

5. CONCLUSIONS

A. If in any area there is a need for a processing method for waste materials in which the aim is a relatively high volume reduction, then the following alternatives should be considered in greater detail:

    (1)   incineration *without* heat utilization

    (2)   incineration *with* heat utilization

    (3)   pyrolysis (assuming that this process is suitable for large-scale application).

B. Attention should be devoted to the combined supply of heat and electricity. There are often quite considerable savings of primary energy in such cases; further, the economic aspects may be favourable compared with situations where no heat or energy is supplied.

C. The alternatives mentioned in A should be compared on the basis of the following parameters:

    (1)   environmental hygiene (emissions to the soil, water and atmosphere),

    (2)   reliability,

    (3)   net energy to be supplied,

    (4)   net operating costs,

    (5)   volume reduction,

    (6)   possibilities of recovering components from waste materials or residues.

D. In order to establish whether particular pyrolysis processes can be considered for large-scale application, the existing processes in the United States of America should be carefully analyzed on the basis of the parameters given in C.

6. REFERENCES

A. Incineration

1. T. Bohn, Probleme zukünftiger Energieversorgung (Problems of future energy supply), *Brennstoff-Wärme-Kraft* **24**, 10, (1972).
2. H. Hondius, Total Energy-systemen in hun toepassingen op grote schaal (Total energy systems and their large-scale applications), *Polytechnisch Tijdschrift*, 5 July 1972.
3. H. Hondius, Aardgas en kernergie voor elektriciteitsopwekking (Natural gas and nuclear energy for electricity generation), *De Ingenieur*, 8 September 1972.
4. F. A. W. H. Van Melick, De elektriciteitsvoorziening in onze samenleving en haar wisselerking met het 'milieu' (The supply of electricity in our society and its interaction with the environment).
5. R. Seldenrath, Nederland energiebeleid (Holland–Energy Management), *De Ingenieur*, 23 June 1972.
6. Elektriciteit in Nederland in 1971 (Electricity in Holland in 1971), *De Ingenieur*, 22 March 1973.
7. H. Kronberger, Seawater desalination process cost comparison and the effect of local conditions on process choice, 3rd Int. Symp. *on Fresh Water from the Sea* **4** 253-264, (1970).
8. G. A. Pieper, Technische en economische aspekten van meertrapsontspanningsverdampers, (Technical and economic aspects of multi-stage relief evaporators), *De Ingenieur* **11**, 15 March 1973.
9. Zoet water uit de zee (Fresh Water from the Sea), Brochure from N.V.Provinciale Zeeuwse Elektriciteitsmaatschappij.
10. P. R. Bom, Waterdestillatietechnieken (Water distilling techniques), *De Ingenieur* **8**, 22 February 1973.
11. G. A. Pieper, Ontzilting aantrekkelijk voor waterproduktie (Desalination suitable for water production), *De Ingenieur*, 24 November 1972.
12. O. Wijnstra, The combined power station and seawater distiller on the island of Texel, The Netherlands. *ibid.*
13. G. A. Pieper and H. W. Kockx, De proceswatervoorziening voor industriële doeleinden in het Botlekgebied (Process water supply for industrial purposes in the Botlek area). $II_2O(6)$ 3, (1973).
14. Central Bureau of Statistics: Statistisch Zakboek 1973 (1973 Statistical Yearbook): Table 16: Basic balance-sheet of energy consumption; Table 18: Electricity balance-sheet; Table 19: Gas balance-sheet.
15. D. G. H. Latzko, Alternativen voor energieopwekking en transport (Alternatives to energy generation and transport). Gas (94) (February 1974.)
16. Energy Conservation: ways and Means, *Stitchting Toekomstbeeld der Techniek*, 12 June 1974.
17. C. W. J. Van Koppen, Energie verbruik in woningen en gebouwen, en in verkeer en vervoer (Energy consumption in houses and buildings and in traffic and transport). *De Ingenieur* **86**, 34, 22 August 1974.
18. G. Stabenow, Betriebserfahrungen mit Müllverbrennungsanlagen in Chicago und Harrisburg/USA (Operating experiences with refuse incineration plants in Chicago and Harrisburg/USA). Mitteilungen VGB, 54th edition **1**, January 1974.

B. *Pyrolysis*

19. G. M. Mallan and C. S. Finney, New techniques in the pyrolysis of solid wastes, *A.I.CL.E. Symp. Series,* **69**, 133, (1973).
20. J. A. Fifes, Solid waste disposal: incineration or pyrolysis *Environmental Science and Technology* **7**, 4 April (1973).
21. Karl J. Thomé-Kozmiensky. Abfallbeseitigung mit thermischen Behandlungsmethoden (Waste removal using thermal treatment methods), *Müll und Abfall,* 6th edition, **6**, August 1974.
22. D. A. Hoffman and R. A. Fitz, Batch retort pyrolysis of solid municipal wastes, *Environmental Science and Technology,* **2**, 11 November (1968).
23. Bureau of Mines, report of investigations 7428: Conversion of Municipal and industrial refuse into useful materials by pyrolysis. (August 1970).
24. E. Douglas, M. Webb and D. R. Daborn, *The Pyrolysis of Waste and Product Assessment.*Warren Spring Laboratory, Stevenage, Herts.
25. J. Menzel, Der pyrolytische Abbau von Kunststoffen in einer Wirbelshicht (The pyrolytic decomposition of plastics in a fluidized bed). *Chemie Ingenieur Technik* **46**, 14 (1974).
26. R. Rasch, Thermische Mullbehandlung unter Luftausschluss (Thermal refuse treatment with air exclusion). *Chemiker-Zeitung* **98**, 5, (1974).
27. R. S. Burton and R. C. Bailie, Fluid bed pyrolysis of solid waste materials, *Combustion,* February 1974.
28. J. V. Henselmans, W. J. A. H. Schoeler and M. Tels, *Pyrolysis of Solid Wastes,* (342 references). Technical University, Eindhoven.
29. SCI/DECHEMA Conf. On the preservation of our raw-material resources, a contribution of chemical technology, Cambridge, March, 1973; see also K. H. C. Bessand and J. J. P. Staudinger, *Chem. and Ind.* **12**, 548, (1973).
30. *Plastics in refuse disposal,* published by the Verband Kunststofferzeugender Industrie (Union of Plastics Producing Industries),Frankfurt, 1973; see: Estimates of the Verband Kunstsofferzeugender Industrie and the project group *Abfallbeseitigung* (refuse disposal) in the preparation of the long-term environment programme of the Federal Government.
31. Plastics waste as a special problem of refuse disposal. Report by the Batelle Instiute Frankfurt/Main. Published by the Federal Ministry of the Interior in: Supplements to *Müll und Abfall* **4**, (1970). See also: *Umwelt und Gesellschaft,* published by W. Bommer, Umwelt + Medizin Verlagsges. m.b.H., Frankfurt, 1973, in particular D. Behrens, 79-100; and *Energie für die Zukunft* (Energy for the future), Umschau, 1974, in collaboration with the Deutsche Forschungsgemeinschaft, (p.80-87).
32. M. J. Spendlove, *Umschau Wiss. Techn.* **73**, 366 (1973); see also W. Herbert, Solid waste recycling at Franklin, Ohio, *Proc. 3rd mineral waste utilization symp.,* U.S. Bureau of Mines and IIT Res. Inst., Chicago, (1972); C. B. Kenahan *et al.* Report of Investigation 7204 (U.S. dept. of the Interior, Bureau of Mines); energy for the future (3b), there lit. to chapter 9.
33. Y. Shimizu, H. Ando, T. Abe, O. Inomata and S. Matsuzawa, *Bull. Nat. Res. Inst. Pollution and Resources* **2**, 1, 43 (1972). Compared with S. Speth, *Chem. and Ind.* 557, (1973) and *Chemie Ing. Techn.* **45**, 526 (1973).
34. J. Menzel, H. Perkow and H. Sinn, *Chem. and Ind.* 570, (1973).
35. H. Perkow, thesis, University of Hamburg, 1974 (in preparation).
36. J. Fritz, Investigations for a thesis, Dept. for Applied Chemistry, Institute for Inorganic and Applied Chemistry. University of Hamburg, (1974).
37. On the problems of incineration slag, see, for example, (a) Solid waste disposal and conversion system, company paper of Andco-Torrax, Buffalo, NY 14225. (b) Process for disposal of refuse, German Offenlegungsschrift 1.508.003, Battelle-Institute, Frankfurt/Main, inventor: F. Fink.

Conservation & Recycling, Vol.1, pp.83–90. Pergamon Press, 1976. Printed in Great Britain.

MODERN TECHNIQUES FOR RECYCLING

MICHAEL E. HENSTOCK

University of Nottingham, England

INTRODUCTION

Any waste or discarded material is worthless if it cannot, in its current form, be used. The value of a waste is potential, and depends entirely on its ability to be recycled. Such value may be economic or social, usually the former.

Recycling may be by means of:

(a) Closed loop methods. Here, the material is refined back to essentially its virgin specification; it may subsequently be used for any purpose appropriate to that material specification, e.g. copper may be refined electrolytically before use in electrical applications.

(b) Open loop methods. The material is here treated as a starting point or raw material for another manufacturing process, e.g. contaminated copper may be used in brass extrusions.

Recycling of energy is topical and the subject of much research, particularly into pyrolysis systems, but these aspects of materials conservation are covered elsewhere in this symposium. This paper deals entirely with the recycling of solid raw materials and is devoted to some of the methods that have been developed to deal with the mixed waste so often encountered. The "value" of such a waste depends entirely on the degree to which it may be split into fractions, each destined for a particular recycling route. It is intended, here, to examine some of the newer separation techniques and the ways in which they have been incorporated into complete Resource Recovery Systems (RRS).

Every waste-producing unit constitutes a separate problem, since the waste flow from each will be different. Metal merchants collecting the waste of industry attempt to segregate, as far as possible, into uniform and usable grades and aggregate the residue. No attempt will be made here to deal with waste streams from individual factories, since the segregation methods applicable to one will certainly be unsuitable for another.

The standard techniques of mineral dressing have been applied and, in some cases, modified to achieve separation of one or more desired components (herafter termed "valuables") from the worthless gangue. It should be noted that worthless is only a relative term; the gangue may be so in the local context but it is arguable that nothing is truly worthless in a global sense. Even locally it is possible that a discard might be used as landfill or to provide heat.

These standard techniques, some of which have been used for many years, include air and water classification, sieving, jigging, tabling, flotation, magnetic and dense-medium separation. All are easily located in the literature[1] and little purpose is served by describing their operation in detail here. Each has been used in some aspect of waste recovery; air classification or elutriation is commonly used to remove the lighter fraction, generally paper and light polymeric film, from domestic refuse[2], and water classification may be applied to the upgrading of the metallic fraction of the mixed non-magnetic portion of shredded automobiles[3]. Magnetic separation is routinely used to extract tin-plate cans from the domestic refuse stream and froth flotation has been applied to the recovery of fine glass from incinerator residues[4].

Each waste-separation flowsheet is designed for a specific application and it would be pointless, as well as impractical, to examine the many published schemes. In general, any separation process works best on a continuous stream of feed material of consistent quality. Since, to need separation at all, the stream must contain more than one component, it cannot by definition be homogeneous

but there should be some consistency between samples taken at predetermined intervals. A waste
from a plant reclaiming copper by chopping discarded cable would comprise finely divided rubber,
polymer and fabric with occasional metallic fragments; it could be considered as a homogeneous
feed. Used consumer durables are heterogeneous, e.g. motor cars, refrigerators, electronic equipment,
etc. but some degree of homogeneity can be achieved by size reduction. The equipment used for this
is known as a shredder or pulverizer, and is considered elsewhere[5]. The output from a shredder is
often fine enough to be treated by an assemblage of mineral-dressing methods. Typically [2], the
lightest paper and polymer is removed by air classification, ferrous scrap by magnets, and aluminium
and heavy organics partially by secondary air elutriation and partially in a water column. There are
innumerable variations on this theme.

The recent literature on waste treatment has revealed a number of new techniques, some apparently developed specifically for recycling, and the remainder of this paper is devoted to consideration of the more significant of these.

Some of the most promising processes currently under investigation include:

1. Electromagnetic or eddy current methods.
2. Float-and-sink, together with its extension to heavy-media separation.
3. Cryogenics.
4. Electrostatics.
5. Glass colour sorting.

Each of these techniques relies on a specific property of the material for identification and recovery.
The success of the process depends upon the accuracy and consistency with which the property can be
detected and used to identify and isolate the product. An optical method might, for example, be rendered inconsistent by surface coatings on the surface of fragments of waste.

Another factor in the ultimate efficiency of a separation process is the uniqueness of the property
selected as the basis for the separation. Should that property be common to one or more other components of the waste stream in addition to the desired material, a mixed product will be obtained; at
least one further separation step will then be necessary.

ELECTROMAGNETIC AND ELECTROSTATIC METHODS

These rely on the response of materials to electrical stimuli where the selection parameter is electrical conductivity; metals generally exhibit electrical conductivities orders of magnitude greater than
other materials, and the selection parameter is thus, for all practical purposes, unique to metals. Two
common components of the municipal waste stream are glass and aluminium; they have similar
densities and are, therefore, difficult to separate by gravity methods. Their electrical conductivities
are, however, very different.

Magnetic separators have traditionally relied on differences in ferromagnetic behaviour; this will
separate most ferrous materials from a mixture with non-ferrous metals. Certain stainless steels are
nonmagnetic and are not removed. Separation is, in any event, generally incomplete since shredding
may have failed to liberate completely the magnetic from the non-magnetic materials. A wide variety
of machines has been developed over the years; they will remove ferrous material too small to justify
prior manual picking. Figures 1 and 2 are typical.

If the voltage impressed on a conductor is induced, by varying the magnetic field, electrical
currents flow within the conductor. Each current is accompanied by its own magnetic field which
opposes the source field and the particle is repelled from the source field region. The ability of the
conductor to sustain the flow of these eddy currents is the selection criterion for identification and
recovery of products.

It has been established[6] that the repulsive force set up by eddy currents is a function of particle
size (Fig. 3); this suggests an optimum shredding procedure.

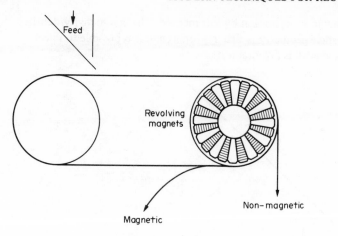

Fig. 1. Magnetic pulley.

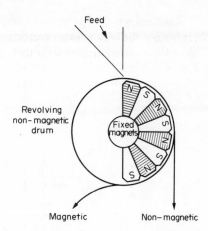

Fig. 2. Drum-type magnetic separator.

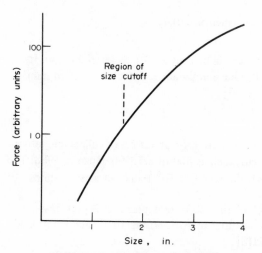

Fig. 3. Eddy current interaction force
dependence upon size.

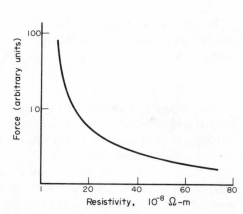

Fig. 4. Eddy current interaction force as a function
of electric resistivity.

The force is also critically dependent on particle resistivity, as shown in Fig. 4. Translated into acceleration and conductivity/density ratio, σ/D, a linear relationship results (Fig. 5). Calculation of this ratio for some common materials yields the following:

Metal	Relative $\frac{\sigma}{D}$
Al	13.1
Cu	6.6
Ag	6.0
Zn	2.4
Brass	1.7
Fe	1.3
Sn	1.2
Pb	0.4

Aluminium is thus particularly amenable to separation by this method. The conductivity/density ratio is not the only relevant factor; particle geometry is also important and it is possible to reject particles of unfavourable σ/D if their geometry is favourable.

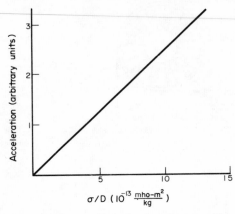

Fig. 5. Linear dependence of acceleration on σ/D, ratio.

The system has been developed in the U.S.A., where several prototypes are under evaluation. Its principle utility seems to be in the recovery of the high-value aluminium can stock fraction in municipal solid waste; recoveries of up to 90% can be achieved[7].

Float-and-sink

The problem of discarded polymeric waste is worldwide; currently, about 2% of collectable refuse in developed countries is polymeric although peaks occur, such as that of 6.7% for Japan in 1968. The packaging industry alone of the US consumed, in 1970, almost 1.8×10^6 tonnes of plastics almost $\frac{1}{3}$ of the total production.

Of the total collectable plastics waste *ca.* 66% is polyoleflin, 20% polystyrene, 11% polyvinyl chloride (PVC) and the remainder is accounted for by all other plastics. Of the 1970 total mentioned above only *ca.* 12% is estimated to have been collected[8].

Methods have been developed to obtain clean fractions of high density polyethylene (HDPE), low density polyethylene (LDPE), polystyrene (PS), polypropylene (PP) and PVC from waste using float and sink techniques. The observed densities of virgin pelletised plastics are given below:

Plastic	*Density* (g/cm^3)
PP	0.90
LDPE	0.92
HDPE	0.94–0.96
PS	1.05–1.06
PVC	1.22–1.38

Mixtures of these can be separated in media including water ($\rho = 1$), water + alcohol ($\rho = 0.93$), brine ($\rho = 1.20$), etc.

The extension into heavy media technology, where separation is made in suspensions of solid particles, is obvious. Much interest has been shown in the recovery, by this means, of aluminium from municipal solid waste (MSW) and from the non-magnetic reject from autoshredders.

The specific gravity of aluminium is 2.7 and this is the medium density at which a split could be made with solid metal. However, small particles may be prevented from sinking by the attachment of air bubbles. A principal source of aluminium in MSW is beverage cans; these are found[9] to settle, in a ferrosilicon heavy medium, at densities as low as 1.7 and as high as 3.0. Behaviour is strongly dependent on shredding characteristics; whole cans or crumpled sheets entrap air pockets or ferrosilicon medium, thus reducing or increasing the apparent density of the fragments.

A possible flowsheet for treatment of shredded automobiles would take the non-magnetic fraction first to an air classifier to remove fabrics, rubber and light polymers. Heavy medium treatment would then remove the aluminium, and the remaining non-ferrous material might be treated pyrometallurgically.

The dense-medium principle has been applied by Warren Spring Laboratory to the residues from municipal incinerators[10]. From them, one fraction assaying 60% Cu and another assaying 95% Al are recoverable, valued (1972) at £203 and £61/tonne respectively.

Cryogenics

Many normally ductile materials become extremely brittle at low temperatures. The fringe of this phenomenon was demonstrated by the wartime Liberty Ships and in the disastrous losses associated with catastrophic fracture. At liquid gas temperatures many metals behave in a glass-like manner, whilst others continue to show ductility. This principle has been used to separate certain mixtures of materials.

Broadly speaking, fcc metals such as copper and aluminium retain ductility at low temperatures, whilst bcc (e.g. iron) or hexagonal metals (e.g. zinc) are embrittled. Scrap such as small motors and generators can be treated with liquid nitrogen and the steel housings then fragmented in a hammer mill[11]. The method is applicable to the stripping of insulated copper wire, in preference to the highly polluting process of cable burning. On a large scale, cryogenics is in Belgium being applied to the processing of baled scrap automobiles; after chilling, the hulks are reduced to coin-sized flakes in a hammer mill in less than 1 minute per bale, and a 370kJ/s (500 h.p.) shredder is claimed to process as much scrap as a 3.7MJ/s (5000 h.p.) shredder operating conventionally.

The method has also been applied[12] to the size reduction of scrap rubber tyres whose transport is, because of their shape, very uneconomical in respect of space.

Electrostatic methods

Electrostatic methods have long been used in the mining industry but they may be adapted to separate streams of mixed refuse. The equipment is shown, schematically, in Fig. 6; operating voltages of up to 200 kV are employed[13]. In separating paper from polymers the former adheres to the drum and the latter is drawn to the electrode. On 2.5–7.6 cm shredded material concentrates averaging 99.4% plastic and 99.9% paper are claimed, with plastics recovery exceeding 99%.

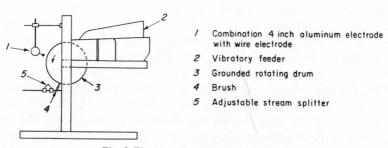

1	Combination 4 inch aluminum electrode with wire electrode
2	Vibratory feeder
3	Grounded rotating drum
4	Brush
5	Adjustable stream splitter

Fig. 6. Electrostatic separation equipment.

Fig. 7. Sortex 962 MC equipment.

The method can thus be used to separate any materials having different electrical conductivities, e.g. metal and plastic wastes.

Colour sorting of glass

The transparency of glass has been made the basis of a sorting method to separate it from stones and other opaque material. A simple adaptation of the optical system enables the device also to grade scrap glass (cullet) into various coloured fractions, e.g. flint, amber and green, and two-stage separation could deliver these end products from the glass concentrate[14]. The equipment is shown in Fig. 7. Commodities to be separated are fed from the hopper by means of a vibrating tray which drops the particles onto an inclined chute, down which they accelerate into the inspection area or optical box. Here, photocell sensors view the particles and the resulting signals are evaluated electronically into accept and reject categories. A reject signal will trigger off a high speed blast of compressed air from the ejector, causing the corresponding undesirable particle to be deflected from the main stream into a separate collecting hopper. The equipment is shown schematically in Fig. 8.

The main application of this system is the removal of stone/ceramic particles from glass cullet and

SCHEMATIC DIAGRAM OF ELECTRONIC SEPARATOR

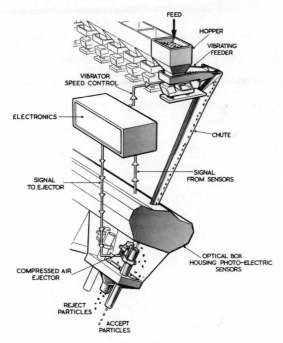

Fig. 8. Operating sequence of the Sortex 962 MC.

its separation into the various constituent colours which are then suitable for recycling.

The system has been described in the context of glass which may be identified by its transparency and separated from opaque particles. The use of electromagnetic sensor heads, however, permits the same basic system to separate non-ferrous from ferrous metals; future developments will probably involve the use of ultra-violet, X-ray transmission and X-ray fluorescence as rejection criteria.

The efficiency of this type of unit diminishes as particle sizes fall and glass fragments smaller than 0.6 cm are best dealt with by other means.

Acknowledgements – Fig. 1 and Fig. 2, after S. J. Truscott, *A Textbook of Ore Dressing,* reproduced by permission of Macmillan (London). Figs. 3–5, after Sommer and Kenney, Ref. 6, *10p. cit.* Fig. 6. is reproduced by courtesy of the United States Bureau of Mines. Figs. 7 and 8 are reproduced by courtesy of Gunson's Sortex (Mineral and Automation) Ltd.

REFERENCES

1. See, e.g. S. J. Truscott, *A Textbook of Ore Dressing,* Macmillan, New York (1923).
2. P. M. Sullivan, Resource recovery from raw urban refuse, U.S. Bureau of Mines, R.I. 7760, (1973).
3. L. J. Troisland, K. C. Dean and C. J. Chindgren, Upgrading junk auto shredder rejects, U. S. Bureau of Mines, TPR 53, (March 1972).
4. B. Morey, Inorganic resource recovery and solid fuel preparation from municipal trash, *Proc. 4th Mineral Waste Utilization Symposium,* Chicago, May 7 (1974).
5. M. W. Biddulph, Principles of recycling processes, *Conservation & Recycling* 1, 31–54 (1976).
6. E. J. Sommer Jr. and G. R. Kenny, An electromagnetic separator for dry recovery of non-ferrous metals from shredded municipal solid waste, *Proc. 4th Mineral Waste Utilization Symposium,* Chicago, May 7 (1974).
7. J. A. Campbell, Electromagnetic separation of aluminium and non-ferrous metals, *Proc. 4th Mineral Waste Utilization Symposium,* Chicago, May 7 (1974).
8. A. J. Warner, Solid waste management of plastics, Research study conducted for the Manufacturing Chemists Association, (December 1970).

9. E. L. Michaels, Heavy media separation of aluminium from municipal solid waste, *AIME 103rd Annual Meeting,* Dallas, TX, February 24 (1974).

10. E. Douglas and D. V. Jackson, Waste reclamation 1: a source of raw materials, *J. Environmental Planning and Pollution Control* 1, 2 (1972).

11. J. H. Bilbrey Jr., Use of cryogenics in scrap processing, *Proc. 4th Mineral Waste Utilization Symposium,* Chicago, 7 May (1974).

12. N. R. Braton and J. A. Koutsky, Cryogenic recycling, *Proc. 4th Mineral Waste Utilization Symposium,* Chicago, 7 May (1974).

13. M. R. Grubbs and K. H. Ivey, Recovering plastics from urban refuse by electrodynamic techniques, U. S. Bureau of Mines, TPR 63, (December 1972).

14. Gunson's Sortex Ltd., Private communication, (1974).

Conservation & Recycling, Vol.1, pp.91–110. Pergamon Press, 1976. Printed in Great Britain.

RECYCLING OF PLASTICS

W. KAMINSKY, J. MENZEL and H. SINN

Hamburg University, W. Germany

Abstract—Considering the shortage of raw materials and environmental pollution, the recycling of plastic waste is a very important topic. Pilot plants for research in Funabashi Japan, Franklin (Ohio) U.S.A., and the R 80-process of Krauss Maffei, W. Germany, have demonstrated the possibility of reclaiming plastics from refuse.

Old tyres and waste from the plastic producing and manufacturing industries are readily available. The pyrolysis of plastic yields gaseous and liquid products, and the exploitation of this cracking reaction has been demonstrated by pilot plants in Japan and Great Britain. Further laboratory scale experiments are taking place in W. Germany.

In continuous fluidized beds and in molten salts, polyethylene, polypropylene, polyvinylchloride, polystyrene and rubber are pyrolysed and better than 98% conversion is obtained. Up to 40% of the feed can be obtained as aromatic compounds, and a pilot plant is under construction. As a first step PVC-containing material can be almost quantitatively dehydrochlorinated.

INTRODUCTION

The production indices of the main industries in West Germany from 1962 to 1971 are shown in Fig. 1. The dynamic nature of the chemical industries is evident, its production doubling in six to seven years, whereas the doubling time of industry in general is ten to twelve years. The relatively high growth rate of the chemical indusrtry is largely due to the very short doubling time of plastics production.

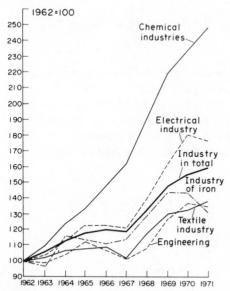

Fig. 1. Production index of the main industries in West Germany.

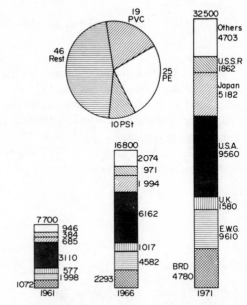

Fig. 2. World plastics production in units of 1000 t/a.

Figure 2 shows world plastics production in units of 1000 tonne/yr. Plastics have the highest doubling rate amongst industrial products, and this can take place in four years, as in Japan for example. On average, though, no industrial nation needs more than five to six years, in spite of the oil crisis.

If the production of plastics is compared with that of ferrous materials, it will be found that the production of both groups may become the same in volume within the next three years. However, on a weight basis, the production of ferrous materials and plastics will become equal in *ca.* 35 years (Fig. 3).

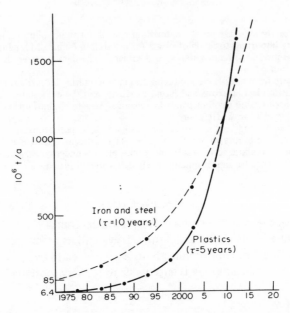

Fig. 3. Foreseeable development of iron and plastics production (by weight) in W. Germany.

About 6.4 million tonnes of plastics and *ca.* 85 million tonnes of steel and iron were produced in the Federal Republic of Germany in 1973. A pessimistic doubling time (τ) of five years in the case of plastics and an optimistic doubling time of ten years in the case of iron is assumed on this graph. One could object that the given doubling rates are not realistic, because increasing oil prices should slow down the growth of plastics production. However, as can be seen in Fig. 4, which demonstrates the effect of the crude oil shortage in 1973, the effect of increased oil prices on the prices of finished plastics products is not very serious.

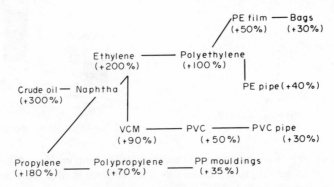

Fig. 4. The effect of increased oil prices on downstream operations:
% increase: Mid 1974 cf. mid 1973.

In general, it is found that the increases for finished plastic components are, in most instances, of the same order as those of competitive finished products made from other materials. This means that, in spite of a reassessment of the competitive position of plastics caused by the dramatic increase in the crude oil price, plastics have been able to remain very competitive. This is because plastics compete with traditional materials not only on a price basis, but in their technical performance, which has a significant bearing on their overall acceptability. The lower density of plastics and their less labour-intensive processing in the production of finished components in relation to other materials are some examples.

Therefore, a major switch to traditional materials from plastics is very unlikely. In fact it is that the high volume plastic materials will benefit more in the future than other materials from cost reducing technological gains, such as, for instance, increased scale of plant, newer production techniques and lower costs for environmental control. This means that further substitution of traditional materials by plastics is even more likely in the future.

Materials	MJ/kg	kWh/kg	MJ/l	kWh/l
Polystyrene	21.35	5.93	22.86	6.35
HD–Polyethylene	27.32	7.59	25.92	7.20
Cement	8.57	2.38	26.82	7.45
Glass	17.39	4.83	45.04	12.51
LD–Polyethylene	53.1	14.75	48.35	13.43
Steel	30.89	8.58	241.88	67.19
Aluminium	169.09	46.97	446.83	124.12
Copper	55.01	15.28	490.10	136.14

Fig. 5. Energy necessary for production of some common materials
(Stanford Research Institute, April 1973).

This prognosis is confirmed by Fig. 5, which shows the demand of energy for the production of 1 kg and 1 l. of some common materials. (In these data the energy demand for distribution is not included).

It can be seen that the energy necessary to produce one volume unit of polyethylene is much less than that of steel. The energy demand ratio of steel to polyethylene is about ten and, even having regard to the fact that about a three-fold volume of plastics is necessary to achieve the strength of steel, the factor of energy saving using plastics instead of steel is still greater than three.

It is also evident that, from an energy viewpoint, an increase in the production rate of plastics relative to that of other materials is to be expected in future. Moreover, it seems that the present competition in growth rate will change into a more intense substitution of traditional materials by plastics.

These facts and prognoses are inducement enough to transfer the techniques of recycling iron scrap, which have been well known for many decades or even centuries, to waste products of the chemical industry, and to the increasing amount of plastic waste in particular. In this connection, Fig. 4 gives possible return lines for the recycling stream. It is important to know where the recycling stream is to feed back into the production process, and the Hamburg investigation will be described later.

Obviously, it makes a difference whether PE-foil, PE, ethylene, naphtha or crude oil can be made out of a worn out PE-bag. Different methods are already under discussion or in operation. Plant internal wastes, for instance, are extruded or remelted and worked up to final products again, while dirty or mixed waste plastics can be worked up by adding fillers and foaming agents to yield downgraded products. Processes like these change the plastics only physically, and these are classified as re-use processes.

Recycling processes imply a chemical change of the waste plastic as well. Here a conversion to the raw material or an intermediate of plastics production takes place. Examples of this kind of reaction are depolymerisation, applicable to only a few types of plastics like polystyrene or polymethylmethacrylate, and the cracking of waste plastics into naptha.

Fig. 6. Collecting and despatch of plastic waste in Funabashi, Japan.

Finally, there are processes for recovery of the heat value alone from the plastics. Although this aims to substitute for an actual raw material, crude oil, this is not a recycling process because the circuit is interrupted by the combustion. Moreover, in the not too far distant future, the value of waste plastics as a source of energy will become less important because of the substitution of conventional by unconventional energy sources like nuclear-, solar-, or geothermic energy. The decreasing amount of crude oil available will make plastic waste more valuable as a source of hydro-carbons and aromatics.

Figure 6 shows how plastics can be collected, a project considered impossible by many people. This picture was taken at Funabashi, Japan, where it has been shown that, by appropriate propaganda and education, consumers can be urged to separate plastic wastes out of the garbage. The waste plastics are collected in small polyethylene sacks, easy to handle even for children.

The percentage of waste plastics in municipal solid waste is, in Japan, 8–12%; elsewhere, it is less. In Germany, in 1974, a plastics content of 5.4 wt %, 17.9 vol. %, was determined at an incineration plant in Hamburg; this collection procedure has been found to be workable in German cities.

A similar result can be reached by other ways of course. Figure 7 shows a layout of a separation process developed by the U.S. Bureau of Mines. For a technologist it is interesting that the old-established processes of ore dressing have found new applications. It is planned to put this process into operation at Reutlingen, a small town in Southern Germany, in 1978. There are, however, some difficulties in crushing the rubbish, and the crusher itself has been known to be wrecked by ex-

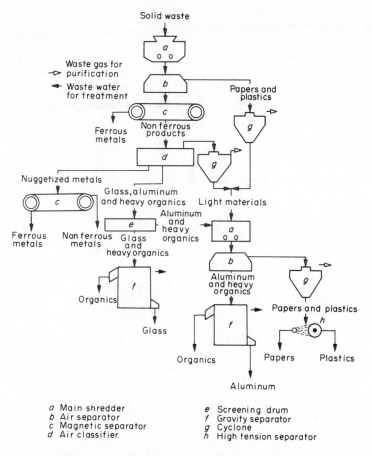

a Main shredder
b Air separator
c Magnetic separator
d Air classifier

e Screening drum
f Gravity separator
g Cyclone
h High tension separator

Fig. 7. Separation of garbage (flow sheet, Bureau of Mines, U.S.A.).

plosions. It should be mentioned that the developers of the process claim that the separation of a fraction with a high plastics and paper content is profitable.

A process recently introduced by Krauss-Maffei, called the R 80 process, has the same result, especially regarding paper recovery. Paper recovery is common in Germany, unlike some other countries such as the U.K. A light fraction is produced which contains paper, plastics and textiles, and this is considered the main and most valuable fraction. This light fraction is mixed with water and stirred in a pulper until all the paper is shredded and can be removed as a slurry. The residue is a mixture of plastics and textiles which can be used as feed for a recycling process.

The plastics content of German garbage rose to 1.1 M tonnes in 1973. By application of one of these collecting or separating processes, it should be possible to prepare and concentrate most of the plastic waste from the garbage for re-use or recycling.

Before discussing the details of some re-use and recycling processes, it is important to realize that there are other, more accessible, sources of waste plastic. The plastics producing and manufacturing industries generate large amounts of waste plastics. Often, purity and high quality allow immediate reprocessing of this material in the same plant. Nevertheless, the quantity of plastic waste to treat is significant. In 1973 German industry accumulated 240 000 tonnes of such waste, which was too dirty to be worked up again. Another problem that can make reprocessing impossible is the presence of thermosetting plastics or of other materials in combined plastics or laminates.

About 20 000 tonnes originate in plastics production (i.e. about 0.3% of the produced plastics), 115 000 tonnes from the plastics manufacturing industry and 105 000 tonnes resulted from the application of plastics. For the disposal of such plastic wastes on a rubbish dump, the factory has to pay *ca.* DM 75/tonne (*ca.* $30), and at an incineration plant the cost may be DM 150/tonne.

Once again it must be emphasized that those 240 000 tonnes of waste plastics are collected already and are available in batches of more than 10 tonnes. Including the 1.1 M tonnes of plastics in the garbage, the quantity of plastic waste totalled at least 1.3 M tonnes in Germany in 1973. The plastic content of scrap cars and the 250 000 tonnes per year of scrap tyres are not included in this amount.

These data once again prove the need for further research in the field of plastics re-use and recycling.

EXISTING RE-USE PROCESSES

Figure 8 shows a plant at Funabashi, where relatively pure plastics are crushed and washed. The separation of glass and metals is achieved by means of air classification. After grinding and magnetic separation the small plastic pieces are washed again.

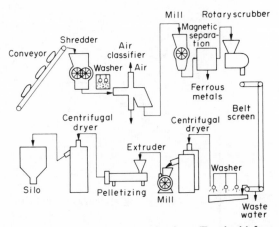

Fig. 8. Flow sheet of separation of garbage (Funabashi, Japan).

The particles are then dried in a hydroextractor, pulverized, extruded and granulated. These granules are processed as usual by an extrusion press or by injection moulding machines.

It is evident that this is acceptable as a method of re-use only when there is a market for products with a poor shock- and tear-resistance. At Funabashi the plastic waste of about 150 000 inhabitants is re-processed to commodities like flower pots and fishbaskets.

The so-called Reverzer was developed by Mitsubishi, and a similar machine, with a throughput of up to 500 kg/h of polyethylene film scrap, is built by Condux in Germany.

Figure 9 shows a cross section of a plant using a Reverzer. Crushed plastic is mixed with an expanding agent and sometimes with a filler, such as sand. Passing the Reverzer the material is compacted and heated, and subsequent cooling and hardening occurs in a mould. In the city of Kusnetsu fence pales are the main products made by this process.

Plants like this are planned to be built all over Japan. A plant with a capacity of 25 tonnes per day needs a site of *ca.* 5000 m^2. In Fig. 10 it can be seen that the processing costs of plastic waste can drop to *ca.* 3.0 cents per kg.* The throughput of 500 kg/h or *ca.* 4000 tonnes per year corresponds to the quantity of plastic waste in a city of more than 100 000 inhabitants.

*At the time of editing U.S.$1 = 300 Yen.

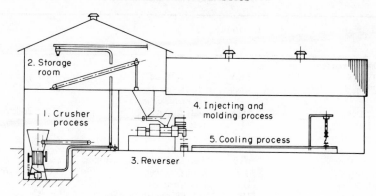

Fig. 9. Plan for Regeneration Systems.

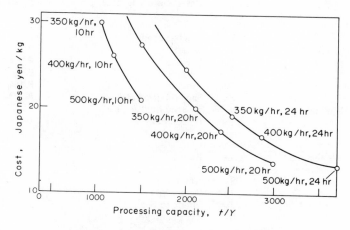

Fig. 10. Cost estimates for Reverzer process.

Further cost reduction by increased throughput seems impossible because of higher charges for transportation, and because of the necessity for the parallel coupling of several Reverzers. At present, plant capacities of about 10 000 tonnes per year for processes like this are considered reasonable in Germany.

RECYCLING PROCESSES

In Fig. 11 some developers and constructors of recycling processes for rubbish, plastics, scrap tyres and scrap are listed.

A pilot plant of the Andco-Torrax-Process is situated at Buffalo. The low-heating-value gas produced is used in a power plant. The main advantage of this process, however is the ecologically acceptable slag, which is produced by sintering at *ca.* 1600°C. A plant of this kind with a capacity of 8.5 tonne/h is under construction in Luxembourg; another will be constructed at Frankfurt.

Another type of shaft furnace is used in the Warren Spring Laboratories at Stevenage, U.K., and is shown in Fig. 12. The organic components of the rubbish are decomposed pyrolytically by heating the furnace externally. Glass and metal are collected in a quench tank. The volatile fractions generated are separated into heavy oils, light oils and gas; the latter can be used as fuel for the furnace. The value of the non-ferrous metals is considered to make this process especially profitable.

Designation	Location	Type	Size	Temperature (°C)
(1) Municipal solid waste				
Andoco–Torrax	USA	Shaft furnace	P 75 t/d	1000–1450
Bureau of Mines	USA	Retort	S	500–950
Fink	D	Arc furnace	L	1500–1700
Garret Res. Dev.	USA	Shaft furnace	P 200 t/d	500
Krauss-Maffei	D	Rotary kiln	P 2 t/d	500–700
Mannesmann	D	Rotary kiln	L	500–900
Monsanto	USA	Rotary kiln	P	1000
National Res. Dev.	GB	Shaft furnace o. Rotary kiln	L	500–900
Pollution Control	DK	Shaft furnace	P 8 t/d	800
Union Carbide	USA	Shaft furnace	P 5 t/d	
University of Cal.	USA	Multiple-hearth furnace	L 35 kg/h	
Warren Spring Lab.	GB	Shaft furnace	L	800–900
West Virginia Univ.	USA	Fluidized bed	P 1 t/d	
Wotschke	D	Reverberatory furnace	P 25 t/d	1600
(2) Plastic waste				
Japan Gasoline	J	Fluidized bed	P 7 t/d	450
Kawasaki Heavy Ind.	J	Retort	P	
Mitsubishi Heavy Ind.	J	Reactor	P 2.4 t/d	500
Mitsui	J	Reactor	P	420
Sanyo Electric	J	Reactor	P 0.4 t/d	400–450
Sumitomo	J	Sand-fluidized bed	P 3 t/d	600
University of Hamburg	D	(a) Sand-fluidized bed	L	700–850
		(b) Salt melt	L	600–800
(3) Tyre				
Bureau of Mines/Firestone	USA	Retort	S	500–950
Cities Serv. Co/Goodyear	USA	?	P	
Hydrocarbon Res. Inc.	USA	Autoclave	L	350–450
Kobe Steel	J	Rotary kiln	P 2.4 t/d	
Nippon Zeon/Jap. Gasoline	J	Fluidized bed	P 5 t/d	
Zeplichal	D	Band conveyor		500
(4) Cable waste				
Ramms	D	Tube	P	500

P = Pilot plant L = Laboratory test plant S = Semi-industrial plant

Fig. 11. Laboratory tests and pilot plants for pyrolysis.

A continuous plant is shown in Fig. 13 which illustrates the kind of information campaign in this field in Japan. It is part of a campaign aimed not at businessmen but rather at the inhabitants of the city. This 5 tonnes per day plant in Japan is built on an area of 500 m^2. The feelings of the inhabitants toward this plant are favourable; in fact they are proud of it.

The plant has been developed in cooperation with Sanyo Electric Co., and is distinguished by microwave heating of the plastics to the melting point. The elimination of HC1 from a PVC-containing feed is also achieved by microwave heating, which in turn is favoured by the carbon-rich residues. of PVC. The molten material then passes a modified screw mixer, externally heated. Here, the degradation into gas and into light and heavy oils takes place at residence times of 10-20 min and at a temperature of ca. 850°C. The oil fractions are collected and sold; the gas is used for the heating of the mixer or is flared.

It should be mentioned that the heating value of the oil fractions produced in this process, or in similar processes using separated plastic wastes in general, corresponds to that of good brands of fuel

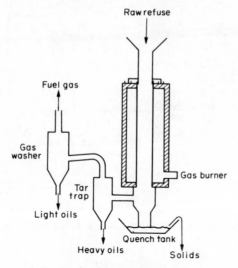

Fig. 12. Pilot plant for pyrolysis of garbage (Warren Spring Laboratory, Stevenage, Herts, U.K.).

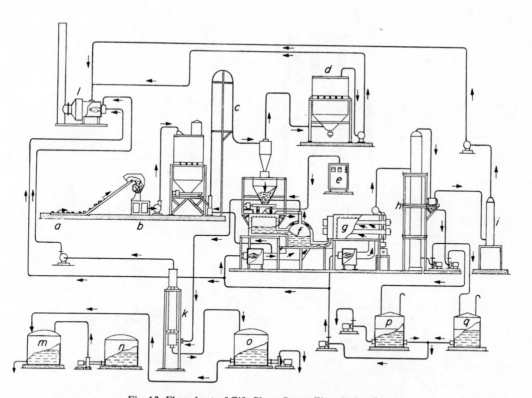

Fig. 13. Flow sheet of Gifu Plant, Sanyo Electric Co., Japan.

(a) Feed; (b) Crusher; (c) Pneumatic conveyor; (d) Sack dryer; (e) Microwave generation, 2450 MHz,
2 x 4 kW; (f) MW-melting vessel for plastic (PVC); (g) Pyrolysis reacter; (h) Cooler and column;
(i) Gas washer; (k) HC1 washer; (l) Combustion tower; (m) Tank for waste water; (n) Tank for NaOH;
(o) (p) (q) Oil tanks.

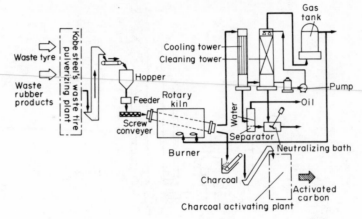

Fig. 14. Flow sheet of KOBE test unit, Japan, for tyre pyrolysis.

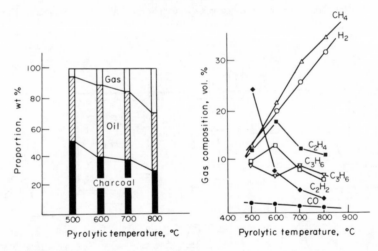

Fig. 15. The effect of pyrolysis temperature on product composition.

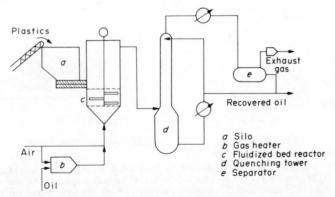

a Silo
b Gas heater
c Fluidized bed reactor
d Quenching tower
e Separator

Fig. 16. Pyrolysis of polystyrene in a fluidized bed, Japan Gasoline Corp.

oil. Oil fractions from pyrolysis of garbage and paper have a rather low heating value and a high oxygen content, and this makes storage difficult.

Figure 14 shows a flow scheme of the well known Kobe test unit, which has been developed for scrap tyre pyrolysis. Shredded tyres with a particle size of *ca.* 1 cm^3, or less than 0.1 in^3, are fed into a rotary kiln, measuring 3m long and *ca.* 0.5 m in dia. The residence time in the pyrolysis zone is *ca.* 20 min. Here again the products are gas and oil, as Fig. 15 shows. In addition the carbonaceous residues are activated by water vapour and sold as active carbon.

A feature of the pyrolysis plant at the Kobe steel factory is the rotary kiln, which is made by centrifugal casting as a single part.

The Japan Gasoline Corp. has developed a recycling process which is shown in Fig. 16. Here, plastics, especially polystyrene wastes, are fed into a fluidized bed which is stirred and heated by the pre-heated fluidization medium and by partial oxidation. It is claimed that the recovery rate for polystyrene is 87%, but the actual yield reprocessable monomer styrene is 50-60% of the feed.

RESEARCH AT THE UNIVERSITY OF HAMBURG

Work has been directed not towards obtaining a superior heat value of the pyrolysis oils, but rather towards establishing the value of the products with respect to their chemical use. Initially, attempts were made to obtain precise information on energy and material balances. Two types of heat transfer to the plastics were investigated, viz. the molten salt reactor and the fluidized bed.

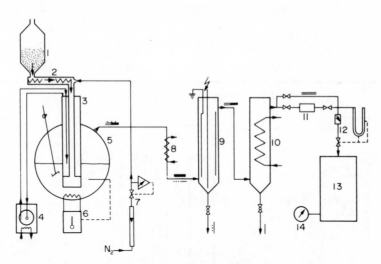

Fig. 17. Apparatus for recycling of plastics in molten salt:
(1) Plastic feed hopper; (2) Screw conveyor; (3) Downpipe with cooling jacket; (4) Thermostat; (5) Reactor flask with stirring mechanisim; (6) Temperature measurement and regulation with electric heating; (7) Rotameter with differential pressure regulator; (8) Cooler; (9) Electrostatic precipitator; (10) Intensive cooler; (11) Gas sampler; (12) Control manometer with throttle and magnet valve; (13) Evacuated gas sample holder; (14) Manometer.

The layout using molten salts as a reaction medium is shown in Fig. 17. The plastics were transported into the heated melt by a screw, where they decomposed and the hot vapours passed to an electrostatic precipitator where paraffin vapours were condensed to form rather pure paraffin waxes. In the intensive cooler a liquid fraction was separated from the hydrocarbon gas. All fractions were weighed and analyzed by gas chromatography (Fig. 18).

Temperature (°C)	640	690	740	790	850
Hydrogen	0.2	0.3	0.6	0.8	1.6
Methane	5.6	9.2	13.7	19.5	23.5
Ethylene	14.0	19.0	22.0	26.6	26.8
Ethane	4.0	5.4	6.8	5.7	4.8
Propene	10.1	14.7	12.4	10.0	4.5
Propane	1.0	1.1	0.5	0.2	0.1
Iso-Butene	2.6	3.1	2.1	0.8	0.4
1,3-Butadiene	3.2	3.3	3.8	2.4	1.9
Pentene-1	1.3	1.2	0.4	0.2	0.1
Cyclopentadiene	1.3	1.6	0.7	0.2	0.1
Hexane	0.8	0.6	0.2	–	–
Hexene-1	2.5	2.1	0.8	0.1	–
Benzene	4.0	4.7	7.3	11.5	11.9
Heptene-1	1.8	0.9	0.7	0.1	–
Toluene	1.2	1.7	2.2	2.4	1.7
Xylene	0.1	0.2	0.3	0.3	0.2
Styrene	0.1	0.2	0.5	0.9	1.0
Indene	–	–	0.1	0.2	0.2
Naphthalene	0.1	0.4	1.3	1.8	3.0
Methylnaphthalene	–	0.1	0.3	0.4	0.4
Diphenyl	–	–	0.2	0.2	0.3
Acenaphthene	–	0.1	0.1	0.2	0.4
Phenanthrene	–	0.1	0.2	0.4	0.6
Carbon	0.1	0.2	1.2	2.3	7.9
Hydrocarbons above C_9	23.2	11.6	5.0	0.8	0.1
Waxes and high aromatics	19.2	12.1	10.2	3.6	3.5
Total	96.4	93.9	89.1	91.6	95.0

Fig. 18. Polyethylene feed stock.

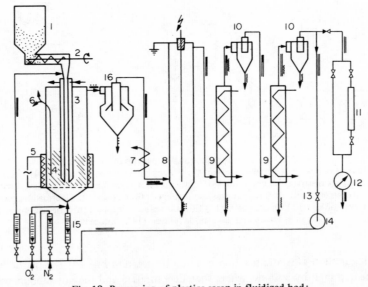

Fig. 19. Processing of plastics scrap in fluidized bed:
(1) Plastic feed hopper; (2) Screw conveyor; (3) Downpipe with cooling jacket; (4) Fluidized bed
reactor; (5) Electric heating; (6) Temperature measurement; (7) Cooler; (8) Electrostatic precipitator;
(9) Intensive cooler; (10) Cyclone; (11) Gas sample; (12) Gas meter; (13) Throttle; (14) Compressor;
(15) Rotameter; (16) Cyclone.

Results of pyrolysis of plastics in a fluidised bed

Input material	Ethylene						Poly-ethylene		Poly-styrene	Tyre rubber		PVC		Naphtha (30–130°C)	
Fluidising medium	cracker gas						N_2	cracker gas	cracker gas	cracker gas		cracker gas		(Industrial cracker)	
Temperature (°C)	740	*	825	*	870	*	740	740	740	740		740	845	750	850
Conversion (wt %)	24.6	*	32.5	*	56.3	*				**					
Hydrogen	0.4	1.8	0.8	2.6	1.7	3.1	0.3	0.5		0.8	1.6	0.7	0.8	0.8	1.0
Methane	3.7	19.8	7.1	23.6	16.9	31.9	7.0	16.2	0.3	10.2	20.4	ʼ2.8	3.0	13.0	17.0
Ethylene	75.4		67.5		43.7		35.1	25.5	0.5	2.6	5.2	2.1	1.7	26.0	32.0
Ethane	4.6	24.4	5.3	18.2	4.2	8.0	3.6	5.4		1.2	2.4	0.4	0.2	4.5	4.5
Propene	3.4	18.3	2.7	9.0	1.5	2.8	22.6	9.4		0.7	1.5	0.4	0.1	20.0	18.0
Isobutene	0.3	1.5					8.7	1.1		0.2	0.4				
1,3-Butadiene	2.6	13.8	1.9	6.4	2.0	3.7	10.3	2.8		0.3	0.5			5.8	4.5
Benzene	1.4	7.5	5.5	18.4	10.7	20.2		12.2	2.1	4.2	8.4	3.5	4.3	5.2	5.5
Toluene	0.5	2.4	1.1	3.5	1.8	3.3		3.6	4.5	3.8	7.6	1.1	1.2	2.4	2.6
Xylene &ethylbenzene	0.2	0.8	0.2	0.6	0.2	0.4		1.1	1.2	1.9	3.9	0.2	0.2	0.7	0.4
Styrene	0.3	1.6	1.0	3.3	3.6	6.8		1.1	71.6	2.3	4.7	0.1			
Indene	0.1	0.5	0.5	1.5	0.8	1.8		0.3	1.4	0.8	1.6	0.4			
Naphthalene	0.1	0.4	0.9	3.1	4.6	8.8		8.7	0.8	0.9	1.8	3.1	2.4		
Methylnaphthalene									2.6	0.7	1.4	1.2	1.0		
Diphenyl									(CH_3-Sty.)			0.8	0.6		
Fluorene												0.4	0.5		
Phenanthrene												0.6	0.8		
HCl										1.6†		56.3	56.4		
Filler										7.9			0.9		
Carbon	0.5	2.5	?		?		0.4	0.9	0.3	42.8		8.8	8.6		
Total hydrocarbon gas + H_2	90.3	79.6	85.4	59.8	70.1	49.9	87.7	61.1	0.9	16.0	32.0	6.4	5.8	77.4	83.0
Longchain hydrocarbons above C_9							10.4	7.3		0.3††					
Total aromatics		3.3	17.9	11.9	40.2	26.5	50.1	0.1	30.1	95.4	30.2	60.4	27.2	27.9	22.6	17.0
Total	94.1		97.3		96.6		98.6	99.4	96.6	98.8		98.7	99.6		

*C_2H_4–free product; **based on rubber content; †H_2S; ††H_2O

On the left the three double columns show the product distribution using ethylene as feedstock (cracker gas in circulation) and in the extreme right double columns are given, for comparison, the results from an industrial cracking plant using low-boiling naphtha as feedstock. The middle columns show the product distribution using polyethylene (PE), polystrene (PS), tyre rubber, and polyvinyl chloride (PVC), as feedstocks. The lower seven lines of figures give the portions of the individual material groups making up the overall balance.

Fig. 20. Pyrolysis of plastics in a fluidized bed.

The layout using a fluidized bed is shown in Fig. 19 and is almost identical. A cyclone connected to the fluidized bed separates solids from the vapours of the hot products of cracking. In the case of scrap tyres as feed, e.g. carbon black and fillers like zinc oxide are collected. The latter can be recovered quantitatively by burning off the carbon afterwards. Again, paraffin or high boiling aromatic fractions are separated by an electrostatic precipitator. Finally, intensive coolers and hydro-cyclones separate a low boiling point liquid fraction from the cracking gas, which is used as a fluidization medium to some extent.

The main products are shown in Fig. 20. The first three columns serve only for comparison and show the behaviour of the circulating cracker gas when using ethylene as feedstock. Conversion of

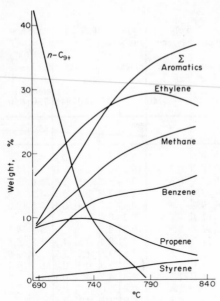

Pyrolysis of polyethylene in a fluidized bed,
recycle gas as fluidizing medium

Fig. 21. Pyrolysis of PE in a fluidized
bed (recycle gas as fluidizing medium)
plotted as wt % against temperature.

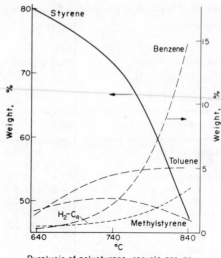

Pyrolysis of polystyrene, recycle gas as
fluidizing medium

Fig. 23. Pyrolysis of polystyrene (recycle
gas as fluidizing medium) plotted as wt
% against temperature.

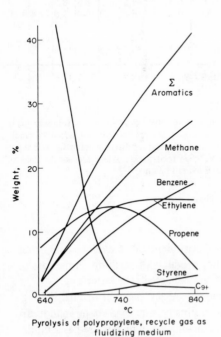

Pyrolysis of polypropylene, recycle gas as
fluidizing medium

Fig. 22. Pyrolysis of polypropylene
(recycle gas as fluidizing medium) plotted as wt % against temperature.

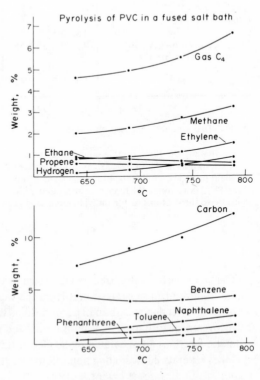

Fig. 24. Pyrolysis of PVC in a fused salt
bath, plotted as wt % against
temperature.

the ethylene proceeded more rapidly with increasing temperature and with the formation of increasing quantities of benzene and methane.

Further examples of cracking experiments show the material balances obtained using PE, PS, tyre rubber and PVC as feedstock.

The table shows the benzene content of the pyrolysis products, for example. The content of aromatics in total is listed in the penultimate line. The pyrolysis of PE can be done by different methods; results in the column obtained by the use of nitrogen as a fluidization medium gave the content of aromatics as only 0.1 wt%. In the column, circulated cracker gas is used as fluidization medium, which increased the aromatics content to 30% at 740°C. In every case more than 97% of the amont of plastic feed material was accounted for.

Figure 21 illustrates the relationship between the pyrolysis products and the reaction temperature. The feed material is PE, and the amount of aromatics increases with increasing temperature, with a production of up to 30 weight % of ethylene at 800°C and a decrease in the yield of paraffin waxes. The relatively large amount of aromatics is built up by condensation reaction of the C_2, C_3 and C_4 hydrocarbons.

In Fig. 22, polypropylene is used as feed material. The decrease of the C_3-fraction by increased aromatics formation at higher temperatures is evident.

Polystyrene is the feedstock in Fig. 23. It can be seen that a high yield of the monomer styrene is only possible at relatively low temperatures. This fact suggests a multistage process with the first step carried out at low temperature. Experiments of this kind are carried out in a pilot scale plant at present.

Figure 24 shows the results of PVC-pyrolysis. The weight percentage of the products is very low, because of the high HC1 content of PVC. The amount of carbonaceous residue is relatively high and increases with increasing temperature.

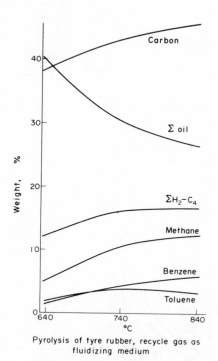

Pyrolysis of tyre rubber, recycle gas as
fluidizing medium

Fig. 25. Pyrolysis of tyre rubber (recycle gas as fluidizing medium)
plotted as wt % against temperature.

Figure 25 shows the pyrolysis of scrap tyres. Here the hydrocarbon portion of the feed is only *ca.* 50%. Half of it, however, can be obtained as a liquid fraction, with a high aromatics content at *ca.* 770°C.

Figure 26 illustrates the possibility of depolymerisation. Some 96 wt % of the feed of PMMA can be obtained as the corresponding monomer in a fluidized bed.

The effect on a plastic granule in a fluidized bed or a salt melt was also studied. In order to study this aspect single granules were inserted into the heat transfer medium in a closed reaction vessel and the pressure was observed. Figure 27 shows the increase of pressure during these experiments. It indicates that the melting period is variable; in fact, it depends on the particle size. In addition, fluidized bed experiments showed that the melting time is reduced by increasing the fluidization. This demonstrates the importance of the mechanical distribution of the molten plastics all over the heat transfer medium. Thereafter, pyrolysis takes place with a constant rate, depending on the temperature.

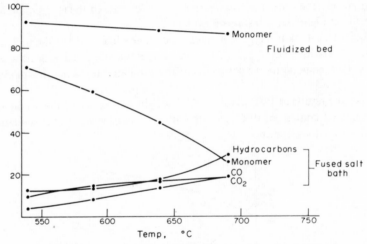

Fig. 26. Pyrolysis of PMMA in a fluidized bed and in a fused salt bath.

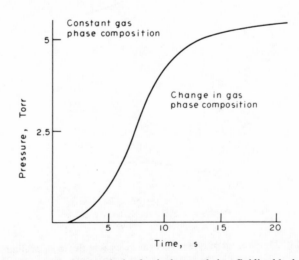

Fig. 27. Pressure changes during pyrolysis of a single granule in a fluidized bed and fused salts.

A third stage follows during which further decomposition of the previously formed products in the hot gas zone occurs at the hot wall of the vessel and at the surface of the bed. From the data determined in laboratory scale studies it was possible to design a pilot plant with a throughput of 10 kg/h.

The development and operation at the University of Hamburg of a pilot plant with such a capacity is part of a research programme jointly sponsored by the Government of the Federal Republic of Germany and by the German plastics manufacturing industries. This programme is divided into the following seven sections:

(1)   Registration and collection of plastic wastes.
(2)   Preparation and concentration of plastic wastes for recycling processes.
(3)   Utilisation of plastic-containing waste by biological degradation.
(4)   Utilisation of plastic waste by pyrolysis.
(5)   Utilisation of plastic waste by other methods of degradation, especially by hydrolysis.
(6)   Technical problems of waste plastic processing for re-use.
(7)   Applicability of products manufactured by methods of Section 6.

At Hamburg University work is proceeding on Section 4.

Charged material	Computed values						Measured values		
	Reaction enthalpy at 25°C		Heat export		Energy consumption		Energy consumption		Deviation
	MJ/kg	kcal/kg	MJ/kg	kcal/kg	MJ/kg	kcal/kg	MJ/kg	kcal/kg	%
Polyethylene	2.17	649	1.84	440	4.55	1089	4.64	1110	+1.9
Polypropylene	2.25	535	1.63	390	3.87	925	3.84	920	-0.5
PVC	0.02	5	0.93	222	1.16	277	1.04	250	-9.7
Polystyrol	1.18	282	1.45	347	2.63	629	2.80	670	+6.5
PMMA	0.68	163	1.57	375	2.25	538	2.42	580	+7.8
Model mixture	2.02	479	1.63	389	3.63	868	3.47	830	-4.4
Tyre rubber	–	–	–	–	–	–	1.75	420	–

Fig. 28. Comparison of measured and computed values of heat balance with pyrolysis in a fused salt bath at 690°C.

Several layouts of the pilot plant have been reviewed especially with respect to the heat supply. In Fig. 28 the third and fourth columns show the calculated and the actual demand of energy for the pyrolysis of 1 kg of plastics. In these data heat recovery is not included. We need ca. 42 MJ (10 000 kcal/h) for the planned throughput of the pilot plant.

Figure 29 shows a possible scheme to heat up a fluidized bed. Beneath the bed is a combustion chamber, where carbon is burned in air. The heat supply for the endothermic reaction of pyrolysis is brought about by the hot CO or CO_2, which simultaneously acts as a fluidizing medium.

Depending on the degree of oxidation, the demand for carbon is ca. 1.2–4.8 kg/h. It is possible, of course, to substitute carbon by gaseous hydrocarbons, generated during pyrolysis. However, this may yield other cracking products, because of the water vapour from the hydrocarbon combustion.

There is also a possibility of direct heat supply by partial oxidation of coal, when the sand of the bed is substituted by slack coal, or by partial oxidation of the plastics feed. Another possibility, the external, indirect heating of the reaction vessel, would create many difficulties in scaling-up.

Figure 30 demonstrates another layout of a pyrolysis process. The first step of the pyrolysis may be performed in such a way that PVC-containing plastics are dehydrochlorinated almost completely

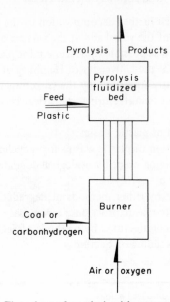

Fig. 29. Flow sheet of pyrolysis with separated heating.

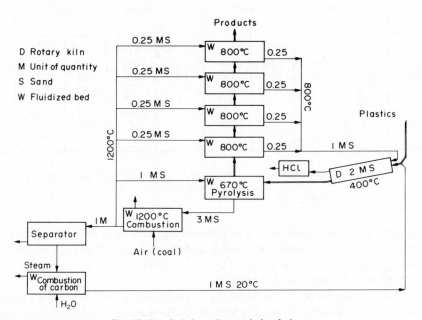

Fig. 30. Pyrolysis by using sand circulation.

in sand as a carrier, at a temperature of *ca.* 400°C and a residence time of 2-5 min. A rotary kiln or a shaft furnace will probably be used for this first step.

The HC1 produced is *ca.* 99% pure and contaminated by only a trace of hydrocarbons. The residue is a pyrolytic, decomposable carbon-rich material. The actual pyrolysis, the second step in this process, is carried out in a fluidized bed. This flow scheme is designed as a five stage bed in order to attain long residence times. The heat supply of the fluidized bed is achieved by using sand or aluminium oxide, which is heated to 1200°C in a third step by burning carbon residues off the sand. As an additional fuel, the use of gaseous hydrocarbons, generated during pyrolysis, is possible.

Sometimes the disposal of special industrial organic waste is difficult and very expensive, because its complete combustion needs relatively long residence times at high temperatures. It will be most advantageous to be able to use this material as a feed in the third stage. Compared with reaction times in flames a much longer residence time will be possible in this expanded fluidizing bed.

In the separator, materials which are not decomposable are eliminated in order to purify the sand, which is continuously circulated. Experiments proved that the transport of a sand-plastics mixture in this process is trouble free at all temperatures so long as the sand:plastics ratio is greater than ten.

Fluidizing gas	Laboratory gas		Prototype (pilot plant)		
	N_2	Cracker gas	N_2	N_2	N_2
Temperature	$740°C$	$740°C$	$710°C$	$770°C$	$820°C$
Hydrogen	0.33	0.53	0.24	0.46	0.67
Methane	6.74	16.12	6.65	9.32	11.82
Ethylene	33.83	25.38	23.94	32.0	36.95
Ethane	3.51	5.33	5.13	4.92	4.86
Propene	21.80	9.32	17.19	19.72	18.05
1,3-Butadiene	9.95	2.81	7.02	7.99	7.12
Butene	11.58	1.53	8.69	6.88	3.87
Pentene	0.01	0.98	9.84	6.95	1.82
Hexene, C_5H_6	0.01	0.98	8.38	3.0	2.36
Benzene	0.05	12.22	1.51	4.73	7.09
Heptene	0.01	1.04	3.33	1.06	0.12
Toluene	0.02	3.59	0.70	1.46	1.92
C_9	1.05	2.22	1.04	1.0	1.13
Rest to 100%	11.11	17.95	6.34	0.61	2.22

Fig. 31. Results of pyrolysis of PE in the prototype.

In the meantime an improvised prototype has been constructed at Hamburg, which has proved to be correctly dimensioned. It does not, however, operate on the basis of sand circulation. Instead, some 30 bent tubes are installed into the bottom of an ash-tub or dust-bin, which is electrically heated. The fluidizing medium is injected through the tubes, thus preventing the escape of sand.

In this improvised prototype, the hydrocyclone, mounted at the end of the cooler, separates the liquids from the cracker gas, which is ignited by the pilot flame of a bunsen burner and flared.

In order to improve the heat transfer and attain higher temperatures in the fluidized bed, flame tubes are used. Figure 31 shows the products pyrolysed in the prototype.

In 1976, a continuous pyrolysis unit will be built in cooperation with Claudius Peters. Although the profitability of a prospective plant cannot currently be assessed with sufficient accuracy, there are hopes that plants with a size of 1-5 tonne/h throughput could prove profitable.

REFERENCES

H. Sinn, Recycling of plastics, *Chemie-Ing.-Techn.* **46**, (14), 579 (1974).

SCI/DECHEMA Conference 'On the preservation of our raw material resources, a contribution of chemical technology', Cambridge, March, 1973; see also K. H. C. Bessant, J. J. P. Staudinger, *Chem. and Ind. (12)* 548 (1973).

Plastics in refuse disposal, published by the Verband Kunststofferzeugender Industrie, Frankfurt, 1973; see: Estimates of the Verband Kunststofferzeugender Industrie and the project group 'Abfallbeseitigung' (refuse disposal) in preparation of the long-term environment programme of the Federal Government.

Plastics waste as a special problem of refuse disposal. Report by the Federal Ministry of the Interior in: Supplements to *Mull and Abfall*, **4**, (1970). See also: Umwelt und Gesellschaft, published by Bommer, Umwelt & Medizin. m.b.H., Frankfurt, 1973, in particular D. Behrens, p. 79-100; and Energie fur die Zukunft (Energy for the Future), Umschau, 1974, in collaboration with the Deutsche Forschungsgemeinschaft, p. 80-87.

M. J. Spendlove, *Umschau Wiss. Techn. 73,* 366 (1973); see also W. Herbert, Solid waste recycling at Franklin, Ohio *(Proc. 3rd Mineral Waste Utilization Symp.,* U.S. Bureau of Mines and IIT Res. Inst); C. B. Kenahan and others, Report of Investigation 7204 (U.S. Dept. of the Interior, Bureau of Mines).

Y. Shimizu, H, Ando, T. Abe, O. Inomata and S. Matsuzawa. *Bull. Nat. Res. Inst. Pollution and Resources* 2, 43 (1972). Compare with S. Speth, *Chem. and Ind,* 557, (1973), and *Chemie-Ing.-Techn.* 45, 526 (1973).

Kobe Steel, Ltd. Tokyo, private communication, 1973.

J. Menzel, H. Perkow and H. Sinn, *Chem. and Ind.* 570, (1973).

H. Perkow, Thesis, University of Hamburg, in preparation (1974).

J. Menzel, Thesis, University of Hamburg, 1974, see synopsis 111, *Chem-Ing.-Techn.* 46, 607 (9174) and microfiche MS 111/74.

J. Fritz, Investigations for a thesis, Dept. for applied Chemistry, Institute for Inorganic and Applied Chemistry, University of Hamburg (1974).

Conservation & Recycling, Vol.1, pp.111–118. Pergamon Press, 1976. Printed in Great Britain.

DISPOSAL OF TOXIC WASTES–1. Electroplating and Electrochemical Machining Wastes

P. J. BODEN

University of Nottingham, England

Abstract–The paper comprises two parts, the first dealing with electroplating and electrochemical machining effluents and the other with poisonous and radioactive wastes.

Some easily recognised pollutants of rivers and waterways are capable of treatment for the profitable recovery of values. Radioactive and certain poisonous substances, on the other hand, are genuine waste products which have to be stored and from which the general public must be protected.

Simple dilution of plating effluents has, until recently, been considered an adequate safety measure, but worldwide experience shows that even diluted effluents can cause serious pollution and contamination. Several methods of control are described. The treatment applied in any given case depends on the policy of local authorities and on the potential savings accruing from extraction processes.

Certain poisonous and radioactive wastes arise as a result of industrial processes and many cannot economically be used again or easily rendered harmless. Their disposal must therefore be permanent and under adequate control. Some suitable storage and disposal methods are described and possible future developments discussed.

INTRODUCTION

Electroplating is an important method of improving the properties of cheap metals such as iron. Thus, resistance to corrosion can be achieved by plating with a more resistant or protective metal. Resistance to wear, greater hardness, and a more attractive appearance may also be obtained by using an appropriate metal coating. More recently, the process of electroforming has developed, so that whole objects are formed by electrodeposition and a great variety of complex shapes can be manufactured without the use of expensive machine tools. The method resembles casting, except that the object is formed at room temperature and at the most 60°C. The metal coatings used to improve iron and steel are generally copper, zinc, cadmium, nickel, chromium and tin, all of which are toxic, even when present in water at low concentration. Furthermore, some of the most successful electroplating solutions are based upon metal cyanides and are therefore highly poisonous. In Table 1, the World Health Organisation's recommendations are given for the maximum concentration of electroplating chemicals allowable in rivers, estuaries and sea water for aquatic life to exist.

Table 1. Maximum permissible concentrations allowable in water to support aquatic life

Metal	Maximum permissible concentration [ppm]
Arsenic	0.05
Barium	1.0
Boron	1.0
Cadium	0.01
Chromium (6)	0.05
Chromium (3)	1.0
Copper	1.0
Nickel	1.0
Lead	0.05
Zinc	5

Electroplating solutions are sensitive to impurities and for good practice the metal articles to be plated must be carefully cleaned, both before and after plating. In order to achieve these high standards a great deal of water rinsing is required and this becomes the source of toxic waste. After plating, the article is removed from the plating bath and droplets of water are retained on its surface and this is known as 'drag-out'. It has been estimated that *ca.* 10–12% of the metal plating bath solution finds its way, by this method, into the rinsing water. To date, clean or potable water for rinsing has generally been sufficiently cheap for the electroplating operators to ignore the cost and large quantities have been used. Control of the level of concentration of toxic chemicals has largely been obtained by diluting the rinse water with fresh water, before discharge to the sewer.

More recently, the rising cost of water has made the electroplating industry use less wasteful methods and internal treatment to remove the toxic substance is becoming widespread. The usual method has been to gather together the rinse waters from all washing operations into one tank and then add lime or caustic soda to precipitate the toxic metals as their insoluble hydroxides. The resulting solid waste, in the form of hydroxide sludge, is allowed to settle in large ponds or the water is filtered to produce an effluent which is acceptable by the sewer operators. The water quality after this treatment is often of greater toxicity than the figures quoted in Table 1, because the toxicity is high even though the solubility of the hydroxide is low, e.g. solubility of cadium hydroxide, 2.6 ppm, maximum concentration permitted 0.01 ppm, but the sewage operator relies on the further dilution of these electroplating effluents by the water coming to the sewer from residential sources. The sludge formed from this treatment is toxic, but is sent to approved dumps. Because of recent changes in the law, the dumping of these toxic sludges in the U.K. is only allowable at approved sites. These dumping sites must be licensed and the operators must apply for consent for all sludges coming to the dump. A more detailed account of the operation of these dumps is given in Part II.

Today, many electroplating plants rely on sludge formation and dumping for disposal of toxic wastes. Present trends, however, are making industry conscious of its involvement in causing pollution of rivers, lakes and estuaries. The metals are valuable materials, and are being disposed in such a way that recovery is not possible at some future date.

Table 2. The size of the metal finishing industry in the U.K.

Metal	Tons per annum
Coppers	2000
Nickel	5000
Chromium	500
Zinc	5000
Cadium	500
Tin	1000
Silver	200
Gold	4
Miscellaneous and alloys	800

The size of the electroplating industry is relatively small, (Table 2), but metal finishing is believed to be a major source of toxic chemicals arriving in effluents discharged to sewage works. In a recent survey [1] in New York City, it was found that the amount of electroplating toxic wastes being delivered to the sewer every day was *ca.* 2000 kg of nickel, 100 kg each of zinc and copper, 700 kg of chromium and 150 kg of cadium.

A detailed survey showed that the 250 electroplating plants in the City were responsible for most of the nickel, 13% of the zinc, and 43% of the chromium contamination. This survey also shows that a relatively small industry is having a large effect on toxic pollution. It is interesting to note that a large amount of pollution by toxic metals was coming from residential waste water. This probably arises from the corrosion of metals, including electroplated articles, e.g. corroding cars, domestic equipment.

In almost all countries the cost of water has increased and this factor is proving to be a great incentive to the recovery and reclaiming of toxic wastes and the saving and recycling of water. The recycling of metals is not usually considered.

SOURCES OF ELECTROPLATING WASTES

Electroplating is a very simple process, involving the passing of d.c. current through a solution of the appropriate metal salt, usually the chloride, sulphate, or cyanide, and the article to be plated is the cathode and for the anode is metal of the type being deposited.

In theory, there is no need to replenish salt solution, since the anode dissolves to replace the metal deposited from the solution. In practice, as much as 12% of the salt solution is lost by the process of 'drag-out'. After plating, the article is removed and it is impossible to drain away all the salt solution, especially from intricate shapes. For flat sheets, drag-out may be as little as 0.2 l. per 10m^3 of surface, but with complex shapes such as nuts and bolts, where capillary action may entrap liquid in the threads, drag-out can be 5–10 1./10 m^3.

The plated article is therefore rinsed and the rinse water becomes contaminated. Furthermore, the rinse water cannot be used successfully for cleaning further articles and must be constantly replaced. One method of economising on rinse water is to have a counter current system as given in Fig. 1. This figure shows that the final water may return to the plating bath containing the most concentrated solution to make up losses due to evaporation, but it is not possible to use this method for all plating baths. For many plating baths, the quality and surface appearance of the electroplate is determined by the low concentration of impurities and the recycling of rinse water can often introduce these undesirable effects.

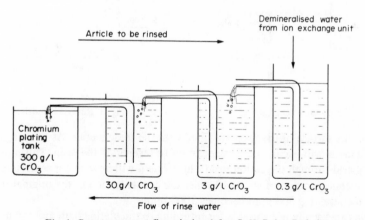

Fig. 1. Counter current flow rinsing (after S. H. Baier, Ref. 6).

For large electroplating plants, where several metals are being plated, the rinse waters are joined together from all the plating baths and sludging takes place with lime in a main tank. The water and sludge separate, the water is often acceptable by the sewage operators and is therefore disposed down the sewer. The sludge is either pumped to a storage lagoon or tanks and some de-watering occurs. Periodically, this is removed to approved dumps.

A typical plant producing 100 000 1. of sludge containing 8% solids, from one week's operation, may dispose of this sludge in any of the following ways:

(a)   100 000 1. carried away by tankers at 8% sludge content to the dump.

(b) Water content reduced by expensive filtration plant to give 20% sludge content, thus 35 000 l. per week is transported by tanker to the dump. Filtered water is used again.

(c) Pumping to settling ponds (large areas of land required). Removed when 20% sludge content by drainage, which may take several months. 35 000 l. per week transported to the dump.

METHODS OF REDUCING WATER CONSUMPTION AND CONCENTRATING TOXIC WASTE

Recently, the cost of water has risen considerably, and many electroplating plants are forced to consider saving water. The cost of water has been higher in Western Germany than the U.K. or U.S.A. and they have long experience of treating electroplating effluents to recycle the water using the process of ion exchange.

The method of *ion exchange* [2] consists of passing the dilute rinse water through an organic polymer resin in the form of small granules. The process resembles a filtration process but the heavy metals undergo a chemical exchange reaction with the ion exchange resin to give sodium ions which are harmless in the water.

There are ion exchange resins for both cations and anions, so that complete demineralisation of the water is possible equivalent to distilled water. Rinse water can therefore be recycled; a typical flow diagram is given in Fig. 2. The ion exchange resin eventually becomes exhausted, i.e. all the

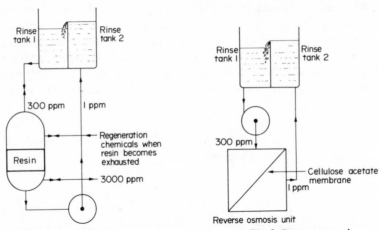

Fig. 2. Ion exchange.　　　　　　　　Fig. 3. Reverse osmosis.

exchange sites on the surface of the resin are filled with the toxic metals. At this stage, no further extraction of the metal will occur, and it is necessary to regenerate the resin. This may be carried out by passing strong acid through the cation resin; the effluent will now be concentrated in the toxic metal ion giving a concentration of about 10 times the concentration in the original rinse water. Thus a typical solution containing 300 ppm becomes 3000 ppm.

These solutions are usually not suitable for returning to the plating bath and the usual method adopted is again to form a sludge using lime. In certain special cases, such as chromium plating rinse waters, it has been possible to re-use the concentrate in the plating bath, because this does not contain special additives. The ion exchange method is used for gold and silver where it is economical to burn the resins in a furnace to leave a concentrated gold or silver residue.

More recently, a process has been developed called *reverse osmosis* [3], and this has been proposed for toxic metal extraction. The advantage over ion exchange is that it acts as if it were a superfine sieve or filter. A membrane of cellulose acetate is used, supported on a filter cloth. The separation of metal cations and anions is by pressure and it is necessary to go to 7000 kg/cm^3 to obtain a reasonable flow rate, see Fig. 3. The membrane eventually becomes saturated just like a filter, but it can be regenerated by a back pressure. The water, obtained by back flushing, again contains a ten times increase in concentration compared with the original rinse water. In many instances, the electroplater treats this with lime to produce a sludge for disposal. The advantage over ion exchange is that expensive chemicals are not required for regeneration and the ion exchange resin is replaced by a relatively cheap cellulose acetate sheet. However, it requires the use of high pressure equipment.

Evaporation

Evaporation [4] by boiling away the water and cooling the steam produces a greater concentration and a pure water product. However, it is very expensive to operate because of fuel costs and because of the capital cost of the high temperature equipment. Much higher concentrations are possible than with ion exchange and reverse osmosis, but in general where it has been used the concentrate is again treated to form sludge for disposal.

The electroplating industry, by means of these various techniques, has been able to save water, but the metals were not recovered but were sent to dumps as sludge.

Reclaiming

The electroplating industry has never had a real incentive to save the metals contained in rinse water because the plating plants are generally small and the capital cost of reclaiming has been too high for a useful profit to be made. Even in large electroplating plants, the cheapest method of disposal was by sludging and dumping. However, with the use of metal cyanides in electroplating baths, it became necessary for electroplaters to have processing equipment on the premises to remove this very dangerous chemical, and discharge was very carefully controlled by the authorities.

Cyanides may be removed by either of two methods. These are outlined in Fig. 4. Cyanide may be processed by (a) complete destruction with chlorine gas and (b) conversion to the less poisonous cyanate. Thus the idea of having chemical processing as part of the plating cycle became more widely adopted, and the industry has become more receptive to treatment of waste at the electroplating plant.

$$\text{(1)} \quad \underset{\substack{\text{Metal} \\ \text{cyanide}}}{2\,MCN} + \underset{\substack{\text{Chlorine} \\ \text{gas}}}{5Cl_2} + \underset{\substack{\text{Caustic} \\ \text{soda}}}{12\,NaOH}$$

$$\rightarrow 2MCO_3 + 10\,NaCl + N_2 + \underset{\text{(gas)}}{H_2O}$$

Non-toxic chemicals and gases

$$\text{(2)} \quad \underset{\text{Cyanide}}{MCN} + \underset{\substack{\text{Sodium} \\ \text{hypochlorite}}}{NaClO} \rightarrow \underset{\substack{\text{Cyanate} \\ \text{less} \\ \text{toxic} \\ \text{easily} \\ \text{oxidised} \\ \text{by air}}}{MCNO} + \underset{\substack{\text{Sodium} \\ \text{chloride}}}{NaCl}$$

Fig. 4. Chemical treatment of cyanides.

Chemical processing of wastes

As more concern has been shown by the general public about the release of toxic chemicals into sewers and rivers, and since the indiscriminate use of dumping has been the subject of more control, then the electroplating industry has been made aware of recovery rather than dumping. Recovery includes both water and the metals. When the process of rinsing was studied, it was found that it was possible to make enormous savings in the use of rinse water by using a chemically treated rinsing solution, i.e. adding the sludge-forming chemicals directly to the rinse water, but of course without the need for any flow. At first, this was a refinement of the sludge-forming process. Chemical rinsing allows the

sludge to form immediately in the rinse tank, and most of the sludge collects in the bottom of the
rinse tank, where it can be periodically removed. No pumps or stirring are usually necessary, but the
process was still one of forming a sludge to be subsequently dumped. The metal article to be rinsed
was placed in a second tank which was used to remove the chemical rinse which by itself was non-
toxic. The dumping of the second rinse tank water was perfectly acceptable by the sewer operators.
The use of chemical rinsing is now being widely adopted, and in some cases this has led to reclaiming.
It was realised that instead of forming the cheap and convenient hydroxides of metals, it was now
possible to form sludges that could be commercially saleable. The best example of this is in the case
of nickel plating baths [7]. By using sodium carbonate in the first rinse tank, the nickel ions in the
drag-out are precipitated as nickel carbonate sludge. This carbonate sludge is a crystalline solid which
separates very quickly from solution compared with the very slow and slimy hydroxide produced in
the usual sludging operations. Thus the nickel carbonate is easily filtered and dried to provide a useful
and saleable product.

The electroplated article has a film of sodium carbonate solution as drag-out from the first chemical rinse, but this may be rinsed away by water in a second tank and the sodium carbonate entering
the rinse water is not toxic.

Thus reclaiming may be achieved and the technique has been applied to several other metals such
as zinc and copper. Unfortunately it has not been possible for a suitable compound of chromium to
be produced in this way. At the moment chromium is converted to a toxic sludge for disposal and
this remains a problem to be solved. The most striking result of chemical rinsing is the enormous
saving in the use of rinse water, and from an economical point of view the process is more than justified
for the saving of water. A typical example [7] may be quoted whereby a nickel plating plant was
converted to chemical rinsing at a cost of £55,000 (tanks, dosing equipment, pump, etc.). The water
consumption was reduced from 140 M l./annum to *ca.* 30 M l. which gave a saving of £6,000
per annum water charges. Chemicals and running costs, including depreciation of the plant, were
£4,000 per annum, but the sale of the nickel carbonate produced at 4 tons/annum (as nickel)
amounted to £6,000. The process was therefore viable and there was a reduction in toxic waste to the
sewer.

Note: Solubility of nickel hydroxide 130 ppm,
            Solubility of nickel carbonate 93 ppm,
            Solubility of zinc carbonate 10 ppm.

Future prospects

The cost benefits of reclaiming seem to depend ultimately on water costs. This is because the
electroplating plants are generally small and therefore the amount of metal to be recovered is small.
In most western European countries and in the U.S.A., there is a movement against the release of
toxic substances entering the sewer. This is because the 'activated sludge' from sewage works may
become an important agricultural material, and at present the level of toxic wastes entering the sewer
is sufficient to concentrate in this active sludge and this product may not be saleable on account of
its toxicity. The problem that faces many electroplating firms is the relatively high capital cost of
recovery plant, but reclaiming would be more economical if the small quantities could be collected
together and processed by a central organisation. In the U.K. a few companies are being formed in
order to deal with these wastes, but transport and handling costs are too high for the collection of
process wastes from a large number of small electroplating firms. It has not been possible to find a
method for extracting chromium from sludges, and this remains a problem. Recently, an attempt has
been made at a co-operative scheme whereby concentrated effluents from reverse osmosis units at
electroplating plants were collected by a reclaiming firm and processed at their site to produce
sodium chromate. This scheme is given in Ref. [5].

Electrochemical machining wastes

The aero engine industry has made extensive use of electrochemical machining and there is some likelihood of its adoption in other large industries such as the car industry. The method of machining is most useful for very hard metals such as the nickel chromium alloys. Very intricate shapes may be reproduced but the process leads to a great deal of waste produced in the form of a hydroxide sludge similar to that produced in the electroplating industry. Because the electrochemical machining method does not allow the machine tools to wear, it is the policy of the machinist to remove large quantities of material by this technique, and thus some 70% of the material may be machined away and this is lost as sludge. In conventional metal machining, this waste would be much less and in the form of metal chips or turnings which could be easily recycled. The electrolytes used in this process are generally based on sodium chloride and sodium nitrate, which are relatively cheap and the urgency to recover them is not great. In these solutions, the nickel and chromium are precipitated as hydroxides and this produces the sludge. Each electrochemical machine has a centrifuge which removes the sludge as a 5% solid–water mixture. In certain large plants settling tanks are used but sludges for dumping contain only 20% solids in water. The quantity produced of nickel chromium sludge in the U.K. is *ca.* 20–30 ton/annum, and a process of recovery has been worked out by scientists at the Department of Industry Warren Spring Laboratory, and this process is given in Fig. 5. The figure shows a diagram of a complex plant which would require a high capital investment and in general the electrochemical machining users do not want to set up in the metal reclaiming business since they have no use for the final product. Furthermore, with only 20–30 tons/annum there is very little incentive to recover because this amount does not produce enough funds to repay the cost of extraction. The process would be economical if some 70 ton/annum were available. Sludges from this process are at present dumped, and there is not sufficient produced per annum to attract reclaimers at this moment in time, although the sludge represents the richest ore in the world. Unfortunately there is not the same incentive for this industry to aim for recovery as has been the case for the electroplating industry.

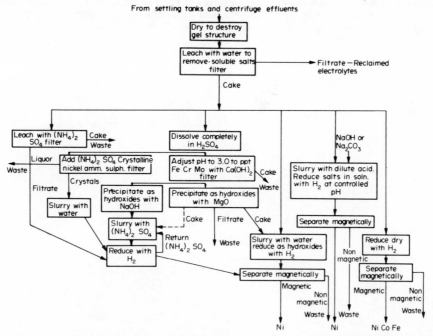

Fig. 5. Department of Industry U.K., Warren Springs Laboratory, scheme for extraction of metals from E.C.M. wastes.

SUMMARY

The reclamation and recycling of wastes from these industries is not as well developed as in other industries. Fortunately external factors such as water shortages and material price rises are encouraging plant operators to take measures towards recovery. It has been difficult in the past to convince industrialists, local authorities and the general public that there should be a charge on the disposal of toxic wastes by dumping to the sewer. Modern trends, which are against this practice, have led to a genuine reduction in costs of electroplating by savings in water charges and materials. The case for this is not apparent for electrochemical machining wastes, but by intelligent dumping procedures, recovery of what may one day be regarded as 'precious metals' will be possible.

REFERENCES

1. Report of the Department of Water Resources, N.Y., U.S.A. (1974).
2. P. R. Price, *Metal Finishing J.* **18**, 279 (1972).
3. Water Pollution Control Research Series No. 12010 D. R. H. Minneapolis, M, U.S.A. (1971).
4. J. M. Culotta & W. F. Swanton, *Plating* **57**, 1221 (1970).
5. A. Golomb, *Plating* **51**, 931 (1974).
6. S. W. Baier, *Practical Waste Treatment and Disposal, Metal Waste Disposal,* (Gen. Ed. D. Dickinson), Applied Science Publ. Ltd. London (1973).
7. R. Pinner, The future of effluent treatment in metal finishing. *Metal Finishing Journal,* Feb (1973).

GENERAL READING

A. Kenneth Graham, *Electroplating Engineering Handbook,* 3rd Edn. van Nostrand, London (1971).
D. Pearson, Economics of Waste Reclamation. *Conf. on Industrial Waste Problems,* 1971 (Factory Equipment News).
A. W. Fletcher, Metal extraction from waste materials, *Chem. Ind.* p. 776, July (1971).
T. J. Kolesav, Closed loop recycling of plating wastes. Abstract No. 74997, PERA Library.
Practical experience in effluent treatment. *Trans. Inst. Metal Finishing* **49**, p. 10, Part I (Spring 1971).
W. E. Beckenn, Treatment of cyanide waste. *Electroplating and Metal Finishing* **25**, 12, p. 20 (December 1972).
R. Pinner and V. Crowle, Cost factors for effluent treatment and recovery of materials in the metal finishing department. *Electroplating and Metal Finishing,* March (1971).

Conservation & Recycling, Vol.1, pp.119–128. Pergamon Press, 1976. Printed in Great Britain.

DISPOSAL OF TOXIC WASTES–II. Poisonous and Radioactive Wastes

P. J. BODEN
University of Nottingham, England

INTRODUCTION

Many industries use toxic chemicals in the manufacture of useful products. For example, mercury is used in the electrolysis of brine, in long life batteries and as a fungicide to prevent the deterioration of seeds. Many toxic heavy metals such as cadium, chromium, lead and zinc are used for electroplating on base metals such as iron. The nuclear energy power stations produce electricity from very small amounts of fuel, but the wastes are very radioactive. The use of specific poisons such as DDT has increased the yield of major crops. Thus Japan produces five times more crops per unit area than Africa or India because it uses ten times more pesticides, see Fig. 1. As a result of these industries,

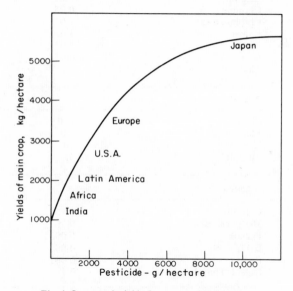

Fig. 1. Increased yields from use of pesticides.

waste products are produced that have to be dumped and they are very toxic. Some of these wastes can be rendered harmless by treatment at the factories and some may be reduced in toxicity by conversion to some other chemical species, e.g. chromium in the hexavalent form is 20 times more toxic than trivalent chromium; thus this conversion to trivalent is carried out in the factory. Cyanides can be converted into less toxic cyanates or even into harmless nitrogen gas and carbonates. Many electroplating plants have facilities for carrying out this conversion.

Methods of disposal

For many wastes, the toxicity cannot be reduced and three methods of treatment are used:
(1)   Dispersal in rivers or the sea to give a low enough concentration so that they can be tolerated.
(2)   Storage, preferably as solids, on special sites, protected from the general public.
(3)   Reclaiming.

Disposal of wastes

Method (1) is used a great deal, and industry is allowed to discharge toxic chemicals at specified low levels into rivers, streams and the sea. The World Health Organisation has given a list (Table 1) of maximum concentrations of heavy metals in effluents that can be tolerated by aquatic life. This presupposes that no concentration of these chemicals will occur. In a few instances this has been found not to be the case. For example, very low activity radioactivity released from a nuclear reactor site was found to be concentrated 100 times in local shell fish! This was traced to the metal zinc.

Table 1. Maximum permissible concentrations allowable in
water to support aquatic life

Metal	Maximum permissible concentration [ppm]
Arsenic	0.05
Barium	1.0
Boron	1.0
Cadium	0.01
Chromium (6)	0.05
Chromium (3)	1.0
Copper	1.0
Nickel	1.0
Lead	0.05
Zinc	5
Anions	
Chloride	250
Fluoride	1.0
Nitrates	10
Cyanides	0.2
Organics	
Chlroform	0.15
Methylene Blue	0.50
Phenols	0.0001
DDT	0.05
Endrin	0.001
Organic Phosphates	0.1

The most spectacular case of the danger of dispersal is that of mercury [1]. Mercury is used in industry in several ways, see Table 2, and enters the waste when batteries are thrown away, or when certain types of paint are stripped off and dumped or when waste brine from electrolysis of sea water is pumped into the sea.

Table 2. Uses of mercury in industry

Chlor alkali industry	58%
Batteries, switches, instruments	26%
Paints	7%
Plastics, dyes, drugs	5%
Seeds, insecticides	4%

Evidence for mercury poisoning came to light when several people died in Japan. Local fish were found to contain 20 ppm of mercury and mud near factories on the coast had as much as 2000 ppm. Since deep water fish contain *ca.* 0.08 ppm, fish with mercury contents above this concentration can be considered contaminated and in turn lead to poisoning of man.

It is interesting to look at the mercury content of fish caught in U.K. coastal waters, see Fig. 2. This indicates pollution of the fish; local fishermen had as mcuh as 0.02 ppm in their bloodstream compared to an average of 0.005 ppm for the rest of the population. The danger limit in blood has been assessed at 0.1 ppm so that the situation is not yet critical. Higher levels have been found in certain lakes in Sweden and in the Great Lakes in North America, with the consequent danger to people eating fish. In certain cases fishing has been banned.

Solid waste disposal

The disposal by method (2) is very important since many industries treat their toxic wastes in the factory by forming solid wastes. In the case of the heavy metals this is comparatively easy and insoluble hydroxides are formed so that liquid effluents can often be pumped, when separated from them, immediately into rivers, etc. because of the low concentrations achieved. The solid wastes are often in the form of slurries, i.e. 10–20% solids in water. These are difficult to filter and are often placed in settling ponds and removed when sufficient quantity has been accumulated, i.e. when transport of a reasonable amount is possible.

In the U.K. the new 'Deposit of Poison Wastes Act' 1972 allows the dumping at specially licensed sites for toxic chemicals but all *radioactive wastes* must be handled by the govenment's own disposal service.

Operation of a toxic waste dump (excluding radioactivity)

The site must be carefully checked by geologists so that *all* water issuing from the site may be monitored by chemical analysis. Ideally the site should be over clay so that surface water is separated from ground bed water (which may be associated with drinking water sources). Surface water dykes or streams can then be monitored.

Such sites are available in the U.K. but they must conform to procedures given in the Act. An industry which wants to use the dump must agree to a 'waste contract'. Before dumping, the waste must be analysed and the dump operator notified of this. The operator then applies for 'consent' for dumping and this must be obtained from the local authority. If consent is given the site operator must agree to keep a record of the amount and whereabouts of the waste and he must not mix together incompatible wastes. For special toxic wastes a separate grave must be dug and this site must be clearly marked. All waters issuing from the dump must be analysed and must conform to the limit set by the World Health Organisation standards (Fig. 2.).

Reclaiming

Reclaiming (method (3)) is in its infancy. Because many industries accumulate relatively small amounts of these wastes it is not often economical to recover them. However, a few organisations are being set up to collect these wastes so that reclamation of a suitable quantity can be carried out. This has been particularly successful in the recovery of organic solvents and the recovery of certain heavy metals such as copper, nickel and tin. At the present time there is no economical method (or incentive) for recovering chromium from sludges, although a recent study suggests that it could be economical if several operators in a large city could collaborate with running a cooperative extraction plant [2]. It should be noted that incineration is a doubtful method for dealing with toxic wastes. At best it can only serve to concentrate the wastes, which still remain to be disposed.

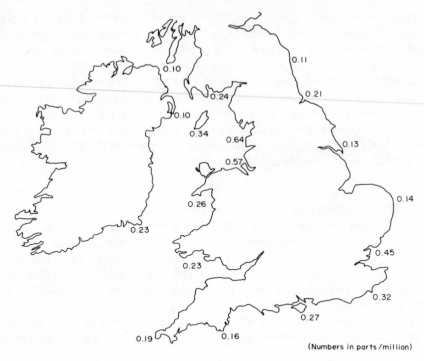

Fig. 2. Mercury content of fish around the coast of Britain, 1971 (see Ref. 1).

Radioactivity from nuclear power stations

In order to understand the special problem of dealing with radioactive wastes it is necessary to understand the source and danger of these substances.

Many engineers and scientists believe that the future prosperity of the whole world depends on a cheap source of electrical energy and one that does not use the world's oil and coal supplies. Thus nuclear energy is to be developed in many countries, and the predictions for this increase in the U.S.A. are as follows;

Table 3. Predicted increase in electricity generation in the U.S.A.

Year	1970	1985	2000
Nuclear power	9 000 MW*	215 000 MW	960 000 MW
Coal, oil and gas	303 000 MW	580 000 MW	760 000 MW
Hydro electric	56 000 MW	120 000 MW	200 000 MW

*MW = megawatts generating capacity.

Nuclear energy is attractive because of the fact that 1 kilogram of uranium can produce the energy equivalent to 3 million kilograms of oil and this means that a vast supply of energy is available from small amounts of nuclear fuels. There is however, a price to pay; high level technology is required, and also good security and safety measures in the handling and disposal of highly toxic radioactive wastes.

Occurrence of radioactivity

Neutron bombardment of uranium 235 (0.17% in natural uranium) splits the atom roughly into two equal parts, but releases a vast amount of heat energy when some of the mass is changed into energy, (see Fig. 3.). The process is known as nuclear fission and the two fission products become the nuclear waste and they are intensely radioactive. What does radioactive mean? Radioactive atoms give off invisible particles or rays which damage animal and plant tissue. There are three types of radioactivity:

Alpha (α)-particles,	essentially electrons that can be easily stopped by simple shielding.
Beta (β)-particles,	these are helium ions, and cause damage to animal tissue, giving burns, etc.
Gamma (γ)-rays,	resemble X-rays and are particularly damaging to living tissue because of their penetrating power.

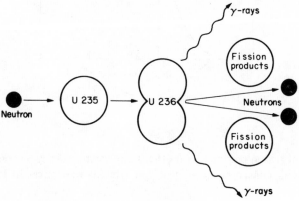

Fig. 3. Nuclear fission.

Measurement of radioactivity

The radioactivity is dangerous because it is invisible but Geiger counters and other devices can . detect it. There are three units of measurement:

(a) the Curie, which measures the number of particles (disintegrations) per second
1 Curie = 1 Ci = 3.7×10^{10} particles/s; 1 μ Ci = 3.7×10^4 particles/s.

(b) the rad, which measures the amount of energy given out by a specific volume of the substance.
(Rad comes from Radiation Adsorbed Dose and corresponds to the adsorption of 100 ergs of energy per gram, i.e. per gram of bone, muscle, skin).

(c) the rem, which is the rad multiplied by an effectiveness factor. This has been introduced because 1 rad of α-radioactivity is less harmful to man and animals than 1 rad of β or γ radioactivity, because of the difference in penetrating power. For our purposes we will consider only β, γ, and 1 rad = 1 rem, i.e. the effectiveness factor = 1.0.

There is some variation in the effect of radiation on humans but the level that will cause death has been established [4]. Figure 4 shows the effect of dose rate. The figure shows that for exposure to 100 rads, no deaths would be expected for normal healthy people, whereas above 600 rads death would be most certain. Exposure to 100 rads may not lead to death but could cause cancer, leukemia or cataracts in the eye. However, exposure at below 25 rads is considered to be safe. At present the average radiation per year from natural sources is about 0.13 rads and nuclear electric power, with the normal precautions, adds about 0.0005 rads. Medical use of X-rays, etc. adds about 0.07 rads and television, high altitude air travel, etc. about 0.02 rads. It is expected that nuclear waste disposal may add 0.0003 to 0.003 by the year 2000 if all the proposed safety precautions can be maintained.

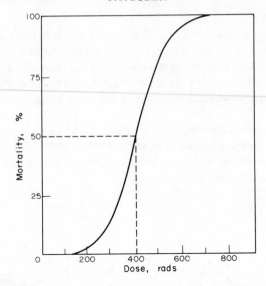

Fig. 4. Effect of radioactivity on human mortality.

Relative toxicity

    The level of toxicity of fission products with other toxic chemicals may be compared by the use of the maximum permissible concentration allowable in drinking water given in Table 4.

Table 4. Comparison of toxicity of poisonous and radioactive substances

	Maximum permissible in drinking water
Material	Concentration in parts per million (ppm)
Lead	0.1
Arsenic	0.05
Fission products Radioactive strontium	0.000000004
Radioactive caesium	0.00003
Plutonium 239	0.00005

Therefore the release of radioactive fission products by dispersal into rivers and streams would not be permissible because of the highly toxic nature of these chemicals.

    The radioactivity does not last for ever but decays. Unfortunately the rate of decay is such that the toxicity decreases by about one half every 30–40 y and they would not be safe for disposal into rivers or the sea for *ca.* 700 y (decay to *ca.* 10^{-16} concentration).

    Another source of radioactive waste occurs, in the nuclear reactor, by the formation of isotopes of elements similar in size to uranium, the so-called actinides. One of these products is plutonium, which may be used again as fuel in nuclear reactors. The maximum permissible concentration in surface water of these nuclear fuel products is of the order of 0.00005 ppm but the decay period, to render them safe for dispersal, is about 25 000 y, i.e. 500 000 y before they have decayed to a safe concentration.

Sources of radioactive wastes

Two types of waste may be identified:

Low level activity. This arises from contamination of materials in the handling of radioactive products. The waste consists of paper, tools, builders rubble, plastics and metal in the form of valves. tubing, etc. Liquid wastes are obtained from washing down contaminated clothing, tools, etc.

High level activity. This consists of the fission products from the spent fuel and the filter material, ion exchange resins, evaporator concentrates accumulated from the 'clean up' of all liquid effluents from the power stations.

Treatment of low level radioactive waste

In the U.K. a special area has been used in Cumberland, where disposal is carried out by burying in the ground. A 250 acre site [5] has been set aside in a remote area and 50 acres in the middle will have trenches. The trenches will be *ca.* 5 m deep, 10 m wide and 200 m long. Such a trench is expected to last *ca.* 20 y and up to 5 more trenches should be possible on the 50 acre site. Careful monitoring of the geology of this area has been carried out and the bedrock is sandstone, overlaid with clay. The clay effectively isolates the groundwater from the water in the sandstone layer and diverts it to a ditch on the site. The water then drains into a tidal section of a river at a distance of 800 m from the site and approx. 800 m from the sea.

The volume of the low-activity waste consists mainly of paper, with some metals and plastics. This is delivered in plastic bags and the unshielded radioactivity does not exceed 750 m rem/h (approx. $5 \times 10^{-3} \ \mu\text{Ci/cm}^2$).

Since 1967, there has been no serious problem; the water from the site is well below permissible levels of radioactivity. Fires have broken out on a few occasions but these have been put out with foam extinguishers. The smoke from the fires has not been radioactive.

It had been found that this is the cheapest and safest way of dealing with the problem. Incineration had been tried but this was expensive, mainly because the gases in this case were radioactive and had to be filtered. A certain amount of plastic occurs in the waste and this proved to be corrosive to the combustion unit.

The combustion process also concentrates the 'radioactivity' in the ash, which makes the disposal more hazardous. Compression and baling had been tried in order to reduce the volume but this proved to be costly in that another process was involved and also contamination of the baling area and apparatus would occur involving more safety precautions.

Treatment of high level radioactive wastes

Wastes from nuclear power station effluent cleaning systems. The liquid effluents from nuclear power stations, such as cooling water, washing water and gas cleaning plant water are passed through various types of equipment to remove solid radioactive materials. Radioactive wastes therefore accumulate as solids on filters and on ion exchange resins and as liquids in concentrates from the bottom of evaporators.

One method of dealing with this waste is to seal it in specially shielded drums or seal it within the drums with cement [6]. The used filters and ion exchange resins containing radioactive waste may be added as a dry solid or as slurries to the drums and if very active may be mixed within the drum with cement to give extra shielding. The activity of each drum is maintained at such a level that the surface radiation on the outside of each shielded drum is below 200 m rem/h. At this level it may be transported by rail. A typical design of such a shielded drum is given in Fig. 5. The liquid effluent from evaporators may be concentrated within the drum by driving off the water by hot air. The concentrated liquid can then be solidified with cement or concentrated as a dry solid. The activity level determines the procedure. The waste can then be removed to a storage site, by rail. For every 1000 MW power station it is expected that 250 m^3 of this type of waste will accumulate in one year.

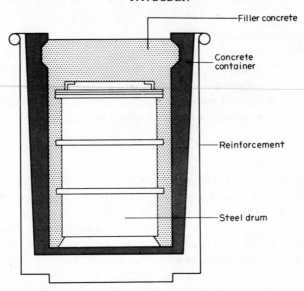

Fig. 5. Shielded drum for disposal of wastes (from Ref. 6).

Deep sea disposal

Many countries are arranging to dispose of radioactive wastes such as these, with methods agreed by the International Atomic Energy Agency.

Special containers will be deposited in designated deep water areas of at least 4 km depth and avoiding telephone cables, fishing grounds. The drums will slowly leak, hopefully over a long period (30–100 y), when the toxicity will have been reduced, and they will be slowly dispersed in the sea water. Concrete mixtures have been suggested so that leaking of the wastes would be very slow.

Wastes from chemical processing of nuclear fuel. When the nuclear fuel is burned up then it must be replaced. The fuel is loaded into the reactor in the form of rods, usually contained in long thin cans of stainless steel. After a certain period, perhaps a year, the used or spent fuel cans are removed and replaced by fresh fuel. The spent fuel is highly radioactive since it contains mainly fission products. It also contains unused uranium fuel and actinides. The latter are atoms formed from uranium by absorbing neutrons to become heavier atoms, the so-called *TRANSURANIC* elements, the most important being plutonium. These atoms can be used again as fuel. It is noteworthy that these new elements are highly radioactive and have very long half lives (25 000 y) but they are worth extracting because they may be used again as fuel. Separation of these elements from the waste would therefore be worthwhile and at the same time remove the disposal problem. Unfortunately it is only practicable to recover 99.5% and the remaining 0.5% renders the waste highly toxic for several thousands of years. The spent fuel at first undergoes chemical processing to remove this fuel and *ca.* 5 m^3 of solid waste per 1000 MW/y is generated for disposal.

The chemical processing consists principally of opening the cans and dissolving the spent fuel in nitric acid solution. The final waste consists of nitric acid solution from which 99.5% of the uranium and plutonium have been removed. If 99.9999% extraction could be achieved then the time that the wastes remain toxic would be reduced to *ca.* 1000 y but the chemical techniques for this degree of separation are not available.

At the present time, the high level radioactive wastes contained in these very corrosive liquids (nitric acid) are stored as liquids, in stainless steel tanks and under strict security, at the processing plants. This is considered to be temporary, until methods of disposal that will be safe for future generations can be carefully worked out. The wastes generate heat (1 kW/m^3) and must be kept cool to avoid boiling, drying out and melting. Utilization of this heat does not seem to be economical because of the relatively small volumes involved.

Proposed future methods of disposal

Discussion of the best method of dealing with this problem has been the subject of great debate for the last twenty years.

A decision on how to deal with the waste is now becoming very urgent because of the enormous expansion being planned for nuclear power throughout the world. In the U.S.A., the installed capacity in 1973 was 24 100 MW but this is expected to be 215 000 MW by 1985 (see Table 1.). In Western Europe 23 500 MW capacity in 1973 is expected to grow to 250 000 MW by 1985 and the total in the world by that date may be as much as 650 000 MW capacity. Thus the nuclear waste would also increase by a 10 fold factor in the next ten years.

The number of possibilities for storage and disposal have been discussed in detail and a useful summary has been made by Kubo and Rose [7]. These authors have set out several methods and have discussed the advantages and disadvantages of each. Their findings may be summarised as follows:

Lowest cost disposal

Melting. This method would depend on the eventual solidification of the wastes by the heat generated. The solid waste would eventually become so hot and melt. This property could then be utilised by putting the waste into deep holes in rock strata (the holes may be created by a nuclear explosion) and the melt would then form a 'glass' with the rock. The waste in this form will not be retrievable by water since such a 'glass' would be insoluble. It could be arranged for the hole to be located in a remote region or on the site of the chemical processing plant; the latter will reduce contamination due to transportation.

The method is attractive but there is some uncertainty about the effect it might have regarding contamination of ground water. The waste would be irretrievable.

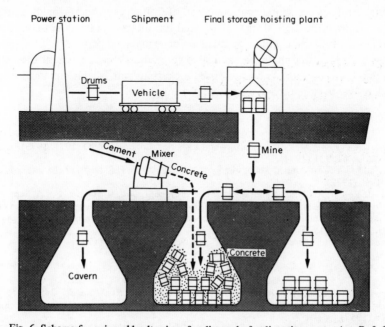

Fig. 6. Scheme for using old salt mines for disposal of radioactive wastes (see Ref. 6).

Underground disposal. Salt mines are considered to be safe geological regions since in the past no water has been present, otherwise the salt would have been leached out, and furthermore, the salt layer has some plasticity and a mine would eventually seal itself. Many old salt mines exist, e.g. in Germany and in the U.S.A. A typical operation is given in Fig. 6. The waste would either be solid or liquid contained in drums, or as a 'glass' manufactured at the chemical processing plant. The glass would prevent leaching if over the centuries the water system changed.

The use of the waste sealed in glass could mean that underground chambers cut into areas of thick granite could also be utilised.

Higher cost disposal

Technology has not yet found a use for the radioactive wastes but in the eventuality that this occurs, storage may be considered rather than disposal.

It has been suggested that 'mausolea' should be erected, probably underground, where containers could be stored indefinitely. This could be expensive as the years go by and the quantity increases. Some 20 000 containers a year are produced but this would be 200 000/y in ten years time. The location could again be underground but storage would have to be in small units and cooling arrangements must be supplied. One method is storage of the solid waste in stainless steel drums and then submersion in flowing streams of fresh water or lakes. There would be cooling of the drums by the water, which would not corrode the steel.

Future possibilities

Because of the heat problem, storage or disposal in the Antartic has been considered. This may be in the frozen ice or in the rocks, at the level where permafrost extends. In both cases water would be absent and so there would be no danger of contaminating the oceans. Greenland is also considered a suitable storage site for these reasons and the ice extends below sea level.

At the moment no nuclear waste can be put in the Arctic or Antarctic because of International agreement.

The proposal is attractive since the region is very hostile and is only accessible to scientifically prepared expeditions. Thus accidental contamination of future generations would be unlikely. If the actinides are *not* removed then safe storage is required for 500 000 y; the doubt comes when estimating whether the ice area would be permanent for such a long period.

Finally, it has been suggested that when a reliable space shuttle has been built these dangerous wastes could be shot into the sun. At present space rockets are not reliable and until these are perfected then this answer to the problem cannot be contemplated.

REFERENCES

1. *Survey of Mercury in Food,* Min. of Agriculture and Fisheries, London HMSO (1971, 1973).
2. A. Golomb, *Plating* **61,** 931 (1974).
3. W. G. Dupree and J. A. West, United States energy to the year 2000, U.S. Dept. of the Interior, Washington, D.C. Report Dec. (1972).
4. P. Lindop and J. Roblat, Radiation pollution of the environment, *Bull. Atom. Sci.* U.S.A. Sept. (1971).
5. H. Howells, Disposal of Radioactive Wastes into the Ground, *Int. Atomic Energy Conf.* Vienna (1967).
6. H. Queiser, Treatment of radioactive slurry and storage of concentration waste, Nuclear Engineering International, **108,** February (1975).
7. A. S. Kubo and D. J. Rose, Disposal of Nuclear Wastes, *Science* **182,** Dec. (1973).

USEFUL READING

T. H. Pigford, Environmental aspects of nuclear energy production. *Ann. Rev. Nuc. Sci.* **24,** (1974).
C. R. McCullough, *Safety Aspects of Nuclear Reactors.* (Geneva Series on the peaceful uses of atomic energy), van Nostrand, NY (1957).
G. M. Masters, *Introduction to Environmental Science and Technology,* Wiley, N.Y. (1974).

Conservation & Recycling, Vol.1, pp.129–136. Pergamon Press, 1976. Printed in Great Britain.

RECYCLING OF PAPER

F. J. COLON

Centraal Technisch Instituut TNO, Apeldoorn, Holland

Abstract—The market situation of paper and of the raw materials for paper production are reviewed, and it is concluded that, in the future, a shortage of raw materials is very probable. An additional source of fibres might be found in municipal refuse if appropriate processes can be developed.

After a short description of the manufacture of paper, the physical basis of separation processes is outlined. The principle of the Zig Zag Air Classifier, an important part of the TNO municipal refuse separation system, is discussed. Some of the results from the system, which is currently undergoing scaling up to 15t/h, will be shown.

INTRODUCTION

The paper industry plays an important role in two fields of the world's community. On the one hand it supplies the materials that are needed for the transport of the thoughts of human beings. On the other hand, it provides the materials needed for the protection of all sorts of goods that must be transported from one place to another.

The demand for paper and paper products is directly related to the level of inter-human relations. As the development of a nation proceeds, the consumption of paper increases. The paper industry fulfils the demand by converting raw materials into the various paper products.

Long ago, textile wastes were the main source of fibres. As there were not enough fibres available, the use of the other cellulose fibres, mainly derived from wood, was developed. The use of waste paper became common practice.

Since the demand for paper is still rising, other sources of fibres must be exploited. One possible source is municipal refuse, if one could separate the fibres from the other wastes. For this reason the Dutch Research Organisation TNO started an investigation into the application of industrial separation processes to separate paper from municipal waste. In the next section, some of the results of that investigation will be given and discussed.

THE MARKET SITUATION OF PAPER FIBRES

The demand for paper is determined to a large extent by the degree of industrial development of a country, as demonstrated by Fig. 1. If world consumption were based on the U.S.A. figures, the normal world resources of fibres would not be able to supply nearly enough material.

The present structure of raw materials supply for the paper industry varies from country to country, depending on its natural wood resources. In Holland, which is short of wood, a high percentage of waste paper is used. The difference in the use of waste paper in various countries is demonstrated by Fig. 3.

The growth of the paper market in the future might be influenced by the development of artificial fibres or sheets of plastics or by other communication methods such as audio visual aids, but it is very difficult to predict the development possibilities in that particular area. Figure 4 demonstrates how the paper market is expected to grow in the Netherlands, assuming that changes in the relation of new communication techniques to paper fibres may be neglected.

The possibilities to meet the growing demand for paper fibres are:

1. Reduce the loss of paper.

paper consumption per capita in 1972

	in kg
USA	279
Sweden	193
Canada	166
Danmark	151
Switserland	144
Finland	140
Netherlands	137
W.Germany	129,9
Great Britain	128,9
Australia	124,8
Japan	123,8
Norway	123
Belgium	118
New Zealand	112
France	104,7
Austria	86,1
Ireland	84,4
Iceland	82
D.D.R.	72,2
Italia	68

Fig. 1. Paper and cardboard consumption
per capita in 1972.

sources of raw materials for the paper production

wood ⎰ ground wood
     ⎱ semi-chemical cellulose
       chemical cellulose

linters

straw / bagasse

waste paper

Fig. 2. Sources of raw materials for paper and
cardboard production.

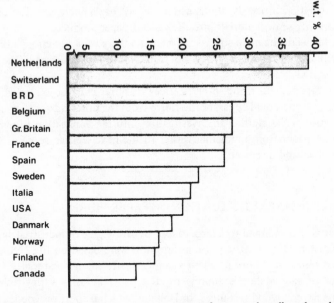

Fig. 3. Collection of waste paper as percentage of paper and cardboard production in 1969.

2. Promote the collection of waste paper from industry and trade centres by waste paper traders and organisations such as the Boy Scouts.
3. Separate paper from municipal refuse.

THE PRODUCTION OF PAPER

Paper is made by suspending fibres in water at a fibre concentration of *ca.* 0.3% (Fig. 5). The suspension is fed on to an endless cloth of a continuous paper machine where the water is drained and

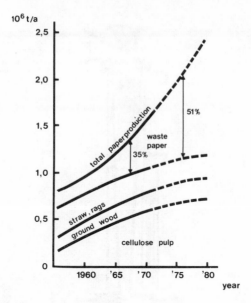

Fig. 4. Paper and cardboard production and raw materials supply in Holland.

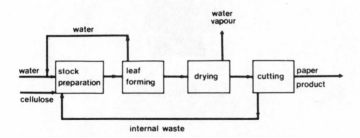

Fig. 5. Simplified flow-sheet of a production of paper and cardboard.

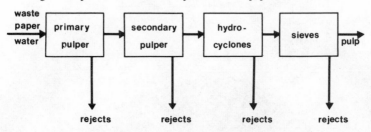

Fig. 6. Flow-sheet of stock preparation using waste paper.

the leaf is formed. The leaf is transported to a drying section where, by means of steam heated drums, it is dried. At the end of the machine the leaf is collected on a roll or cut into sheets.

When waste paper is used as the raw material the preparation of the suspension takes place in a series of processes as indicated in (Fig. 6). In the pulper, a round tank of 10-15 m^3 capacity, the fibres are freed from the paper structure in water by a mixing rotor. At the bottom of the tank is a perforated sieve plate to reject the coarse material. The pulping is repeated in a second pulper of a different construction. Higher shear rates and finer sieves are applied. The resultant pulp is cleaned by passing it through hydrocyclones and sieves (Fig. 7). Sand, dirt and fine fibres are rejected. A view into the pulper is shown in (Fig. 8).

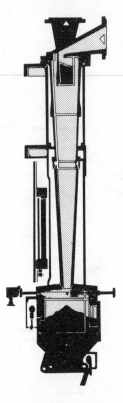

Fig. 7. Hydrocyclone.

Fig. 8 View inside pulper.

ADDITIONAL FIBRE SUPPLIES FROM WASTES

In order to use the paper content of domestic refuse, it is necessary to develop processes to separate the paper from the other wastes. In the past, hand picking of paper from waste was sometimes practised, but hygiene and labour costs make this impractical nowadays.

Separation systems

The separation systems described in the literature may be divided into two groups:
— separation of fibres after mixing up domestic waste with water
— separation without water addition.

A wet separation system is under development by Black Clawson Co. [1], who have constructed a semi-industrial plant at Franklin, OH, U.S.A. The Black Clawson process is based on the paper production process. Instead of cellulose, however, the pulper is fed with domestic waste. Of course the greater part is unusable and has to be drained. The disadvantage is the difficult processing of these wet waste residues. Moreover it creates a large quantity of waste water. The dry separation systems in development are based on separation by means of air separators, ballistics, screens or a combination of these. Piloting is going on, for instance, at:
— Stanford University, U.S.A. (2)
— Bureau of Mines, Pittsburgh (3)
— Forest Products Laboratory, Madison, U.S.A. (4)
— Franklin Institute, Philadelphia, U.S.A. (5).

It is concluded from available information that in the Netherlands the 'dry system', both environmentally and economically, has good prospects. Without further work, the application of American data to Dutch waste is impossible. The composition of American domestic waste completely differs from Dutch waste. For instance, it contains almost twice as much paper as that in the Netherlands. Extensive examination of dry separation methods with normal Dutch domestic waste seemed to be desirable.

PHYSICAL PRINCIPLES OF SEPARATION PROCESSES

Separation processes in waste technology are mainly based on the following properties:

1. Magnetism
2. Falling velocity
3. Density
4. Particle size
5. Conductivity
6. Reflectivity.

In the case of paper, separation properties 2, 3 and 4 are of importance. Two unit operations are mainly involved—sieve machines and air/water classifiers. In the sieve machine the size of the particles is the dominant parameter. The classifiers are based on the difference in falling velocity of the particles. In theory, falling velocity

$$V = \frac{\Delta \rho g}{18 \eta} d^2,$$

where
$\Delta \rho$ = difference in density of particle and medium
g = acceleration due to gravity
η = viscosity of the medium
d = particle size.

This is Stokes Law. In practice, however, with waste materials separations, the definitions of the characteristic size and density are impossible so experiments must be made to determine the separation conditions.

Principle of the TNO separation system

Based upon present knowledge of separation techniques, complete with data from literature, TNO studied the possibilities of a dry system for domestic waste. During the separation of the mixture containing different materials present in domestic waste, the differences in physical properties of the materials are utilised. This system is shown in (Fig. 9).

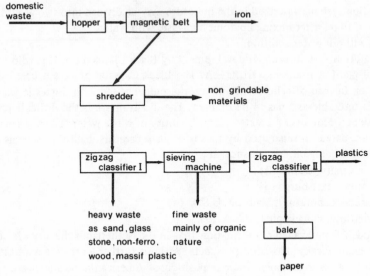

Fig. 9. Flow diagram of TNO separation system.

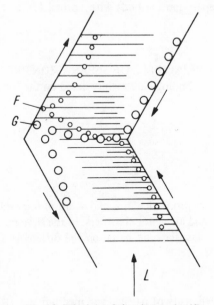

Fig. 10. Principle of the zig-zag classifier.

Primary separation of paper and residue waste is possible by shredding the waste, in the right way, into pieces of about 10cm in size. The paper achieves a different velocity by the size reduction of the remaining waste components. Separation based upon falling velocity is executed in a zig zag classifier (Fig. 10). The mixture to be separated using velocity is fed into a vertical channel, provided with a number of bends. Air is blown up the channel with a fixed velocity. Small particles (F) are carried up by the air current, heavy particles (G) falling down along the wall. On the bend, the heavy waste crosses the air current, causing a separation once more. The quality of separation can be raised by using more channel units similar to the plates of a fractionating column. In 1932, Stebbins in the U.S.A. took out a patent of this type of unit. When supplying shredded waste to a well-designed classifier, paper leaves the classifier at the top together with the air current. This paper fraction still contains plastic films and fine waste. By screening and sifting a paper product is obtained which has possibilities as a raw material for the paper industry.

State of development of the TNO system

In 1972, a pre-examination at laboratory scale took place at the Central Technical Institute TNO. By means of a plant with a capacity of 100kg/h domestic waste, a paper product was separated and the Fibre Institute produced experimental paper sheets. The cardboard industry considered the

Fig. 11. Zig-zag classifier of 1t/h capacity.

quality of the fibres as usable for cardboard production. Then a pilot plant with a capacity of 1t/h was designed and built. Figure 11 gives an impression of the Classifier 1 of that plant. The pilot plant has been built in the Municipal Waste Disposal Plant at Haarlem. The city of Haarlem has shredded refuse for composting purposes since 1967, and has a total capacity of 50 000 t/a. The pilot plant was fed with a part of the refuse directly after the shredder (GONDARD).

After an investigation period of about six months, experiments have ended and the design of a separation plant with 15t/h capacity started, with completion expected by mid 1976.

SOME RESULTS OF THE PILOT PLANT STUDY

The separation of the Haarlem waste resulted in:

     3% iron
25–35% heavy fraction
25–35% fine fraction
20–30% paper
     5% plastic.

A study concerning the economics of the process is being carried out by the Dutch Institute for Waste Disposal and the results will be published in the future.

Some 4 tonnes of the paper product were transported to a paper machine factory, and there processed in the same way that mixed waste paper is normally processed. Figure 12 gives a flow sheet of that system. The difference from a normal stock preparation system is that the pulp is thickened on a drum type filter to *ca.* 70% wt. moisture and heated to 100°C. This is done for two reasons; homogenistation of waxy contaminants and killing of pathogens.

The results of this experiment were such that it was decided to build the 15t/h plant and to carry out an evaluation of the paper product in a small cardboard factory.

Acknowledgement—The author wishes to acknowledge the help given by Ir. G. H. van Dorth of the Dutch Fibre Institute TNO in connection with the details of paper production.

REFERENCES

1. W. Herbert, *TAPPI,* **54** (10), 1661-1663.
2. A. Boettcher, *ASME*–PUBL. 69–WA/PID–9 (1969).
3. C. B. Kenahan, Bureau of Mines Inf. Circ. No. 8529 (1971).
4. W. F. Carr, *Paper Trade J.* **17,** 48–52 (1971).
5. Franklin Institute Research Labs. No. 1-2911-02 (Rev. 1).

Conservation & Recycling, Vol.1, pp.137–147. Pergamon Press, 1976. Printed in Great Britain.

THE RECYCLING OF METALS—II. Nonferrous Metals

MICHAEL B. BEVER

*Department of Materials Science and Engineering, Massachusetts
Institute of Technology, Cambridge MA 02139, U.S.A.*

Abstract—This paper deals primarily with the recycling of copper, aluminium, lead and zinc and also with some aspects of that of other nonferrous metals. Nonferrous metal recycling is highly developed. Home scrap, prompt industrial scrap and old scrap are recovered. Old scrap is most important for metals such as copper which have been in use for a long time. Nonferrous scrap is beginning to be recovered by auto shredders. The recovery of nonferrous metals from municipal solid waste will mainly involve aluminium.

The nonferrous secondary industry collects, sorts and physically processes scrap. Some scrap, in particular copper and lead, is metallurgically processed either in primary or secondary circuits; others, such as aluminium, are usually recovered in separate secondary circuits. The purity of the scrap determines the extent of processing carried out. Alloys are largely recovered as alloys. The secondary metals produced may be of the same quality as primary metals but some are of lower quality and are used in appropriate applications.

Prompt industrial and old scrap make appreciable contributions to supplies; they are *ca.* 50% of current consumption for copper and lead and *ca.* 20% for aluminium. Secondary production of nonferrous metals is less capital-intensive, consumes less energy and tends to be less polluting than primary production.

GENERAL CHARACTERISTICS OF NONFERROUS METALS RECYCLING

This paper is primarily concerned with the recycling of copper, aluminium, lead, and zinc. The recycling of these metals has many features in common with that of other nonferrous metals. Much of the following discussion, therefore, is also applicable to tin, nickel, titanium and the precious metals. On the other hand, the metallurgical processing characteristics of secondary metals differ so much that only general principles of processing will be discussed.

The recycling of nonferrous metals is probably more highly developed than that of any other class of materials. There are several reasons for this. The price of the precious metals, tin, titanium, nickel and copper promotes recycling. Another favourable factor is the prevalent use of nonferrous metals in durable goods. This is especially true of copper. The relative indestructability of many nonferrous metals compared with iron and steel also favours their recovery after use.

The recycling of nonferrous secondary metals differs in many respects from that of ferrous scrap, which is the subject of a concurrent paper.[1] The capital requirements for the physical and metallurgical processing of nonferrous scrap are lower than those for the recycling of ferrous scrap, especially by steel plants. Consequently, entry into the nonferrous secondary metals industry is comparatively easy. This has resulted in the fragmented nature of the industry, which still comprises many small local units. There is, however, an international market for nonferrous secondary metals. [2]

Economic factors such as economies of scale and the costs of pollution abatement favour sizeable secondary metals firms. [3] As automobile shredders are becoming a source of nonferrous metals, an increasing number of large firms are engaging in nonferrous metals recovery. [4,5] Primary producers can process some secondary nonferrous metals and as a result these integrated firms are active in nonferrous metals recycling.

TYPES AND SOURCES OF NONFERROUS SCRAP

Nonferrous scrap is of three types: home scrap (or revert scrap), prompt industrial scrap (or new scrap) and old scrap (obsolete or post-user scrap). These three types are recycled through loops (1), (2), (3), (2′) and (3′) in the generic flowsheet in Fig. 1. 'Purchased scrap' designates prompt industrial and old scrap combined.

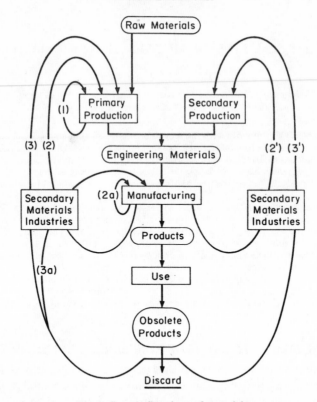

Fig. 1. Generic flowsheet of materials.

The amount of home scrap generated depends on the metal and the product. For example, in the production of aluminium sheet an appreciable amount of home scrap is generated in the form of edge trimmings. As a related matter, the melting of aluminium and the handling of the molten metal result in the formation of drosses, which are difficult to recycle. Melting losses can also be significant in the processing of other nonferrous metals.

Prompt industrial scrap is generated in different amounts by various manufacturing industries. Scrap generation ratios were collected and analyzed for copper, aluminium and iron and steel in 1954. [6] The spread of these ratios ranged from 4.9% for electrical welding apparatus to 47.3% for screw machine parts in the case of copper and from 5.4% for vacuum cleaners to 48% for screw machine parts in the case of aluminium. While such large spreads were found for various products the overall scrap generation ratios were nearly the same for aluminium and copper—20.5% for copper-base products and 18.4% for aluminium products. These percentages compare with 19.4% for iron and steel products. Scrap generation for titanium in the production of jet engines and aircraft structures is high. [7, 8]

Most prompt industrial scrap is recovered by primary or secondary producers as shown by loops (2) and (2′) in Fig. 1. Some prompt industrial scrap, particularly brass and aluminium, however, is recycled within the manufacturing sector as indicated by loop (2a). Statistical information on this type of recycling is limited.

Nonferrous old scrap is derived from many sources, which depend on the metal. For example, large amounts of copper scrap originate in obsolete electrical and telecommunications equipment. Aluminium scrap may arise from products with life cycles of 30 y or more, e.g. 50 y for electrical applications [9] but an appreciable fraction of post-user aluminium scrap arises from packaging applications with very short life cycles.

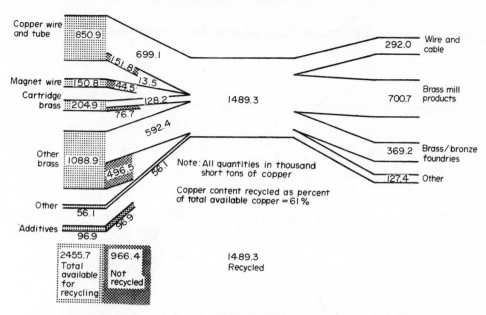

Fig. 2. Flow of recycled copper, 1969, (1,000 short tons). Source: Ref. [9].

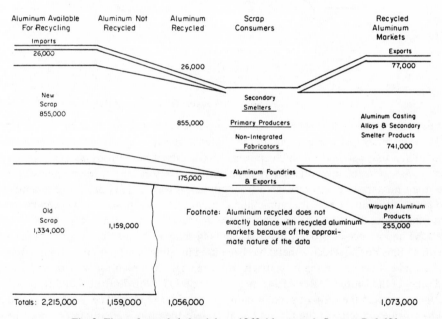

Fig. 3. Flow of recycled aluminium, 1969 (short tons). Source: Ref. [9].

The sources of old scrap in the United States in 1969 are shown in the flow diagrams for recycled copper, aluminium and lead (Figs 2–4). Junk automobiles are becoming significant sources of secondary nonferrous metals, which can be recovered from the nonmagnetic fraction of auto shredder outputs. [5] The major metals recovered from this source are zinc, aluminium and copper. Junk automobiles are already an important source of secondary zinc. [4] Stainless steel (which as a secondary material is classified as 'nonferrous') is also recovered by auto shredders.

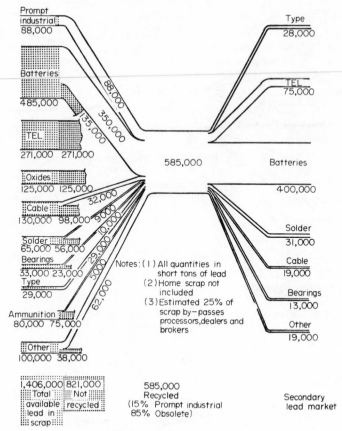

Fig. 4. Flow of recycled lead, 1969, (short tons). Source: Ref. [9].

Municipal waste is a potential source of nonferrous scrap although the amount recovered will be limited. The total municipal waste stream in the United States is currently estimated as somewhat under 100 million tons per year of which approx. 1% consists of nonferrous metals. [10] Not all of these wastes originate in communities likely to support recovery facilities. Aluminium will be the most important nonferrous metal recovered from municipal wastes. [11] Special programmes for aluminium can collections reduce the aluminium content of the waste stream. Tin can be reclaimed from cans which enter the magnetic fraction of resource recovery systems. [10]

The relative importance of prompt industrial and old scrap differs for different metals. One factor is the length of time during which a metal has been used in appreciable amounts. Copper has a long history of use and old copper scrap is relatively important; it accounted for approx. 45% of all recovered scrap in the United States during most of the period 1966-75 (calculated from data in Ref.12). For aluminium the ratio of prompt industrial to old scrap is still *ca.* 3 : 1. Titanium is expected to provide old scrap in the future, but at present the ratio is greatly in favour of new scrap. [7, 8]

THE INDUSTRIAL ORGANIZATION OF NONFERROUS METALS RECYCLING

The generic flowsheet of the materials industries (Fig. 1) shows alternative paths for recycling scrap: prompt industrial scrap and old scrap may be routed to primary plants (loops (2) and (3)) or to secondary plants (loops (2′) and (3′)). For some nonferrous metals, both alternatives are possible but others can only be processed separately in a special secondary circuit. The next Section will consider these alternatives further.

Secondary nonferrous metals are identified and traded by grades. In the United States the National Association of Recycling Industries (NARI)—formerly the National Association of Secondary Material Industries (NASMI)—has developed schemes for copper (over 40 grades), lead, zinc, aluminium (approx. 25 grades), nickel and stainless steel. These grades are based on composition, physical characteristics and type of product. [2]

Secondary metals which are processed in the primary metallurgical circuit become comingled with the primary metals produced from ores. They cannot be identified in the final product. Some secondary metals processed in separate circuits are of a quality equal to the primary metals and can be used interchangeably. Other recycled metals, however, cannot meet primary specifications. Special secondary alloys have been designed based on the compositions resulting from typical scrap charges. Such alloys are intended for applications in which looser composition specifications are acceptable. An example of this is the use of secondary aluminium alloys in die casting and foundries. [13] Some alloys made from aluminium scrap, however, are used in mill products, especially by non-integrated producers.

PHYSICAL AND METALLURGICAL PROCESSING OF NONFERROUS SCRAP

Prompt industrial scrap is sold through middlemen or directly to the processing plant, either a primary or secondary metal producer. Most old nonferrous scrap passes through more complicated paths and undergoes extensive preparation. This scrap has to be collected, sorted, separated and in many cases physically processed before metallurgical treatment. The separation and other preliminary processes are becoming increasingly complex and capital-intensive.

Coarse scrap is comminuted by cutting or shredding whereas fine material is compacted by briquetting. The non-magnetic shredder fraction may be processed by heavy-media separation. [5] Systems for separating aluminium from municipal waste based on electromagnetic interaction ('aluminium magnets') are being developed. [10]

The alloy content of scrap governs its processing: it is general practice as far as possible to recover alloys as alloys. The outstanding example is brass since brass mills consume large amounts of brass scrap. It has been stated that approx. 40% of the zinc in the brass produced in the United States is derived from brass scrap. Lean copper alloys are also generally recovered as alloys. As a result less than one-third of the copper recovered in the United States is recovered as the pure metal. [2] Over 90% of secondary aluminium is recovered as alloys. [14]

As mentioned in the preceding Section, some nonferrous scrap, for example, copper and lead scrap, can be processed in either the primary or secondary production circuit. In such cases geographic location and quality of the scrap determine which circuit is chosen.

Secondary copper may enter the primary circuit at three points: the purest grade ('No. 1 copper') may be added to the wire bar furnace, less pure material ('No. 2 copper') to the anode furnace and material of still lower quality to the smelting circuit at the converting stage. It can be seen that this routing has been designed so that the greater the impurity content of the copper the more processing it receives. Secondary copper recovered in primary plants becomes part of 'refined copper' and is marketed as such. If secondary copper scrap is processed separately, various types of equipment such as a cupola or blast furnace are used, sometimes followed by treatment in a converter. [2, 4, 15, 16] Copper scrap is also treated by leaching. The choice of process depends largely on the impurity content and available equipment.

Secondary aluminium is not processed in the primary circuit because the equipment used in the Hall-Héroult process is unsuitable for dealing with aluminium scrap. However, primary aluminium producers use high-quality scrap, in particular home scrap, which is melted in special reclaimation furnaces and combined with primary metal for casting ingots. Less pure aluminium is processed separately in secondary plants and the resulting product is identified and marketed as such. [13]

There is a tendency for the best aluminium scrap to be consumed by the primary industry whereas the lower grades of material are processed by independent secondary producers.

Currently available technology for the refining of aluminium is limited because it is more reactive than most of its common impurities. These impurities, therefore, cannot be removed by selective oxidation. Magnesium can be removed as the chloride, but this creates a pollution problem in addition to wasting a useful alloy element. Magnesium-bearing alloys are segregated and used in the production of aluminium magnesium alloys.

Titanium provides another example of the separate recovery of scrap. Titanium scrap, including industrial scrap, must be carefully segregated and identified. Otherwise it is likely to be so contaminated that it cannot be added to the primary circuit for producing aircraft-grade titanium. Such titanium scrap, however, can be processed and combined with sponge titanium [7]; the resulting product is considered as secondary titanium.

There are definite trends toward improving secondary processing operations. The handling and charging of scrap and the casting of metal produced are being mechanized. Furnaces of large capacity are being installed and increasing attention is being paid to their thermal efficiency.

CONTRIBUTIONS OF RECYCLING TO THE SUPPLY OF NONFERROUS METALS

The amounts of scrap used in the United States in the production of aluminium, copper, lead and zinc from 1950 to 1975 are shown in Fig. 5 together with the amounts of ores and imported materials. [17] In this figure scrap refers to old scrap only.

The amount of scrap used can be expressed as a percentage of total consumption. This percentage—which has been called scrap consumption ratio—is shown in Fig. 6 for the four major nonferrous metals in 1960 and 1970 in France, Germany, Italy, Japan, the United Kingdom, the United States and the Western World. [18] In this figure scrap refers to purchased scrap (old and prompt industrial scrap combined).

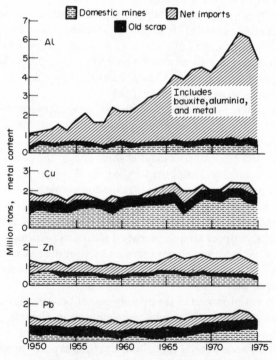

Fig. 5. The supplies of major nonferrous metals in the United States 1950–1975. Source: Ref. [17].

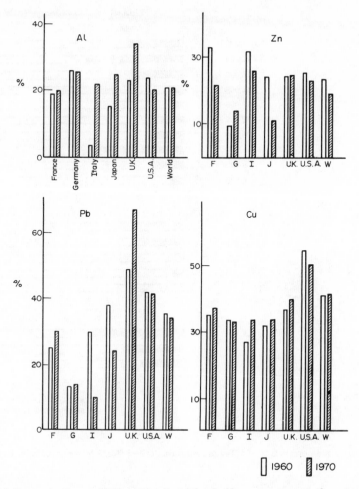

Fig. 6. Domestically supplied prompt industrial and old scrap as percent of consumption for selected countries in 1960 and 1970. Source: Ref. [18].

Old scrap is the really critical item for materials conservation. Old scrap as a percentage of consumption in the United States in 1975 is shown in Fig. 7.

The scrap consumption ratio of aluminium for both old and prompt industrial scrap is *ca.* 20% in most of the countries covered in Fig. 6. Old aluminium scrap accounts for only 5% in the United States (Fig. 7). Such a small contribution to current supplies is characteristic of a material which has undergone rapid growth and has not yet accumulated a large pool of old scrap: the quantitative relations involved will be discussed below.

Recycled old zinc scrap makes a minor contribution to the consumption of zinc, similar to the pattern for aluminium scrap (Fig. 7). The explanation of this small contribution of zinc, however, is different from that for aluminium. Zinc usually is not recovered from galvanized ferrous products. Much zinc in die castings has been lost in the past but some is now being recovered from auto shredder output. [4] Zinc is recovered extensively through the recycling of brass. Also, increasing amounts may be recovered in the course of recovering other metals: in particular, in the smelting of copper scrap zinc can be recovered in the flue dust; similar recovery from fumes in steelmaking processes may be developed.

144   MICHAEL B. BEVER

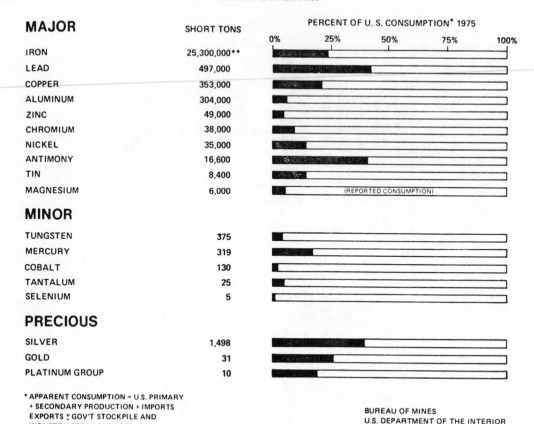

Fig. 7. Tonnages and percentages of U.S. consumption derived from old scrap. Source: Ref. [17].

Scrap plays a major role in the supply of lead as shown in Figs. 5-7. This is true of purchased scrap (Fig. 6) and old scrap (Fig. 7). The recycling of batteries, especially in the United Kingdom and the United States, is a major factor in the supply of old lead scrap. The large percentage of recycled lead in the United States is remarkable in view of the fact that large quantities of lead are currently consumed in dissipative uses, in particular, as gasoline additives. [19]

Copper is recycled very effectively in the United States and the United Kingdom. Prompt industrial and old copper scrap contribute approx. 50% to United States supplies (Fig. 6) and old scrap alone 20-25% (Fig. 7).

The contributions of old scrap to the supplies of other nonferrous metals, in particular, tin, nickel, chromium and magnesium are shown in Fig. 7. Old scrap makes a very large percentage contribution to the supply of antimony, which can be explained by the extensive recovery of antimonial lead from batteries and type metal. This is a case of co-recovery whereby one metal is recovered in the course of the recovery of another. [19]

The percentage contributions of old scrap to the supply of precious metals (Fig. 7) are lower than may be expected in spite of the incentives for recycling these metals and the convenient opportunities for doing so. In part this is due to the dispersive or dissipative nature of some uses of precious metals such as plating and photography. Programmes for recovering silver from photographic processing solutions are being conducted.

The percentage contributions of old scrap to the current consumption of metal is necessarily small if the volume of consumption has grown rapidly and the metal is used in products with a long average life cycle. This relationship is shown schematically in Fig. 8. This figure applies to various nonferrous metals including the precious metals and is particularly pronounced for aluminium (see also Fig. 5).

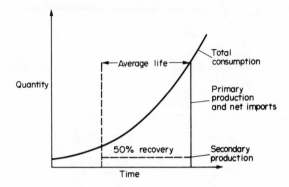

Fig. 8. The relation between the average life of goods, secondary production and total consumption.

The amount of scrap recycled can be expressed as a percentage of the amount potentially available. These potentials can be estimated by assuming average life cycles of major classes of products and using consumption data for the years when the life cycles began. [9] This method of estimation has been applied to a number of nonferrous metals; some results are shown in Table 1.

Table 1. Recycled nonferrous metals as a percentage of available potential

	Recycled (1 000 sh t)	'Available' (1 000 sh t)	Per cent Recycled
Copper	1,489	2,456	61
Aluminium	1,056	2,215	48
Lead	585	1,406	42
Zinc	182	1,271	14
Stainles steel	378	429	88
Precious metals	–	–	75

Year: 1969
Source: Battelle Memorial Institute (Ref. 9).

The potential of a metal available for recycling is related to the cumulative pool of the metal in use. This pool can be estimated from total past production statistics corrected for imports and exports. The qualitative relations between material in use, the accumulated pool of obsolete material, material recycled and material lost in dissipative uses are shown in Fig. 9. This figure refers to lead but may be applied to other materials.

BENEFITS OF RECYCLING NONFERROUS METALS

The recycling of nonferrous metals is carried out in the market economies by private firms which collect and process scrap and market the recovered metals. The driving force for these activities is profit. At the same time recycling serves social objectives. These objectives are the conservation of resources and the protection of the environment from the pollution of primary production. Recycling conserves resources by saving raw materials and reducing metallurgical processing requirements and energy expenditures. In contrast to ferrous metals [10], the recycling of nonferrous metals makes

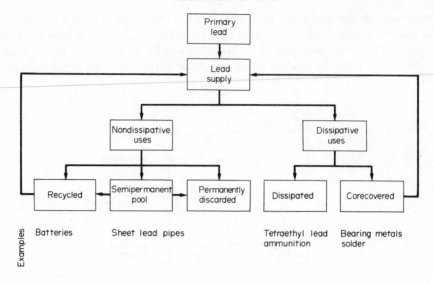

Fig. 9. The life cycle of lead. Source: Ref. [19].

only minor contributions to the disposal of municipal waste because nonferrous metals make up only a small fraction of the waste stream.

Production of metals from scrap reduces the drain on ore deposits and decreases the demand for mining and smelting operations. Recycling also saves the indirect materials required by some production processes. For example, the production of aluminium by the Hall–Héroult process uses large amounts of petroleum coke which are not needed in the processing of secondary aluminium.

Recycling provides the only indigenous sources of metals in industrialized countries that lack ore deposits. The contribution of scrap metals to supplies, expressed as the scrap consumption ratio is discussed in the preceding section. In addition to increasing the supplies of materials, recycling benefits the balance of payments of resource-poor countries.

Secondary raw materials are more concentrated and purer than primary raw materials. Scrap is already in the metallic state and generally needs only refining and, in the most favourable cases, only melting. The recovery of secondary metals, therefore, can be carried out with fewer and simpler processing operations and usually less pollution than primary production.

Since secondary production usually requires less extensive processing than primary production, the use of scrap results in equipment savings and increases production capacity. Also the capital costs of secondary processing equipment are appreciably lower than those of primary processing equipment. For example, the costs of equipment for processing secondary aluminium are of the order of 10–15% of the costs of primary production equipment. [14] The operating costs of secondary production are also generally lower although some secondary operations are labour-intensive. Some of the savings of metallurgical processing costs, however, are presumably expended on collection and physical processing. Little information is available on the comparative costs of secondary and primary nonferrous production.

Secondary metals processing avoids much of the air and water pollution often caused by primary production. [4] Also, the recovery of nonferrous metals from scrap does not involve the disposal of mineral wastes associated with production from ores. It does not incur the need for the extensive pollution abatement measures required increasingly for the smelting of ores, particularly sulphide ores. Secondary production, however, can cause unacceptable levels of pollution, especially because secondary producers are generally located in densely populated areas. The necessary abatement measures can be burdensome. [3, 4]

The energies required for the metallurgical processing of secondary metals are lower than for primary production. A thermodynamic analysis of the production of five major metals has shown that the theoretical energy requirements of secondary production relative to primary production can be as low as 2% for magnesium and 5% for aluminium. [20] This analysis assumes ideal conditions and does not take into account process inefficiencies or the energy requirements of collection and mechanical processing. According to another estimate, the recycling of nonferrous metals requires approx. 20% of the energy of primary production. [21]

Very little is known about the energy consumed by the collection, transportation, physical separation, and mechanical processing of secondary metals. The nature and location of old scrap determine the amount of energy expended in collection and transport. The energy consumed in mechanical processing of scrap metals can be evaluated, but this has not yet been done. The energy and labour that must be expended on the recovery of scrap increases with the degree of its dispersion. Because of the resulting constraints, the optimum amount of recycling will always be smaller than the physically possible maximum. [22]

Acknowledgement—The author is grateful to Marion G. Bever for much valuable help in the preparation of this manuscript.

REFERENCES

1. M. B. Bever, The recycling of metals—I. Ferrous metals, *Proc. Conf. on Recycling and Disposal of Solid Waste*, Inter-University Centre of Post-Graduate Studies, Dubrovnik, Yugoslavia, 7–11 April 1975 and *Conservation and Recycling* **1**, 137–147 (1976).
2. P. Fine, H. W. Rasher and S. Wakesberg, Operations in the nonferrous scrap metal industry today, National Association of Secondary Material Industries, Inc. (1973).
3. Economic impact of air pollution controls on the secondary nonferrous metals industry. U.S. Department of Commerce (1969).
4. J. S. Jacobi, Recovery and reuse of metals in: *Minerals and the Environment, Proc. Int. Symp.* London, 4-7 June 1974, (Ed. M. K. Jones) The Institution of Mining and Metallurgy, pp. 291-301 (1975).
5. L. R. Mahoney and J. J. Harwood, The automobile as a renewable resource, *Resources Policy* **1**, pp. 253-265 (1975).
6. Industrial scrap generation: iron and steel, copper, aluminum. A statistical study. U.S. Department of Commerce (1957).
7. J. J. Gray and P. McIlvoy, A summary of the secondary titanium market, Bureau of Mines, Information Circular 8532 (1971).
8. J. R. Doyle and K. T. Love, Recent technologies and an overview of the reclamation of titanium alloy scrap, *Metall. Soc. AIME* (1976).
9. Battelle Memorial Institute, A study to identify opportunities for increased solid waste utilization (1972).
10. Resource recovery and waste reduction, 3rd Report to Congress, U.S. Environmental Protection Agency (1975).
11. S. T. Abbate, Use of aluminum recovered from municipal solid waste in: *Resource Recovery and Utilization*. (Ed. H. Alter and E. Horowitz) American Society for Testing and Materials, pp. 106-113 (1975).
12. Copper Development Association, Annual data 1976, copper supply and consumption 1956-1975.
13. D. L. Siebert, Impact of technology on the commercial secondary aluminum industry, Bureau of Mines Information Circular 8445 (1970).
14. Utilization of nonferrous scrap metal, United Nations Industrial Development Organization, Report of the Expert Group Meeting on Nonferrous Scrap Metal, Vienna 25-28 Nov. 1969, United Nations, N Y (1970).
15. M. J. Spendlove, Methods of producing secondary copper, Bureau of Mines, Information Circular 8002 (1961).
16. D. Davies, Secondary copper recovery, *Resources Policy* **1**, pp. 246-252 (1975).
17. Status of the mineral industries, Bureau of Mines (1976).
18. J. A. Clay, Future developments—a primary view of the secondary non-ferrous scrap industry in: *Discussion on Scrap Recovery, Inst. Metals,* 20-22 March (1973).
19. J. R. Alward, J. P. Clark and M. B. Bever, The dissipative uses of lead, *Proc. Council Econ. AIME* (1976).
20. J. C. Bravard, H. B. Flora, II and C Portal, Energy expenditures associated with the production and recycle of metals, Report No. ORNL-NSF-EP-24, Oak Ridge National Laboratory (1972).
21. G. A. Lincoln, Energy conservation, *Science* **180**, pp. 155-162 (1973).
22. M. B. Bever, Raw materials: energy and environmental constraints, *Science* **185**, p. 99 (1974).

Conservation & Recycling, Vol.1, pp.149–159. Pergamon Press, 1976. Printed in Great Britain.

RECYCLING OF GLASS

OLE H. WILLERUP

Pollution Control Ltd., Copenhagen, Denmark

Abstract—Household refuse generally contains 5–10% of glass. *Per capita* production of refuse in Denmark is about 300 kg per annum of which an unusually low percentage comprises beer and soft drinks bottles in a country where the tradition persists of using returnable containers. Further, government legislation permits brewers to sell only up to 4% of their total consumption in non-renewable bottles. The arguments for and against non-returnable beverage containers are discussed and a continuing trend towards shorter trippage noted in some countries. The results of a Swedish study are reported where the energy consumption is considered in respect of a returnable bottle, a non-returnable PVC bottle, a non-returnable steel can and a non-returnable glass bottle. The results are reported of British, Danish and Swedish test collections of paper, glass and metal. Re-use procedures are described for collected glass.

1. INTRODUCTION

Since the end of the Second World War, and particularly during the last decade, there has been an increasing 'throw away' tendency. In the European countries the amount of household waste has increased to more than 1 kg per person per day on average, and in some states in America the amount is as high as 2½ kg per person. The composition varies from country to country, but the tendency is the same everywhere: more paper, more plastic, more valuable metal and glass, and less ash.

The increasing amount of waste from households is not only due to an increasing standard of living, but also in many countries a result of a change in the familly model. Nowadays a lot of women work outside the home part-time or full-time, and this leaves less time to purchase food and other goods. The supermarkets with their pre-packed goods meet this demand, and the result has been an increasing amount of packaging and nonreturnable cans and bottles in the garbage can.

It has been known for several years that the world has a limited supply of raw materials, but nevertheless it has seemed impossible to organise any kind of resource recovery if it was not immediately feasible. However the energy crisis has awakened many people to the realisation that recovery systems should be considered even if they are not profitable at present.

2. EXISTING RECOVERY AND RE-USE OF GLASS SCRAP

2.1 *Dumping and sanitary landfill*

Most refuse today is simply brought out of town and dumped on to a convenient piece of land. Unfortunately convenient areas of land are becoming more and more difficult to find, and we are being forced to face the severe problems of urban refuse.

The reaction of many people to this problem has been to look for better and more efficient ways of disposal such as ocean dumping and sanitary landfill, but none of these solutions strike at the heart of the problem, namely that valuable resources are being thrown away forever. In a small country like Denmark, with 5 million inhabitants, 100 000 tonnes of glass are thrown away every year, and in the United States, for example, the yearly amount is 15 million tonnes.

2.2 *Glass in household waste*

In most countries the percentage by weight of glass in household refuse is between 5 and 10%. In Denmark each person produces *ca.* 300 kg of household refuse per year and consequently throws away *ca.* 20 kg of glass per year. The main part, approx. 12 kg, consists of wine and spirit bottles. Approximately 6 kg are glass for preserved goods and only 2 kg are bottles for beer and soft drinks. The unusually low percentage of bottles for beer and soft drinks in Denmark is a consequence of the tradition of using returnable bottles. This will probably not change in the very near future, because the Government has settled regulations which only permit the breweries to sell up to 4% of the total consumption in non-returnable bottles or cans.

2.3 *Glass scrap (cullet)*

The resource implications and industry structure for glass fabrication are very different from those of the aluminium and steel industries. Glass is made from sand, soda ash, lime or limestone, and in many cases supplied with cullet, which means crushed glass. Sand or silica do not normally cause any resource problems and supplies of both soda ash and limestone appear ample for all foreseeable requirements. Because of the ready availability of raw materials, glass plants tend to be located near their customers. For example, there are over 100 separate plants located throughout the United States and the effect is that potential markets for glass-scrap or cullet exist in most metropolitan areas.

Glass scrap is not simply a competitive material with raw materials, but it is a complementary part of the manufacturing process. This both aids and complicates the possibilities of recycling in the glass industry. Glass batches usually contain a specified addition of cullet which, because of its lower viscosity, speeds up the mixing and reaction of raw materials and also reduces the energy consumption. For this reason, glass industries usually produce a supply of their own cullet which, because of its known quality, is preferred to purchased glass scrap of unknown quality and composition.

2.4 *The industry's own re-use*

Generally there is no problem for a glass industry in re-using its own cullet; consequently the main problem concentrates on the most efficient re-use of the consumers' glass waste. This has been important in the past, and will be more important in the future as the percentage of non-returnable containers increases.

3. RETURNABLE OR NON-RETURNABLE CONTAINERS FOR BEER AND SOFT DRINKS
3.1 *Development*

The first efforts at a market conversion to one-way non-returnable containers were made by the steel industry in the late forties and early fifties. Together with the major can companies, they viewed the beer and soft drinks market as the last major expansion area for steel cans. With returnable bottles averaging *ca.* 30–40 trips from the consumer to the bottler, it was clear that 30–40 cans would be needed to replace each returnable bottle over a period of 6–8 months. Aluminium companies made a successful entrance into the market in the mid-to late fifties by introducing the all aluminium beer can, but aluminium has since only appeared in the top of the steel cans to facilitate opening. A surprising early success for cans was found in the ghetto areas of major cities, where consumers generally buy small amounts of food due to limited storage and cooling space. Consequently they often purchase one cool package per visit to the market and a 3–4 cent deposit per single returnable bottle lacks the appeal of the purchase of non-returnable bottles. There was also reluctance on the part of the retailer to accept returned bottles, because of diminishing retail storage space. In the United States, for example, in 1960, 40% of the supermarket space was devoted to non-selling storage and in 1970 only 10% of such space was for storage.

Since the makers and bottlers of beer and soft drinks were not selling containers to the public, they were indifferent to the needs of the steel and can industries. Nevertheless, wholesalers and retailers have their own inducements towards conversion of the market to throw-away containers. The reduction of storage space and the elimination of the labour of sorting and stacking returnables has an obvious appeal. At about the same time, glass bottle manufacturers realised the impact of cans on their market, and competition began. With pressure from both sides, the bottlers revised their bottling lines to handle throw-away containers. Therefore the decline in return rate and retreat from the market place of the returnable is not caused by bottle fragility, but is due to general affluence, competition from other packages and advertising, and the capacity for change in consumer habits. The result of this development has been that in the United States only 30% of soft drinks today are delivered in returnable bottles. This percentage was 98 in 1958.

While less returnable containers are being sold nowadays, those which are used make fewer trips to the bottler. From 40 return trips per soft drink container, for example, the national average in the United States has declined to *ca.* 15 trips. In Denmark returnables still make 35–40 trips, but as mentioned before Denmark has a very high percentage of returnable bottles. In many other countries, the non-returnable bottles cover more than 30% of the beer and soft drink packaging.

It seems to be accepted that beer and soft drink bottles have the same shape and appearance, although a few companies base their marketing on different and special shapes. However, this is not the case for wine and spirit bottles, which at the present makes it very complicated and difficult to return them. Consequently wine and spirit bottles in most countries are non-returnable and only a European or worldwide standardisation may change this.

3.2 *For and against non-returnables*

Limited energy and raw material resources have focused attention on non-returnable bottles and a lot of organisations producing and manufacturing non-returnable bottles or selling beer or soft drinks in these bottles have contributed with literature towards a better understanding of the various considerations affecting their use.

The following definitions may be given:

A returnable bottle is a glass container made strongly and precisely enough to be used several times as a container. Often a deposit is charged by the supplier to the retailer and passed on by the retailer to the consumer.

A non-returnable bottle is designed to make only one trip from the bottler to the consumer via the outlet where the product is purchased. The non-returnable bottle is made of light-weight glass which makes it technically impossible to re-use it as a container.

As the situation now has developed, a large number of shops and stores which sell soft drinks would have great difficulty in handling returnable containers of any sort. If soft drinks were only available in returnables, many retail outlets, and certainly most self-service supermarkets, would probably be unable to stock soft drinks and beers. The only alternative would be the introduction of extra staff and handling systems to cope with the returnable bottles and/or the use of glass crushing facilities at every store. This would, of course, result in a heavy cost increase which would have to be passed on to the consumer.

Almost every one of the approx. 5000 different lines in a modern supermarket is packed in non-returnable containers. Products in glass such as jams, sauces, coffee; products in cans such as soup, fruit, baked beans and other foods; products in plastics and paper like frozen foods, cigarettes, eggs, etc.

The non-returnable glass industry claims that the transportation, labour, energy and technical resources needed to re-use a returnable bottle are costly. The process involves:

Storage while awaiting collection.

Transportation back to the bottler (petrol, oil, traffic).

Optical inspection (difficult when bottle surface becomes marred by re-use).

Sterilization (four different stages).

Quality control checks.

The processing of returnables uses large quantities of hot water and water is becoming an increasingly limited resource. Furthermore the washing process also creates considerable effluent.

Different governmental institutions for environmental control all over the world have tried to figure out the difference between returnable and non-returnable bottles. It seems difficult to reach the truth because the problem is very complex and a price has to be put on factors such as environmental control, traffic, etc.

3.3 *Swedish comparison of 4 types of bottle*

A very detailed study has been worked out by Mr. Sundstrom in Sweden. The report compares the energy use for four different types of beer bottle, namely a returnable bottle, a non-returnable PVC bottle, a non-returnable steel can and a non-returnable glass bottle. The report calculates the kWh per litre of beer and differentiates between disposal of the packaging by incineration and by controlled tipping after pulverisation.

The calculation covers the energy consumption in all stages, including digging and transport of sand, chalk, soda ash, energy consumption by production of labels and caps, etc. The result of these investigations have been the following energy consumption measured in kWh per litre of beer:

Returnable bottle (8 trips)	1 2298 kWh
Returnable bottle (19 trips)	0 9375 kWh
Non-returnable bottle—PVC	1 3288 kWh
Non-returnable steel can	2 2188 kWh
Non-returnable glass bottle	3 2341 kWh

These figures have been found when the methods of waste disposal is incineration. Similar figures have been calculated by landfill, but the difference in energy consumption by the two waste disposal systems is not very great.

The different materials flow for glass bottles and PVC bottles are shown in Figs. 1 and 2.

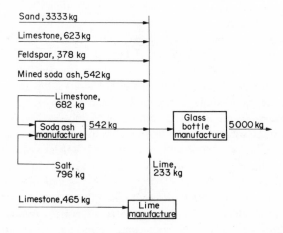

Fig. 1.

It seems reasonable to concentrate on energy consumption when comparing returnable and non-returnables, especially when the comparision is between returnable and non-returnable *glass* containers, because the raw materials are available and because the waste disposal of glass very seldom causes environmental problems.

Where a well established system of returnable bottles exists, this should, in my opinion, be kept. A typical example of loss of energy and resources was the change from returnable milk bottles to paper

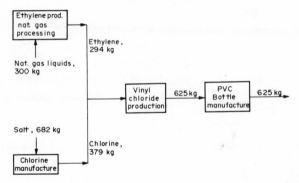

Fig. 2.

packaging in Denmark. It was splendid marketing from the industry who sells this packaging and the small dairy was happy to avoid the space of washing facilities, the technical problems and the problems of the necessary employees for sorting, controlling, etc. However the consumers have paid the bill in higher prices for container and disposal costs.

4. RE-USE OF WINE AND SPIRIT BOTTLES

In the case of wine and spirit bottles, it will probably be much more difficult to change the present situation regarding returnables and non-returnables than it was for milk, beer and soft drinks. Wine and spirits are usually delivered in non-returnable bottles but, nevertheless, it is still possible to organise an efficient return of these bottles. First of all a standardisation of the bottles would help very much and secondly, a high enough deposit for each bottle has to be carried through.

4.1 *British study of return of wine and spirit bottles*

A group in England, (P.E. Consulting Group Ltd.) has studied the possibilities of wine and spirit bottle recovery.

There seems to be *ca*. 2000 different wine and spirit bottles in England and if all these bottles should be returnable, the sorting problems would be tremendous. But *ca*. 100 types of these 2 000 types cover more than 70% of all bottles. The group suggests that these 100 types of bottles should be given a returnable symbol, and the established collecting points would pay 1 penny for each bottle bearing the symbol. A network of regional depots operated by the recovery organisation would collect empty bottles for preliminary sorting for returnability. A transport organisation would collect the bottles from the depots and collecting points and deliver them to the processing factories. The factories would be responsible for washing and packing the recovered bottles and deliver them to the bottlers.

On the basis of an assumed recovery rate of 45%, a total of *ca*. 260 million bottles would be recovered for re-use. The cost per recovered bottle delivered to the bottlers would be in the range of 4-5 pence and the total capital cost of establishing the scheme would be *ca*. £20 million.

If the concept of returnability symbol was not accepted the effect would be to impose a cost premium, resulting in a cost per bottle of 5½-7 pence. The price for a new bottle is, on average, *ca*. 4 pence today. Consequently the returnability symbol has to be accepted if the scheme is to be feasible.

About one third of the total amount of 600 million wine and spirit bottles comes from private homes and the other two thirds from pubs, hotels, clubs and restaurants. The study group has estimated the recovery rate to be 50% of bottles consumed in the home, 75% of bottles used in pubs, and

50% of bottles used in hotels, clubs and restaurants. Personally, I think that the recovery rate for bottles consumed in the household is over-estimated in spite of the payment of 1 penny per bottle. Many households have no space for collecting bottles. It will, of course, be of interest for schools, churches and voluntary organisations to gather bottles for cashing in at the local centre. The study group suggests a total of ca. 300 local collecting points staffed by one man whose duties would be to receive bottles, pay for them and make a rough sorting into five main groups of bottles. He would be provided with a small crushing machine to deal with unwanted bottles. The cost of the collecting points has been calculated at 1 penny per bottle plus, of course, the penny paid per bottle.

The number of regional depots operated by the recovery organisation, which would provide a service to the unlicensed trade, would be ca. 30–40 depots. They would provide a service to the trade, collecting cartons of empty bottles when requested, probably in stipulated minimum quantities of 10 cartons per call. The overall average cost per bottle for those retrieved from the trade via the regional depots is estimated to be 1½ pence. The recovered bottles would be transported from the collecting points and the regional depots using trailers which could be left at the regional depot for loading by the depot's staff and, when filled up, transported by a contractor. Presuming that there would be four processing factories at London, Birmingham, Manchester and Glasgow, for example, the transport cost is quoted at 0.3 pence per bottle.

At the processing factories the bottles would first be sorted into five main categories which could be normal whisky bottles, normal gin and other spirit bottles, and finally litre bottles. After sorting into all categories it is proposed to store dirty bottles on pallets until an adequate quantity of particular bottle-type can be accumulated for economic processing. The cost of processing per bottle would be ca. 2 pence and the transport to bottlers would be ca. 0.5 pence. The total operating costs of the recovery organisations will, as mentioned before, be between 4 and 5½ pence depending on the collection being via regional depots or collecting points. Figure 3 shows the two different calculations.

	Via collection points Pence/bottle	Via regional depots Pence/bottle
Collection and initial sorting	2.0 — 2.5	1.5 — 1.9
Transport to factory	0.2 — 0.4	0.2 — 0.4
Processing and delivering	2.0 — 2.6	2.0 — 2.6
Mangement charges	0.1	0.1
Interest on working capital	0.2	0.2
Total	4.5 — 5.8	4.0 — 5.2

Fig. 3.

In many ways the scheme seems to be realistic but the group agrees that some important practical points have not been taken into account, for example the question of the bottles' strength in relation to re-use, the effects of dimensional variations and the need to use labels suited to bottle re-use. National considerations such as environmental factors and social benefit have not been taken into account either.

4.2 *Future legislation*

According to the above-mentioned considerations about returnable and non-returnable containers, governments in many countries will probably decide to reverse the tendency of the increasing non-returnables and certainly favour returnable packaging by legislation in the future. They may succeed, but never completely, and it will consequently still be of interest to develop efficient methods of recovery of non-returnable glass containers.

5. COLLECTION OF GLASS FROM HOUSEHOLDS

Two different principles regarding collection exist, namely separation in the households and separation by the waste disposal plant. Considering separation in the home, several studies and practical tests have been carried out. Some of the methods have been:

Separation of clear and coloured glass into two paper sacks collected once or twice a month.

Separation of the household garbage into three sacks, namely one for paper, one for metal/glass, and one for the rest of the household refuse.

Collection by placing containers locally, for example, for glass, metal, newspapers and cardboard.

5.1 British test collection of glass

The first category has recently been tried by the Redfearn National Glass Co. in the city of York in England. During May and June last year, the company, in conjunction with the city of York District Council, ran a campaign in a selected are of *ca.* 100 households to examine the feasibility and cost of household collection of used glass containers. Two large paper sacks, one for clear glass and one for coloured glass, were delivered to each household, and the publicity programme advised the householders to remove metal and plastic caps and lids, to separate glass by colour in the two paper sacks and to avoid disposing of returnable bottles, old window glass, mirrors, bulbs, etc. Every fortnight the cleansing department removed the used sacks and delivered new sacks. An analysis and research excercise was undertaken together with a check on the efficiency of separation, cleanliness, the amount of non-returnable containers and the number of contaminants such as lids and caps. Initial reaction from the public who were to take part in the programme ranged from good to very enthusiastic.

The first collection was particularly satisfying, because the people had stored bottles following the scheme's advance publicity. They had also taken the opportunity to clear out cupboards, garages and sheds. Towards the end of the campaign there was a reduction in the quantity collected, but more noticeable was the decline in quality because closures had not been removed from containers and, in some instances, sacks contained waste matter other than glass. Returnable bottles, some of which carried deposits of five pence, made up a surprising percentage of the glass containers collected despite the request that these should be returned to the point of purchase. The last collection brought in returnable bottles with deposits to the value of £12. Householders expressed concern regarding the lack of storage space and the potential danger to young children from glass that may be broken during storage around the house.

The number of sacks returned during the test period was between 25 and 50% of the sacks delivered, presumably found useful for storing other materials. Although the idea of the scheme was enthusiastically received and a large number of glass containers was collected, the results were disappointing, the company claims, not only because the householders did not accept the rules of the game, but also because the economy was very bad. Whereas the estimated quantity of glass from refuse analyses was five tons/week, a total of 11 tons of glass for recycling was collected during the two months period and the cost for the glass came to £35 per ton. The Readfearn National Co. agreed to pay £5 per ton for coloured glass and £7 per ton for clear glass, which left a difference of *ca.* £30 per ton. The city engineer found it impossible to asses the relatively small saving per ton that resulted from not having to pass the glass through the council's incinerator plant and tipping as residue. The resultant figures do not take into account the cost to the company of supplying 10 000 paper sacks at 4 pence per sack or the cost of publicity necessary to obtain the best possible participation.

Analysing the results of the programme, the city engineer drew up another plan, but estimated figures indicated that a deficit would occur even if labour and transport costs were eliminated by using a trailer behind the normal collection vehicle.

Based on a collection round of 5000 properties, the expenses for one week would have been:

Bonus for collectors	£5.00
Running costs, trailer	£3.00
Hire and emptying	£7.00
5000 sacks	£185.00
Total	£200.00.

Assuming 11 tons of glass at a price of £10 per ton, this would consequently still result in a loss of approx. £90 a week. Furthermore, it has to be emphasised that, had a glass factory not been within the city, labour and transport costs would have been much higher.

The most important conclusion to be drawn from the York project is that it is too expensive to reclaim glass packaging in isolation from household waste. House-to-house collection when it involves collection from household waste is only likely to be feasible if other materials are reclaimed such as paper, metal and plastics, as well as glass. The analysis of the York pilot scheme confirmed the view that deposits charged on bottles are not the answer to recovery and return problems. Sections of the public will throw away returnable bottles rather than take the time and trouble to return them and reclaim their deposits.

5.2 *Swedish test collection of paper and glass*

Besides the U.S.A., Sweden started early trials of sorting useful waste materials in households. A very famous test was carried out in Gothenburg from April 1973 to January 1974, involving *ca.* 7400 apartments corresponding to 18 500 people. 200 containers of 150 l for glass and 200 containers of 300 and 400 l for paper were placed with the normal garbage cans.

The Gothenburg Cleansing Dept. collected during the test period 4.1 kg of glass per person (calculated on a yearly basis; 5.7 kg per person) and 15 kg of paper per person (calculated on a yearly basis; 21.2 kg per person) which corresponds to *ca.* 10% of the normally collected household refuse. The income from sales of glass and paper (average 60–80 S.Kr. per ton), together with the saved costs by incineration, (85 S.Kr. per ton), gave 7.10 S.Kr. per apartment. The collecting and transport costs were 12.90 S.Kr. per apartment so the loss in the test period was 5.80 S.Kr. per apartment.

A balance or profit can only be obtained if the sale price of the raw material increases to almost double the above mentioned, but if this happens, labour and transport costs at the same time certainly increase. The cleansing department claims that the rate of service has to be decreased in order to obtain balance, for example by increasing the number of apartments over the 35 used in the test period per collecting depot.

5.3 *Danish test collection of paper and glass/metal*

In Denmark quite a number of trials were started in 1974, but a final conclusion has not yet been reached. In Birkerod, near Copenhagen, 5000 households participate in a project where paper is separated in one sack and glass/metal in another sack, collected separately every fortnight. During the first five months, *ca.* 8 kg of paper and 5 kg of glass/metal have been collected per household, which covers between 15 and 20% of the total amount of household refuse (see Fig.4). Again the

	Participa-tion	Recoverd materials, tonnes					Recovered refuse excl. recovered materials
		Paper	Glass/metal	Total	Private homes	Commerce and industry	
Sept.	70%	42.7	32.0	74.7	64.7	10.0	405
Oct.	80%	82.0	45.5	127.5	103.0	24.5	436
Nov.	83%	64.5	33.0	97.5	75.1	22.4	395
Dec.	90%	51.0	23.4	74.4	51.6	22.8	414
Jan.		240.2 75.0*	133.9 50.0*	374.1 125.0*	294.4	79.9	1650
Total		315.2*	183.9*	499.1*			

*Estimated figure

Fig. 4.

economy is very doubtful because of the high cost of two extra sacks per fortnight and the high collection and transport costs. Unfortunately, as regards the economy of the test, the waste paper prices have decreased very much during the last year. In evaluating the different projects mentioned, it has to be taken into consideration that most of the tests have been started and carried through by companies and industries who have a special interest in succeeding. As an example, it may be mentioned that the trial in Birkerod is started by a company who normally get all their profits from the sale of paper sacks.

5.4 *Centrally-placed containers*

Personally, I do not believe that sorting and collection by households has a future, but I believe that there may be some feasibility in organising centrally placed containers for recovered material. This method will save the cost of the sacks or containers at the homes, and it will save the professional collecting and transport costs. I agree that the amount of recovered material by this system will decrease, but there may be a possibility of increasing the amount by paying for delivery of sorted waste materials such as newspapers, magazines, cardboard, white glass, coloured glass, etc.

5.5 *Recovery from raw refuse*

At the present time a number of research programmes on raw refuse separation are being carried out. The highly sophisticated machines which have been developed for particular purposes in the mining industry, for example, have been tried successfully, but they are not always usable for sorting garbage. Consider a typical item of refuse, for example a beer can. It may have a paper label or be printed, it may be all aluminium or have a steel body and aluminium ends and it may be half full of left over beer or rain. A strong magnetic separator may decide that this item is ferrous. A meter sensing its surface characteristics only may code it as paper. Other equipment will probably decide that something having so high a water content must be fruit. All this is supposing that the can could be measured alone. It may well be wrapped in paper or a plastic bag or in a nylon stocking or have some butter paper stuck to it. Consequently it is necessary to pulverise the refuse material before sorting, and sometimes to pulverise in two stages.

Having established a recovery plant for raw refuse including shredding, the sorting of glass will not give severe problems. Crushed glass may be removed from shredded refuse by screening. It will occur in a mixture of sand, dirt, rock, and a relatively small amount of miscellaneous material such as wood chips and small metal objects. The glass may be coated with moisture and organic material. Fine screening and filter sand washing techniques may be used to refine and recover the glass within a desired size range. The National Center for Resource Recovery in the United States has made studies of glass particle sizes from different shredding operations. The data suggest that the particle size will usually range between 40 mesh, the lower range of coarse sand, to 1 cm, the upper range of fine gravel. An electronic colour sorting is available* for sorting glass scrap into coloured and colourless glass. This may be done with cullet from pulverised raw refuse or cullet recovered from incinerated glass.

6. RE-USE OF GLASS SCRAP

6.1 *Established glass production*

The most obvious method of recycling glass is for the manufacturer to recycle it back to the glass furnace. This is easier said than done, however, and the reason for the difficulty lies in the glass making operation itself. As mentioned before, glass is mainly sand or silica, 70-75%, but it also contains limestone and soda ash in exact predetermined amounts to make large quantities of a uniform quality and colour. For special product manufacture, for example glass wool, other ingredients such as boron are added. The materials are blended in a mixer and the batch goes to the glass furnace, which can be compared with a huge pot or tank. Flames form at openings in the walls and across the top of the batch. The temperature reaches *ca.* 1200°C. After it is melted, glass flows into a refining chamber and then drops to automatic feeders where it is finally formed into the required shape.

Although 200 tons per day of glass is the capacity of the average furnace, the operation is still rather delicate. Glass has to be at an exact temperature to form and the ingredients must be in the correct proportion. Adjustments have to be made with each variation or the resulting glass may have flaws. Although flaws may be merely visual, the quality and saleability of the container may be lowered since a shopper is less apt to purchase preserved vegetables if the glass container has unsightly spots or bubbles.

Glass furnaces operate continuously around the clock. In fact it takes almost a week to properly shut a furnace down or start up. Also recipes for glass may vary from furnace to furnace and glass from one plant may not combine correctly with glass from another plant.

All glass manufacturers practise internal recycling where containers failing quality control inspections are crushed and returned to the furnace from which they came. In those cases 30-50% of a batch may consist of internal rejects and the glass manufacturers prefer at least 10-15% cullet.

Problems may, however, occur when glass from recycling centres or municipal separation systems is combined with raw materials for use in the furnace. Reclaimed glass could originate from anywhere in the world and may have been formed according to numerous different methods. Any foreign material introduced into a particular factory mixture may cause results that manufacturers are not always able to predict.

Aluminium, ceramic and metals settle to the bottom of the furnace, interferring with furnace operation. The percentage of glass containers produced as coloured glass or flint glass varies, of course, from country to country, but on average about half of all glass containers are flint or clear glass. The remaining containers are of glass that can be amber, green or a number of colour variations. Colour is produced by glass chemically reacting with sulphur, carbon or chromium or iron oxides among others. Once in the glass, colour cannot be removed and therefore coloured glass cannot be successfully used to make flint glass. Since a number of chemicals produce the same colour, the delicate balance of ingredients could again be upset by adding reclaimed glass to batches of coloured glass. A company specification for cullet is shown in [Fig. 5].

There are many different opinions of the percentage of recycling. An average percentage may be as follows:

Green glass   50% totally, of which 15% is internal recycled glass,
Amber glass   30% totally, of which 15% is internal recycled glass,
Flint glass   25% totally, of which 15% is internal recycled glass.

*Sortex Colour Separator.

1. All glass should be typical soda–lime–silica bottle glass.	
2. Contamination by liquids.	The sample should show no drainage
3. Contamination by organic substances	0.5% maimum, as determined by ignition loss
4. Contamination by magnetic materials.	0.05% maximum, with a maximum size of 13mm
5. Contamination by non–magnetic metals.	0.05% maximum, with a maximum size of 6mm
6. Contamination by refractory materials.	Nil
7. Contamination by other solid inorganic materials.	0.1% maximum with a maximum size of 6 mm

8. Contamination by glass of other colours:

Main glass	Contaminants
White flint cullet	0.5 % maxium amber or Non–chrome green glass Nil–chroium green glass
Amber cullet	10% maximum white flint 10% maximum green with 10% maximum white and green combined
Green cullet	35% maximum amber 15% maximum white

All results to be calculated on a dry basis.

Fig. 5.

The energy consumption for the production of glass from pure raw materials is approx. 8000 kJ/kg while 6000 kJ/kg is enough by melting of waste glass. On average 15–25% of the energy can be saved by melting raw materials with cullet.

6.2 *Other purposes of re-use*

For the above reasons, local conditions existing in the glass industry may make it desirable to use glass scrap for other purposes.

Crushed glass can be substituted for a major portion of the clay in brick without changing the essential characteristics of the brick. The Bureau of Mines has investigated the possibilities and the work resulted in the development of some glass clay bricks made from 70% waste glass and 30% clay. This product does not require a raw material glass feed of the purity required for cullet. This is also the case when using crushed glass in the so-called 'glass phalt' paving mixtures. The research team found that a high level (17%) of foreign matter such as metals, bones, plastics and stones can be tolerated in crushed glass used for glass phalt.

The future may show if some of these possibilities of re-use are feasible. I still think that the amount of waste glass in most countries will be too low to build up new products from waste glass.

NEW PRODUCTS FROM WASTE

MICHAEL E. HENSTOCK

University of Nottingham, England

INTRODUCTION

The term recycling is often taken to indicate the transformation of a used product, via some process of grading and refining, to a new product of the same kind, e.g. a lead accumulator's being reprocessed into an identical form. The refining operation signifies a high-purity product, suitable for any use calling for that material. Electrolytically refined copper, for example, may be used for any application of the element; thus, the purchaser has flexibility, but that flexibility is purchased only at the cost of the energy involved in refining the metal to electrolytic grade.

Copper for electrical use must be of high purity, especially in respect of high-valency contaminants. There are, however, many applications, e.g. brass extrusions or horticultural products, that do not demand copper of such purity and for these it would be extravagant to use electrolytic grade. Raw materials for applications such as this cost less than those of high purity but the flexibility is lost; contaminated metals can be used only for selected and non-critical purposes.

The changes in value of an article at the various stages of its life and during subsequent recycling have been considered by Alexander[1] and are illustrated in Figs. 1 and 2.

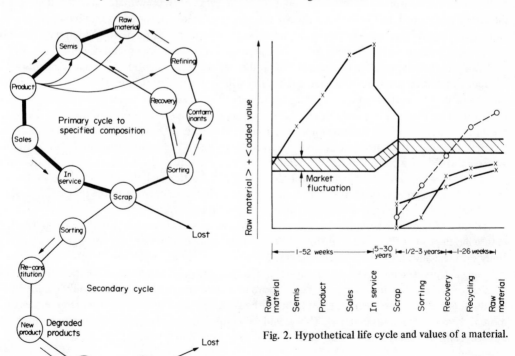

Fig. 1. Open- and closed-loop recycling of materials.

Fig. 2. Hypothetical life cycle and values of a material.

During progression along one of these cycles, time is a variable, the greatest interval being the useful life of the product, i.e. anything from a few weeks to many years. By comparison all other time stages are relatively short, and a delay before recycling can have a very important bearing on whether or not scrap can economically be recycled. Secondly, the value of any raw material increases as it is processed to a finished product. Immediately a product is sold and enters use its value starts to decrease until, at some time between one and, say, 30—50 y later, the article is scrapped and it reverts to zero value. Unless it can be used for some purpose *without* work input, its value *must* be zero. It then starts to acquire some value again, because of the work, i.e. energy, put in on collection, sorting, segregation etc. of each material. Decisions must be made concerning whether these operations and the final refining make the total added value higher than the cost of the raw material; in such a case it is clearly uneconomic to recycle it in the closed loop because no purchaser would come forward. The objective, therefore, is to ensure that, having recycled to the stage where the material can meet a particular compositional specification, it still has a monetary value less than the value of the raw material.

Therein lies the key to the whole problem of recycling of materials.

This problem is shown schematically in Fig. 2. If the economic or cost cycle cannot be completed, the only way in which this equation of simple economics can be resolved is by subsidy to ensure that the disparity between the total added value of collection, etc., recovery and, possibly, refining of scrap can be done for less than the original raw material value. The decision to apply such a subsidy will be made on non-economic, e.g. social grounds. It must, however, be borne in mind that recycling is an economic proposition for over half of the metal scrapped throughout the world in any one year.

It should also be noted that much depends upon the value of the raw material at the time when the article is scrapped; in Fig. 2 this is shown as a spread of values in the form of a band. If, as happens cyclically, raw material prices are low, scrap can be stored for a period which may run into years before rising prices once again attract the attention of a secondary metal dealer.

The alternative approach is to degrade the product or the scrap recovered to some secondary product which is so contaminated that, although it will perform a useful function in some different form, is often not worth another recycling because its value is zero and an excessive amount of work would be required to purify or rectify it. The material would, therefore, ultimately be lost to the entire system, a practical illustration of Clausius's statement of entropy. This loss may be from a variety of causes; the corrosion of iron and steel causes losses amounting to several million tonnes per year on a world-wide basis, and the incineration of domestic refuse also accelerates production of metal oxides, which are subsequently easily lost. Any metal article, whether a single lead shot embedded in the ground or an entire 50 tonne tank abandoned to corrode in the jungle, increases global entropy, i.e. the irreversible dispersion of our metal resources.

Refining of materials from the concentration, relative to average crustal distribution, in which nature has deposited them is a reversion of Clausius and can be achieved only through inputs of energy — mechanical, thermal, electrical, etc. When we mix, for example, metals into alloys we are reversing the process and reverting to a system of greater disorder. Similarly, a component made of a number of different materials approaches a disordered state and can be separated only by energy inputs. It is arguable that mankind would better be served by making articles from large pieces of more or less homogeneous material. This would, of course, imply a large initial investment in material, but recycling would thus be very much easier and recovered values would finance the reclamation operation.

There is little point in dwelling gloomily upon this inevitable outcome of the laws of thermodynamics; study and awareness of the laws serve to remind that recycling can never be 100% efficient. The best we can do is to devise methods whereby contaminated materials may be re-used at different levels of purity for different applications and, as purity falls, at lower and lower prices. Refining would be carried out only when the material was scrapped from its lowest state of purity.

An attractive viewpoint is to regard waste as a potential raw material, albeit one with limited application. This is not a new idea. Winemakers have for centuries thrown water on the husks of pressed grapes and, from the pulp, distilled a variety of potent liquors, e.g. Marc, and gardeners have long used soot as a soil conditioner. Many cases of this type may be cited but, latterly, a greater awareness of the finite nature of the earth has stimulated much research into possible uses for discarded materials.

This paper, which might be subtitled "Waste: a low-cost raw material" will not attempt the comprehensive coverage achieved elsewhere[2] in considering the broad field of materials and possible use cycles. It will, instead, seek to examine some cases where the fairly low value of some discarded materials dictates that new uses must deliberately be invented as a means of solving a disposal problem of the kind that would never arise in the case of economically attractive materials such as massive copper, lead or zinc.

Metals

The dramatic increase in the cost of energy has focused attention as never before on its consumption in the production of aluminium. The industry has reacted swiftly and predictably to charges of energy extravagance, pointing out that careful choice of application for this lightweight metal can quickly recoup the energy invested in its production; such an application is in transport, where weight saved by replacement of steel by aluminium can, over the life of the vehicle, save hundreds of times the initial energy investment[3].

The high energy content of aluminium makes it a particularly attractive material for recycling since it can, under favourable conditions, be recycled at an energy cost of only 2–5% of the original extraction requirements.

Whatever the cost of aluminium, in energy or any other commodity, it is clearly logical to ensure that maximum use is made of it. Drosses produced in the process of aluminizing contain, typically, 56% Al, 31% Fe, and 7% Si and these are found to possess deoxidizing potential in the finishing of steel[4]. In this capacity it is as effective as aluminium wire. Such an application of a cheap, low grade product that, on this occasion, adequately replaces an expensive, high grade product represents an economic gain.

Scrap PVC may be used in a rather similar manner; the purification of liquid tin involves the generation of bubbles of chlorine. Stabilization of PVC is accomplished with lead or tin; thus, addition of the tin-stabilized variety generates chlorine bubbles and the tin released from the PVC joins the bath.

These two uses of waste products conserve primary resources but are fairly minor. Of much greater potential is the attempt to supply the growing demands of the powder metallurgy industry by the direct production of iron powder from iron and steel scrap[5]. The waste is dissolved in hydrochloric acid and ferrous chloride is crystallized and hydrogen-reduced to metal powder.

Glass

The potential for abandoned glass is enormous. In 1972 it was estimated[6] that almost 14 million tonnes of glass was annually discarded in municipal wastes in the U.S.A. Of this, only ca. 2 million tonnes passed through incineration and was thus, potentially, recoverable by existing technology[7].

Studies on the waste glass fraction remaining after free metal and cullet grade glass have been removed from incinerator residues reveal a fraction so contaminated as to be worthless for recycling as cullet. Bonded with some 30% of common plastic clay it is, however, transformable into face brick of good colour and high quality. The fine glass acts as a flux, the slag darkens the colour, and the ceramic and stone materials act as inert fillers; contemporary costings indicated a saving on conventional bricks of comparable grade. The differential is largely explained by the greatly reduced firing temperatures of the glass bricks, some 200–260 K below those of conventional brick bodies, making possible a 23–30% productivity increase[8].

Another product of the current high price of fuel, together with the growing awareness of the pernicious long-term effects of noise, is likely to be an upswing in the use of glass wool for insulation. Its thermal and acoustic properties result primarily from the physical structure of the mixtures of fibres and air, which produces a series of insulating air pockets. The properties are therefore critically structure-dependent but this structure is attainable within wide limits of chemical composition.

Glass fibres can be made[9] from mixtures of the glass incinerator residue mentioned above with dolomite and alumina, and simple variations in technique permit production of both coarse and fine fibres.

A minor potential market exists in the production of micro-sized glass spheres for reflective paint but demand is too small to be of real consequence. A more esoteric suggestion[10] is that waste glass be mixed with animal dung to produce ceramic titles.

Polymeric materials

Waste thermoplastic generated during manufacture presents no problem and is simply remelted, provided it has been segregated from other types and colours. If mixing has occurred the waste may be turned into non-critical packaging where the mixture of colours might even be thought attractive and, for that reason, command a premium. Alternatively, multi-coloured tiles and light-duty board may be fabricated for a limited market.

At the lower end of the purity range, waste thermoplastics and thermosetting materials may be handled by a means such as the Mitsubishi process. This is claimed to process all types of polymers, clean or contaminated, turning them into non-critical components such as fence posts, rain guttering, dustbins, etc. The dominant question concerns the size of the market for such commodities.

Sulphur

One predictable result of antipollution legislation was the closure of old or near-obsolete smelting plants whose productive efficiency would not support the capital investment needed to meet the new emission requirements. The shutdown of smelters in, for example, the lead industry, has increased pressure on the larger and more modern installations, usually heavily committed to the treatment of concentrates from the mine to which they are attached. For this, and possibly for other, more sinister, reasons the small mine operator experiences difficulties in selling his concentrates or in securing custom smelting facilities. The situation is exacerbated by rapidly rising transport costs which preclude shipment of the concentrates to more distant smelters.

Air pollution control regulations already implemented or planned in the U.S.A. require substantial investment capital for removal of sulphurous fumes from copper, lead and zinc smelter gases. It seems inevitable that there will be attendant increases in production costs and ultimately in metal prices. Total investment and resultant metal price increases will depend upon the control regulations ultimately adopted by individual states, and controversy has already arisen between the metals industry and governmental control agencies regarding the ability of industry to control sulphurous emissions to the degree proposed by some of the more stringent regulations.

Several states have established a limit of 10% of the percentage of the total sulphur charged to the smelter that can be emitted as oxides. It is felt that, in order to comply with this standard, companies may be obliged to install capital equipment that has not yet been demonstrated on a commercial scale, and may, within a few years, be faced with having to operate new plants using obsolete, outmoded, or otherwise non-competitive methods. Sulphuric acid production seems to be the only proven technology for removing oxides of sulphur from smelter gases, and most plants plan to use this route. However, acid production is only practical from the converter gases; tightly hooded converters can capture 50–70% of the sulphur oxides at best and, in order to achieve the 90% removal required by law, the dilute gases generated in the reverberatory furnace will also have to be incorporated. Processes under consideration are the Asarco brimstone process to produce elemental sulphur from gas containing 14% or more of sulphur dioxide[11]. Other possibilities include methods for separating and concentrating sulphur dioxide by scrubbing with absorbants such as ammonium sulphite-bisulphite or anhydrous dimethylaniline.

Many processes have been proposed for the removal of sulphur dioxide from smelter gases; of these comparatively few have been sufficiently rigorously tested to provide data for cost estimates under a variety of smelter conditions.

Use of sulphur products

Depending upon the technologies and processes adopted for removing oxides of sulphur, products will be sulphur, sulphuric acid, concentrated SO_2, ammonium sulphate or solid sulphur-bearing compounds. Existing technologies for sulphuric acid production will probably establish it as the major product. From the point of view of the smelting industry, marketing of by-products is essential in order to offset some at least of the control costs. It is anticipated that production of sulphur products from smelter gases will have a profound effect on the national sulphur oversupply situation when the element is already being recovered in increasing amounts from natural gas in the United States and Canada. De-sulphurisation of residual petroleum stocks and products is increasing, and sulphur recovery from fossil fuel-fired generating plants is imminent.

United States domestic demand for sulphur was, in 1972, 9266 x 10^3 tonnes, i.e. little more than the potential primary production, by the Frasch process, of 7984 x 10^3 tonnes. A surplus of potential supply over demand of 15 991 x 10^3 tonnes is indicated and this is projected to increase to 18 560 x 10^3 tonnes by 1980. It is possible that the entire supply–demand structure of the domestic sulphur industry could drastically be altered by the dumping of large tonnages of sulphur or its compounds on the market, and the complete disappearance of the Frasch sulphur industry is not inconceivable.

Nationally, the production of sulphuric acid from smelter gas in the U.S.A. will be uncompetitive because of transportation costs to the major markets. The principal industries using sulphuric acid include fertilizers, paper, cellulose fibre and petroleum refining, the plants for which are mostly located remote from the smelters. Thus, sulphur in excess of local demand will have to be disposed of or stored in some environmentally acceptable manner, and this is most easily done in the elemental form, which may be shipped economically or stored readily without major effect on air and water. Whether all this will actually happen is speculative but, should the legislation be enacted, sulphur would become relatively cheap and there is even a good possibility that substantial quantities of the element would have to be discarded as a waste product. Hence, the Bureau of Mines at its Boulder City Laboratory has investigated new uses for sulphur based upon a greatly reduced price. One notes, however, that the market price of sulphur approximately tripled over the year preceding October 1974 and, far from there being a sulphur glut, there was at that time something of a shortage.

Areas investigated could each possibly consume more than 1 million tonnes of sulphur annually[12]. Experimental asphalt paving mixtures have been prepared by substituting local sands, or copper mill tailings, and sulphur for ordinary aggregate. Road paving mixtures were then made with asphalt cements and results, particularly in respect of anti-skidding properties, look promising. There is no obvious technical reason why sulphur should not be used as a substitute for dense graded aggregate should the latter happen to be in short supply.

Another possible new use is in the stabilisation of copper tailings to wind and water erosion[13]. Such tailings comprise the bulk of mineral wastes that are not amenable to plant growth in the arid climate of the United States southwest. The large areas of finely divided dry mill tailings become airborne with the slightest breeze. Initial research using sprayed coatings of pure molten sulphur showed that the coatings started to disintegrate after weathering for *ca.* one week. This was believed to stem from thermal cycling and from the allotropic transformation from monoclinic to ortho-rhombic form, and research continues to develop a suitable stabiliser. The most promising mixtures have been those containing 92–94% sulphur, 1% dipentene and 5–7% dicyclopentadiene. These organic modifying agents are available in commercial quantities at costs ranging from $0.11 – 0.26kg.

Sulphur formulations with talc, fibreglass and·dicyclopentadiene have also been found effective in constructing impervious linings for ponds and tanks. Although thermal cycling cracks have been observed in those regions above the water line where temperature variations are greatest, the ponds have successfully contained liquid for over nine months. The formulation appears to be non-toxic, supporting both fish and algal life. Bacterial conversion of sulphur to sulphuric acid does not take place since the pH of the water remains constant.

Sulphur-containing coatings have been applied to cinderblock buildings both internally and externally. The coating is attractive in appearance but thermal cycling again limits its use, since it cracks on ageing. Scope exists for research into suitable stabilisers; the slight sulphurous odour apparent at low temperatures can become fairly powerful in very warm weather. Sulphur coatings have been used to retain moisture during the germination period of seed beds. Coating stability can be so adjusted that coatings disintegrate after a time sufficient to allow the young plants to withstand exposure to sunlight.

SUMMARY

The foregoing is almost a random consideration of some possibilities for new uses. No attempt has been made at completeness; much could be written on the potential for rubber, paper and fabrics, areas that have here been ignored.

The possibilities are almost limitless if the collection area is sufficiently large. It is, however, significant that most new use cycles are in low-value applications; in cases where waste products are competing with low-value raw materials the economics of transport and handling etc. must be considered with particular care.

Acknowledgements – Figures 1 and 2 are reproduced by kind permission of Professor W. O. Alexander.

REFERENCES

1. W. O. Alexander, contribution to *The Recycling and Disposal of Solid Waste,* (Ed. Michael E. Henstock), Pergamon Press, Oxford (1975).
2. W. O. Alexander, *ibid.*
3. C. N. Cochran, *Automotive Engineering* **81**, 6 (1973).
4. H. V. Makar and P. J. Gallagher, Deoxidation of steel using waste aluminizing dross: A feasibility study, U.S. Bureau of Mines, TPR 55, (July 1972).
5. P. C. Finlayson and A. P. Morrell, *Power Metallurgy* **11**, 22, p.224–232 (1968).
6. M. E. Tyrrell, Fabrication and cost evaluation of experimental building brick from waste glass, U.S. Bureau of Mines, RI 7605, (1972).
7. P. M. Sullivan and M. H. Stanczyk, Economics of recycling metals and minerals from urban refuse, U.S. Bureau of Mines, TPR 33, (1971).
8. M. E. Tyrrell and A. H. Goode, Waste glass as a flux for brick clays, U.S. Bureau of Mines, RI 7701, (1972).
9. A. H. Goode, Glass wool from waste glass, U.S. Bureau of Mines, RI 7708, (1972).
10. The Midwest Research Institute, *The commercial potential of ceramic tile made with waste glass and animal excreta,* The Glass Container Manufacturers Institute, Inc.
11. U.S. Bureau of Mines, Control of sulfur oxide emissions in copper, lead and zinc smelting, IC 8527, (1971).
12. U.S. Bureau of Mines Research 73: A summary of significant results in mining, metallurgy and energy, (1973).
13. T. A. Sullivan and W. C. McBee, Sulfur utilization in pollution abatement, *Proc. 4th Mineral Waste Utilization Symposium,* Chicago, (May 1974).

SUPPLEMENTARY REFERENCE LIST

Some Recent Selected References

S. T. Abbate, Use of Aluminium Recovered from Municipal Solid Waste, in *Resource Recovery and Utilization,* H. Alter and E. Horowitz, eds. Amer. Society for Testing and Materials. Philadelphia, Pa., 1975, pp.106-113.

J. G. Abert, H. Alter and J. F. Bernheisel, The Economics of Resource Recovery from Municipal Solid Waste, *Science,* Vol. 183, pp. 1052-1058 (1974). Also in: *Materials: Renewable and Non-renewable Resources,* P. H. Abelson and A. L. Hammond, eds. Am. Ass. Adv. Sci., Washington, D.C., 1976, pp. 54-60.

H. Alter, K. L. Woodruff, A. Foodson and B. Rogers, Analysis of Newsprint Recovered from Mixed Municipal Waste, *Resource Recovery and Conservation,* Vol. 2, pp. 79-84 (1976).

H. Alter, Energy Conservation and Fuel Production by Processing Solid Wastes, *Environmental Conservation,* Vol. 4, pp. 11-19 (1977).

H. Alter, S. L. Natoff and L. C. Blayden, Pilot Studies Processing MSW and Recovery of Aluminum Using an Eddy Current Separator. *Proceedings Fifth Mineral Waste Utilization Symposium,* E. Aleshin, ed. III Research Institute and Bu. Mines. Chicago, Ill, 1976, pp. 161 - 168.

H. Alter, S. L. Natoff, K. L. Woodruff and R. D. Hagen, *The Recovery of Magnetic Metals from Municipal Solid Waste.* Report RM 77-1, National Centre for Resource Recovery, Inc., Washington, D.C., 1977.

J. R. Alward, J. P. Clark and M. B. Bever, *The Dissipative Uses of Lead,* Proc. Council of Economics, AIME, 1976, pp. 17-26.

P. E. Becker and H. J. Pick, Resource Implications of Material Waste in Engineering Manufacture, *Resources Policy,* Vol. 1, pp. 142-153 (1975).

M. B. Bever, Recycling in the Materials System, *Materials and Society,* Vol. 1, pp. 167-176 (1977).

M. B. Bever, Resource Recovery, in *Resource Recovery Implementation: Engineering and Economics,* Proc. Conf. Engineering Foundation, Rindge, N.H., July 1976, U.S. Government Printing Office, Washington, D.C., 1977.

M. W. Biddulph, Cryogenic Embrittlement of Rubber, *Conservation and Recycling,* Vol. 1, p. 169 (1977).

M. W. Biddulph, Cryogenic Embrittlement of Steel, *Conservation and Recycling,* Vol. 1, p. 221 (1977).

S. L. Blum, Tapping Resources in Municipal Solid Waste, *Science,* Vol. 191, pp. 669-675 (1976). Also in: *Materials: Renewable and Non-renewable Resources,* P. H. Abelson and A. L. Hammond, eds. Am. Ass. Adv. Sci., Washington, D.C., 1976, pp. 47-54.

G. F. Bourcier and K. H. Dale, The Technology and Economics of the Recovery of Aluminum from Municipal Solid Waste, *Resource Recovery and Conservation,* Vol. 3. In press, 1978.

A. Buekens and J. Schoeters, *Assessment of Current Technology of Thermal Processes for Waste Disposal, with Particular Emphasis on Resource Recovery.* EEC Report, Contract No. 282-76-9EC1-B., 1977.

H. H. Dreissen and A. T. Basten, Reclaiming Products from Shredded Junked Cars by the Water Only and Heavy Medium Cyclone Processes, Fifth Mineral Waste Utilization Symposium, Chicago, USA (April 1976).

E. J. Duckett, The Influence of Tin Content on the Re-use of Magnetic Metals Recovered from Municipal Solid Waste, *Resource Recovery and Conservation,* Vol. 2, pp. 301-328 (1977).

J. F. Elliott and F. E. Brantley, Future Raw Materials Needs of the American Steel Industry, *Iron and Steelmaker,* April 1975.

J. J. Emery, New Uses of Metallurgical Slags, *CIM Bulletin,* December 1975.

D. N. Fan, On the Air Classified Light Fraction of Shredded Municipal Solid Waste. I. Composition and Physical Characteristics. *Resource Recovery and Conservation,* Vol. 1, pp. 141-150 (1975).

J. J. Harwood, Recycling the Junk Car - A Case Study of the Automobile as a Renewable Resource, *Materials and Society,* Vol. 1, pp. 177-181 (1977).

M. E. Henstock, Realities of Recycling. Symposium: Recent Advances in the Recovery of Useful Materials from Industrial Waste, London, The City University, March 2, 1976.

M. E. Henstock, The Conflict between First Cost and Recyclability in the Design of Manufactured Goods, *Proc. Resources Policy '78 Conference,* Christchurch College, Oxford (March 20-22, 1978).

M. E. Henstock, The Contribution of Secondary Materials to the Conservation of Energy, *Proc. International Conference "Energy Use Management",* Tucson, Arizona (October 20-28, 1977).

D. Hollely, Cryogenic Grinding of Rubber and Plastics, *Recycling and Waste Disposal,* Vol. 179 (Sept. 1977).

D. V. Jackson, The Recovery of Metals - General Considerations, *Chemistry and Industry,* December 6, 1975.

R. S. Kaplan and H. V. Makar, Use of Refuse Magnetic Fractions for Steelmaking *Resource Recovery and Conservation,* Vol. 3. In press, 1978.

D. Klumb, Union Electric Company's Solid Waste Utilization System, *Resource Recovery and Conservation,* Vol. 1, pp. 225-234 (1976).

L. R. Mahoney and J. J. Harwood, The Automobile as a Renewable Resource, *Resources Policy,* Vol. 1, No. 5 (September 1975).

H. V. Makar, R. S. Makar, R. S. Kaplan and J. Janowski, *Evaluation of Steel made with Ferrous Fractions from Urban Refuse.* U.S. Bureau of Mines, RI 8037, 1975.

T. S. McKey and S. Bergsoe, *Smelting of Unbroken Batteries.* Lead-Zinc-Tin Session, Amer. Inst. Min. Met. and Pet. Eng. 106 Annual Meeting, Atlanta, 1977.

E. L. Michaels, K. L. Woodruff, W. L. Freyberger and H. Alter. Heavy Media Separation of Aluminum from Municipal Solid Waste, *Soc. Mining Engrs. AIME Transactions,* Vol. 258, pp. 34-40 (1975).

J. R. Miller, Changing Patterns of Demand for Iron and Steelmaking Metallics in the 1975/1985 Decade, *Proceedings of the Council of Economics,* pp. 177-192 (1975).

H. D. Moran, Substitution - Some Practical Considerations, in *Engineering Implications of Chronic Materials Scarcity,* Proc. Conf. Eng. Found., August 1976, Office of Technology Assessment, Washington, D.C., 1977, pp. 281-298.

Resource Recovery and Waste Reduction. Third Report to Congress, U.S. Environmental Protection Agency, 1975.

Resource Recovery and Waste Reduction. Fourth Report to Congress, U.S. Environmental Protection Agency, Washington, D. C., 1977.

C. E. Seeley, Glass in Solid Waste Recovery Systems, in *Resource Recovery and Utilization,* H. Alter and E. Horowitz, eds., Amer. Society for Testing and Materials, Philadelphia, Pa., 1975, pp. 114-121.

H. P. Sheng and H. Alter, Energy Recovery from Municipal Solid Waste and Method of Comparing Refuse-Derived Fuels, *Resource Recovery and Conservation,* Vol. 1, pp. 85-94 (1975).

P. M. Sullivan and H. V. Makar, Quality of Products from Bureau of Mines Resource Recovery Systems and Suitability for Recycling in *Proceedings Fifth Mineral Waste Utilization Symposium,* E. Aleshin, ed., III Res. Inst. and Bu. Mines, Chicago, Ill., 1976, pp. 223-233.

C. A. Verbraak and G. Dapper, Recycling of Tin from Secondary Waste, *Proceedings of the First International Tinplate Conference,* London, October 5-8, 1976.

INDEX